INDIA:
THE ELEPHANT'S
BLESSING

by

Aline Dobbie

Published by

**MELROSE
BOOKS**

An Imprint of Melrose Press Limited
St Thomas Place, Ely
Cambridgeshire
CB7 4GG, UK
www.melrosebooks.com

FIRST EDITION

Copyright © Aline Dobbie 2006

The Author asserts her moral right to
be identified as the author of this work

Cover designed by Sophie Fitzjohn

ISBN 1 905226 85 3

Printed and bound in Great Britain by:
CPI Bath, Lower Bristol Road,
Bath, BA2 3BL, UK

Also by the same author:

India: The Peacock's Call

India: The Tiger's Roar

Further details about the author can be found on:

www.thepeacockscall.co.uk

Dedication

This book is dedicated to all the children who so tragically lost their lives in the Asian Tsunami on 26th December 2004, children from all parts of the world who were also on holiday in affected areas as well as the local children who were innocently enjoying a new sunny day of holiday and festival; most especially my heart goes out to those children who are orphaned as a result of this tragedy in all the countries touched by this terrible natural disaster. Their lives have been abruptly and cruelly changed for ever.

Aline Dobbie
May 2006

Acknowledgements

I would like to thank my husband Graham for all of his love, help and support throughout the research and journeys that have made this third book possible. In these last ten years he has come to know and also love the Land of my birth and so enjoy revisiting India. To all of the many people who have helped me for nearly a decade, my heartfelt gratitude for their friendship and hospitality in homes, hotels, planes and other forms of transport. I hope very much that the next generations of our family will come to know and love India as we do.

Aline Dobbie, June 2006

Contents

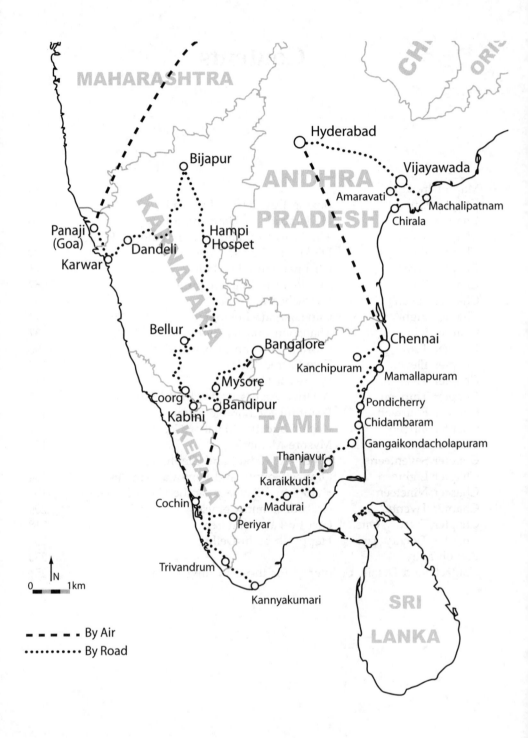

By Air
By Road

Chapter One

Boxing Day 2004 – Tsunami

Christmas 2005 has come and gone and provided a happy peaceful family time; now on the fourth of January 2006 I too am settling down to write as indeed so many people have returned to their own form of work. It is a frosty silvery-white world here in my beloved Tweeddale so it will be no hardship at all to cast my mind back to the start of a wonderful journey through sunny and warm southern India. The pheasants in our garden are croaking at me once again to remind me that I am their food slave and the garden birds are frantic on the bird table which Graham has thoughtfully filled before going off to work. Raju my adored little black cat is curled up on my bed having completed his morning meander. I shall keep a keen eye on him however, he has a tendency to feel hungry and quietly slink off, go hunting and return stealthily, if I am not totally vigilant, with some poor unfortunate prey that he proceeds to devour on my side of the bed! Sometimes the terrified little creature is unharmed and is therefore let loose in our bedroom. What follows is a complete hiatus until I secure the wee thing in a jug we keep especially for these occasions, then I take it outside and gently let it go; Raju all the while looking bored with the whole caper. The low weak winter sun is shining into my study and thus filling me with optimism and the thought of spring and indeed yet another possible trip to the land of my birth – India.

My very clear memory of Boxing Day 2004 is of me standing at the window looking out onto the snowy scene; I marvelled at the full moon low and huge in the western sky, and how it lit up the whole vista in front of me. The sky was still dark but with that first tinge of blue that the dawn brings; the beautiful full moon was ringed in the way that only a cold moon can be and I cast my mind back to the previous year's Christmas moon when we had been cruising in the Arabian Sea en route to Sri Lanka. I thought with a smile of the balmy night air on deck and the wonderful sunrises and what a lovely experience it had all been.

The bedroom radio had come serenely to life with some evocative Christmas music, and then there was a silence punctuated by the staccato voice of a newsreader: "We are receiving reports of a huge tidal wave in the Indian Ocean that has caused death and destruction to all the countries surrounding the Indian Ocean." As I listened in absolute horror I looked up at the moon, this beautiful tranquil silver orb and realised that whereas I was at the start of a pleasurable Boxing Day, 26th December 2004, the area in the world that I had been visiting exactly a year before was undergoing a dreadful natural disaster. We raced downstairs to put on the 24 hour television channels for a detailed update. The news continued to worsen with appalling images on screen and the western world started to come to terms with a colossal unfolding tragedy.

Woodenly we went about preparing for a happy family day, only too well aware how fortunate we were to have our son Stewart and his new bride Corinne back just days before from their honeymoon in The Maldives. The areas of Sri Lanka that we had so happily visited under a year ago were totally devastated and there was the sobering realisation that had we been there we too might be dead. Indeed, our own holiday in The Maldives in September 2004 to Hakuraa Hura became very vivid in our memories and both Graham and I were saddened subsequently to hear that the tiny island had been decimated and the manager of our resort was dead. Galle, Trincomalee: all these lovely places in Sri Lanka were the scenes of nightmare in the unfolding drama on the world's television screens. The Indian coast of Andhra Pradesh and Tamil Nadu also were greatly affected and of course we know of the coast of Thailand and Bandeh Aceh's huge devastation.

By the first of January 2005 I had received two government invitations to visit India and very soon resolved to go to southern India and research the four states of Andhra Pradesh, Tamil Nadu, Kerala and Karnataka for a third book. I had been in Goa previously and also experienced the west coast of Maharashtra and Karnataka, so I felt that this would be useful work to complete a trilogy on India.

2005 has also been a year of great natural disasters in both North America and also yet again in the Indian sub-continent; As I write I am constantly thinking of the poor people in Pakistani Kashmir and the surrounding areas who are suffering so badly after the devastating earthquake at the end of 2005. It is going to be a freezing night here in Scotland and I think of them on cold hillsides and damp valleys; orphaned children, old women and injured people left with nothing, their security and their futures destroyed without home or possessions, many of them still dreadfully injured and traumatised. Their tragedy could in fact swamp the fatality figures of the tsunami if practical help is not brought to them in sufficient quantity. Truly it has been a year of government ineptitude, be it Indonesia, Thailand, Sri Lanka or India, the United States and now Pakistan. Millions of pounds have been donated but we the donors are left frustrated with the inertia that abounds in many of these places and the negativity that swamps their respective politicians and administrations.

I was also filled with total cynicism about the United Kingdom's initial response to the tsunami disaster. It seemed that Christmas had 'got in the way' of Christian thinking with some of our politicians. The curious case of usually camera happy leading members of the government, who court the camera to issue sound bites, were being bashful in the Egyptian sun and their underlings voiced complacent statements that they had to retract or embroider when the public's response, and then disgust with their government's tardy response, became apparent. Then we were told the British Government would match with an equal amount that which the public donated. "To give and not to count the cost", Oh! what a noble sentiment, but one that on this developing occasion British people and their western allies aspired to generously and led the way for their more pusillanimous governments, which then proceeded to compete as governments with other western governments, and indeed shamed some of the Middle East into digging into their respective national pockets.

The Indian Government had a cabinet meeting within hours of the wave striking and decided that they did not wish outside help or interference; they quickly gave help to their neighbouring countries however but very soon realised that perhaps their initial response was ungracious and short sighted. It was probably driven by the idea that India wished to demonstrate that she is perfectly capable of handling emergencies. India is now the fourth largest economy in the world, well on the way to being an economic giant of this twenty first century. Nevertheless, it was unfortunate because ordinary people would ask me, "But why is India turning down offers of help...?' and in the long run of course they have accepted help from the big well-run charities and non-governmental organisations. When the hand of friendship and human brotherhood is extended it is foolhardy for a nation's government to respond ungraciously. The Asian Tsunami did more than anything to bring people of the world together; mourning their loved ones and trying to help the living. Western nations who hitherto had been rather inward looking and complacent gave and thought differently when their own tourists were involved; it was brought home all too vividly on our television screens that whilst we as travellers and holiday makers might be in complete shock and mourning, those alive would at least return home to order and stability whereas those hospitable people in the various affected countries would never be the same again. Greedy governments who could only think of their country's coffers behaved outrageously towards their survivors. Visitors to Thailand were appalled by some of what they saw and experienced, and Sri Lanka continues to fester in its internal politics which impacts heavily with government inertia on its people.

Thousands of Sri Lankans have not received aid and expressed their disgust by refusing to vote in the 2005 November elections; in the end because of this boycott Sri Lanka elected Mahinda Rajapakse president. He is a hardliner who has promised to tear up the Peace agreement with the rebel separatists, known as the Tamil Tigers, provoking fears of a return to the horrible civil war that has taken nearly 65,000 lives and lasted 22 years. For the ordinary western traveller, who loves Sri Lanka and its friendly people and absolutely beautiful island, it is so depressing. There is no doubt in my mind that because of the Sri Lankan Government's stubborn refusal to allocate the charitable funds and help the victims as soon as practicable, westerners are experiencing an inertia in their normally generous giving to the earthquake victims of Kashmir; they feel that their money will remain idle in some government bank account or be the victim of administrative venality.

Having been invited out to India, by not only the Indian Government's Tourism Ministry but also the Tamil Nadu Government, I was determined to try and see for myself what had happened and how the survivors and their families were being treated. Putting my trip together was to say the least very frustrating. Normally when we go to India as a couple it is a totally private endeavour and thus I do not have to consult anyone. On this occasion though, having responded to two invitations, I too was the victim of the infamous Indian inertia and inefficiency.

I chose an Emirates' flight from Glasgow to Dubai and then on to Hyderabad, the capital of Andhra Pradesh. Emirates have had the foresight to provide connecting flights from its hub in Dubai to most of India's burgeoning cities. We have flown on Emirates many times now and particularly recommend their Business Class. It is excellent; however having also flown their Economy I have to say that it is rather disappointing but proving very popular on the Glasgow route with another starting from Edinburgh I believe this year. Within the last year both Jet Airways, a privately owned airline in India, and BMI have inaugurated long haul flights between London and India and those along with the choice that already existed are making the fare to India a great deal more competitive. Now this January Air Sahara, another of India's domestic airlines has launched its long haul flights between London and Delhi at very low prices. This will be very helpful to us all, now however Air Sahara's attempted takeover by Jet Airways has fallen through at the very last hurdle.

Flying Emirates gives the traveller an opportunity to visit Dubai. We had done this in 2003 and found it both interesting and enjoyable. On that occasion we elected to stay at Le Royal Meridien Beach and Spa Resort on Jumeirah Beach. This is a first class hotel with every attention to detail and the most wonderful staff, most of whom come from the Indian sub-continent or Sri Lanka. The facilities are excellent and its position on the beach is the best as it has been there the longest of all that new breed of total luxury hotels for which Dubai is justly famous. The Meridien Group have now also opened The Grosvenor very close by which apparently has even more to offer; we made a point of visiting many of these now world famous hotels and resorts and had a thoroughly enjoyable three days. It has to be said that the Burj Al Arab is strikingly beautiful from the outside but appallingly garish and full of 'bling' within. Dubai is an amazing place in that it is so new and opulent and has so many lavish facilities. I quite understand that it is a desirable destination for shopping and living in luxury. This is very acceptable for a few days, and indeed for the keen golfer that could be stretched into a holiday for several days, but I personally think a visit of more than four or five days would begin to pall. Desert safaris are quite an attraction with the opportunity to dune drive and sand ski, which is exhilarating, ride camels, explore the wadis and eat desert banquets. There is also now the most fabulous artificial snow ski resort, about twenty minutes drive from the centre of town so one can spend a day in the desert and another in the snow! Lavish for the sake of lavish is not something with which I am totally comfortable. I also found the lack of history, which though understandable, leads to everything being very shallow and that, coupled with the fact that the locals do not actually do any real work, made me feel uncomfortable. Graham and I have subsequently spoken to Indians, and indeed seen them on flights to India, the workforce of Dubai without which it could not operate. I have heard some of the miserable stories of exploitation and cruelty with which these wage earners are treated; it is thoroughly unpleasant and a harsh reminder that in London too there are many many people also being exploited, of foreign origin, who are treated almost as slaves by wealthy Middle Eastern people who reside in the UK. The world over and throughout history there have been migrant workers who have had to forgo family life and companionship to earn a decent wage and provide for their respective families. It is calculated that one in four families in south India has a male relative working in the Arabian Gulf. That is understandable but harsh exploitation of these people in this century is not something that we in the West find

5

commendable be it Filipinos, Indians, Bangladeshis, Sri Lankans or Pakistanis. Find yourself on a plane returning from India to Dubai with the Economy seats full of returning workers who look so miserable and dejected and vulnerable in many instances, particularly the very young and it makes you think about what is worthwhile in life.

Thankfully India is now emerging as a major economic power and generating greater business within itself and many who would have had to take this lonely road to earn a wage are finding that employment in India is now possible. Those at the lower end of the economic and social scale are the ones that are still vulnerable; we have evidence of similar situations regarding migrant workers from Eastern Europe within the U K.

Whilst on the subject of the Middle East, it is worth writing about Oman where we visited by cruise ship in 2003, having set sail from Dubai. This short visit was a fascinating insight into the real Arabia. I thoroughly enjoyed the few days and noticed with amusement that in an autocracy even the motorway undersides (as indeed in Dubai) are painted white and the roundabouts are themed with things like coffee pots and other household items. In Oman one can be fined for having a dirty car, so I would be in trouble in 'Toy Town' in Muscat, but then again in their clear bright sunshine my old Ford would not be mud encrusted from country roads in Scotland! Oman's civilization is thousands of years old and the Sultan and his government have preserved and restored their heritage and the country has over 500 forts and towers across the country. Its 1,700 kilometre coastline is famous for its whales, dolphins, turtles and other creatures and the country is fast becoming a worthwhile destination for diving.

We had the opportunity to visit places deep in the interior which was intriguing and showed us the austere beauty of the country with its harsh mountain ranges and wadis. The entry by ship to Muscat's harbour was special and as it is all so beautifully maintained and very pleasing to the eye with the originally Portuguese forts of Mirani and Jalali guarding its entrance; these are floodlit at night. I rose very early and went on deck to watch the sunrise above the mountains which was stunning and then a submarine quietly entered harbour under our interested gaze; it did not fly a flag and was not one of the Royal Navy's. We were berthed very close to the Sultan's yacht – he seems to have two, one which is used I gather as a security back up, but as the Sultan himself is not fond of sea travel I think the vessel stays most of its time in berth. This Sultan had been through Royal Military Academy Sandhurst and served in the Cameronians, a very proud Scottish regiment which was sadly disbanded in 1968, an event which my family and I witnessed with sorrow.

Watching the dhows entering and leaving port one was reminded of the antiquity of seafaring and the fabulous tales of Sinbad the Sailor. Sur, the capital of the Eastern Region is one of the few surviving ports worldwide where traditional dhows continue to be made in the traditional way. We were able to visit Nahar and its desert oasis farm and watch camel racing and also see some wonderful horseflesh. Bedu women came to show us their colourful and enveloping traditional costumes and the benefits of the falaj watering systems were demonstrated to us and explained.

Driving along the Corniche at Muttrah and visiting its famous Souq was very enjoyable too and most of the traders, yet again, seemed Indian or of Indian origin. The Souq had masses of shops selling braids and piping and fringes and sewing aids which presumably the local women use to alleviate the gloom of their outer garments. I bought some perfume from a traditional perfumer and love it. The little bottle stays in my travelling wash bag and is a constant reminder of a happy visit. It has to be said that if one is serious about gold both Dubai and Oman are places in which to buy it. I bought a lovely gold chain in the famous Gold Souq in Dubai which I treasure, but I like rich gold whereas a great many people prefer white gold. This too is available but the Arabian Souqs are famed for what is really gold in colour and form.

I have deliberately mentioned both Dubai and Oman because they are such obvious places to visit on the way to or from India. Because so many Indians live and work in both these states it seemed natural to mention them in my third book on India. I would recommend a visit to both countries; both these destinations are safe which is important, but do be careful about any medication that you have with you entering Dubai. Ensure that it is in the appropriate bottle in which it was dispensed and if necessary have a repeat prescription form with you as Dubai officials can be very autocratic. The international airport at Dubai is truly wonderful and in the middle of the night is a blaze of lights and activity with some very good shopping and one or two very comfortable business class lounges in which to while away the transit times between your flights. Arriving on the first occasion at sunrise it was like looking down on a white 'Legoland' set amidst the desert sands, and the drive from the airport was entrancing. Indeed for those who only like to travel to neat and shiny destinations both Dubai and Oman would suit very well; I however have a deep love for India with its antiquity, multicultural history, tolerance and amazing contrasts.

Kripa Kurien, who owns a small business called Saffron Route, is a young Keralan whom I had met at the World Travel Market in London. It was to her that I turned to help me plan and organize our journey to southern India. Kripa is married into a family with many large business interests and her husband is a doctor. I subsequently had the pleasure of meeting both her father and mother in Chennai and her father very sweetly gave up a day to helping me look round Chennai. Kripa would be able to advise anyone wanting to make a journey to southern India; she has a sweetness and a sensitivity that western travellers would benefit from; she understands perfectly, as she lives in England, that we by and large appreciate good and immediate service, attention to detail and dealing with someone who does not try in any way to pull the wool over one's eyes. She too becomes irritated with her native Indian lethargy and inefficiency.

March is a good month in India; spring is there and though it is quite hot the blue skies and flowering spring blossom with the last of the winter's colour in the garden gives one an immediate good feeling on arrival. I should explain that in winter India is ablaze with lovely annual flowers that we associate with our summer in the West – dahlias, larkspur, chrysanthemums, gladioli, roses, verbena, hollyhocks and others. Poinsettia is another wonderful addition to the Indian winter garden and obviously lovely freshly cut and the stems burnt for putting in decorations over the Christmas season.

Flying into Hyderabad early in the morning whilst the sun was rising gave me a real feeling of anticipation – here I was back in India in a city that I had not visited since 1958 as a child. Looking down as the aircraft made her final approach on the city and its many lakes in the pink tinged dawn I so hoped that there would be no feeling of disappointment. Hyderabad had been a place that enchanted me as a child. I had visited it for a week when out in India for a long summer holiday with my parents after a first and challenging year at boarding school. That first visit in its own way was a growing up sort of experience because I had been away from beloved India – my home for a whole year. At that time I did not think of Britain as 'my home'. That long summer holiday was the second time I lived in and visited southern India. My father had been posted to Andhra Pradesh in his work and our home was in Guntur, a regional head office for the company's tobacco leaf growing district. We made huge, long car journeys to visit all the places he needed to be and to provide some fun and interest for me.

Here then was I arriving again, after an interval of nearly fifty years but by plane; truly it was the finest entry to India that I have experienced recently! Hyderabad's airport is still very small, based on the military airport that is practically in the centre of the city. Comparatively speaking everything is on a miniature scale – sadly not for much longer – a new big airport is being constructed for this great developing place – maybe the fastest growing city in India. Within 45 minutes we had landed, been collected by car and driven to our hotel and I was luxuriating in a hot shower and contemplating a good breakfast. The idea of a large slice of fresh papaya followed by a tomato omelette and some fresh fruit juice spurred me on and prevented me from the temptation of a quick lie down on my bed; we had so many people to meet, places to visit and things to do. A quick shut eye – not even to be contemplated!

Chapter Two

Hyderabad – the happening City!

Looking down in the morning sunlight on the Hussain Sagar Lake from our executive suite I again felt that Hyderabad must have been a city of dreams and splendour. You see in British India Hyderabad was one of the greatest and indeed the wealthiest of states in India with the actual city as its nucleus. Its ruler was His Exalted Highness the Nizam who had a permanent salute of twenty-one guns, and he was at one time the richest man in the world. He exerted full sovereignty within the state, including the right of life and death over his inhabitants and the power to grant honours and titles. The state had its own coinage and postal system, ran its own broad-gauge railway, and maintained a standing army of which 1,052 men were for imperial defence. The state as it was equalled the size of Italy, with an area of 82,000 square miles and a population of about 14,500,000 in 1937 now that has risen to nearly 76,000,000.

We were staying at the Kakatiya Sheraton & Towers which is a flagship property of the ITC-Welcomgroup. I particularly wanted to stay there as my late father had worked for ITC after leaving the Indian Army as a colonel in 1947. My childhood, apart from its first year, had been spent as a child of ITC enjoying all the comfort and privileges that came with working for such a developing group. The hotel's breakfast buffet beckoned; I love breakfast in big luxury hotels in the East. There is such an amazing choice of foods and the chefs stand ready to execute your order of eggs or fresh noodle soup, if in the Far East, exactly to your liking. The fruit platters are bountiful with fresh exotic choices and there is also some really wonderful yoghurt or local porridge from which to choose. Here in south India the additions are Idlis and Dosas. Idlis are a sort of rice cake steamed into a mound; they are delicious with a ladle of curry. Frankly that is too much for me at that time of day; it was still only eight o'clock in the morning! I particularly love Dosas which are also made of rice but are flat, huge, thin, delicate pancakes made freshly in front of you which are super just plain or rolled with something savoury inside or indeed with jam. Because I am now wheat intolerant these rice based dishes are a huge boon. These days I have to gaze forlornly at wonderful croissants or fresh toast, all of which would spell disaster. Dosas make a perfect snack at any time of day. It has to be said though that nothing beats a good tomato omelette with just a hint of green chilli! The waiters were eager and friendly and responded to my Hindi and rushed away to find some fresh little limes for the papaya. Graham and I find at this stage in a journey that we are pinching ourselves to check we are actually here in this far distant place with the sunshine, the raucous song of Indian birds and the *mali* (gardener) outside sweeping the paths and the delightful prospect of a dip in the pool. The blossom of the trees in the hotel's garden was superb; flamboyants, laburnums and vibrant bougainvillea creepers lined the drive.

Naturally for me in my mind's eye I was taken back to that holiday in 1958 when this sort of luxury hotel had not even been thought about. The India of the 1950s was still a post-imperial country coming to terms with itself and indeed the state of Andhra Pradesh only came into being in 1956 to replace what was Hyderabad state. When one travelled in the hinterland the only solution was staying with friends or colleagues, or in some rather modest and very simple hotel or in the *dak* bungalows strategically located all over India. The dak bungalows

Charminar, Hyderabad

were nationally owned, belonging to the postal service. Obviously the really major cities had fine hotels but Hyderabad was still regarded as an ancient city full of antiquity – I do not think anyone then could have foreseen the place that would evolve in twenty-first century India. It always gives me a good feeling to see how India is developing and leaping forward – that, added to happy memories of family times past, made me look forward to this huge journey ahead of me.

Now Hyderabad is referred to as 'the much happening city' and thankfully the governing powers have had the wisdom to see the vital importance of heritage preservation. Historically Hyderabad, which was founded in 1591 by Sultan Mohammad Quli Qutub Shah, was originally known as Bhagynagar in honour of his lady love Bhagmati. The founder of Hyderabad decreed that it should be 'a replica of heaven and unparalleled in the world'.

'The city is verily a paradise,
There is nothing that is not to be found here.
If an old man hurries to the city
He would recover his youth.
Everything that is good is found in
Hyderabad in plenty,
We find in the city all
That is fortunate and nothing that
Causes pain or sorrow...'

This little verse is to be found in the Tarekh-e-Qutub Shahi, a history written about twenty-five years after the foundation of Hyderabad.

Modern Hyderabad, the city I had not visited for nearly half a century, is growing fast but from what I could see well and with foresight. High tech companies like Microsoft are located just outside the city and along with various well known banks like HSBC and GE Capital Bank have major centres providing work and research within its perimeters. Cyberabad is now its other name, and it is so well placed in the centre of India, just a little to the south, that I am in no doubt it will overtake cities like Bangalore in the actual south. I was worried that the almost fifty year interval since I had been there would have shrouded it in shabby over-population and the detritus that is almost inevitable with population pressure and the poverty that is intrinsic to that. Not so; Hyderabad is alive and well and looking beautiful. Its previous chief minister apparently had been a man of clear foresight and made sure that the city has a private cleansing contract and what a difference this does make. It was obvious wherever one drove that daily maintenance was undertaken.

This might sound a silly thing on which to harp, but for one who knew these various great cities half a century ago it is often deeply depressing to see them now mired in effluent and litter and all the tangible detritus of a struggling, even if valiant, population. Admittedly India as a whole knows that this is a huge and challenging problem which she has to conquer, or at least try very hard to overcome but here was the positive result if there is a determined commitment to do it. When I lived in India in the late 1950s and early 1960s the population was about half a billion people. Now it is over a billion and rising. The same land mass, the same streets, parks, ancient historic sites, wildlife parks, rivers, lakes and valleys now have twice the number of people. Here in Scotland we have in this tiny country about five million people with a declining population which will lead to some serious demographic problems within twenty years. Should somehow magically the population double to ten million people in a decade I can just imagine the chaos in our infrastructure, schools, hospitals, roads and leisure facilities. Unless a country has almost unlimited wealth the decay of urban pressure begins to show very quickly. Now, thankfully in India with its burgeoning economic wealth maybe there will be a reversal of this sad downhill struggle. Authorities and public bodies recognise that antiquities and heritage sites have to be renovated and maintained; in this huge journey we saw masses of Indians really enjoying their heritage which was heartening; they may not as yet all understand the importance of it and how they can play a part in its maintenance but definitely there were plenty of Indians enjoying palaces and forts, temples and ancient cities as well as strolling in public gardens and enjoying family leisure time.

The hotel itself was a sheer pleasure to be in with thoughtful décor, not the usual 'bog standard' type furniture throughout. Right from the start the hotel group has carved out a distinctly Indian identity. Each of its hotels is rooted in the soil, culture, history and ethos of its home. I have now visited or stayed in all the major five star properties and they each have an unmistakable personality and presence. They are named after the various dynasties of the region – the famous dynastic names of Chola in Chennai, Maurya in Delhi, Mughal in Agra, Kakatiya in Hyderabad, Maratha in Mumbai and Rajputana in Jaipur. In each hotel the décor and artefacts adorning it are designed around the historical details of each of these dynasties.

The welcome was superb and the facilities excellent. US President Bill Clinton, Russian President Vladimir Putin, Tony Blair and other European leaders plus business luminaries like Bill Gates regularly stay in these hotels, and indeed President George W Bush was due to stay in The Maurya Sheraton on his visit to Delhi in March. I could

Charminar, Hyderabad 2

understand why; our welcome and the service shown to us were warm and friendly. There are a number of restaurants and the three I sampled in the Kakatiya were my favourites. Bukhara provides the best of north Indian tandoori cuisine based on flesh baked in the tandoor. You see the chefs cooking it in front of you and the tastes and flavours are sublime. 'Bukhara' has now become a brand which was voted the Best Indian Restaurant in the world by Restaurant Magazine in 2003. Graham and I made the Peshawari restaurant in the Kakatiya our first port of call for lunch on our first day; just writing about it makes my mouth water. The food is so fresh and simple – char-grilled lamb and chicken or seafood on skewers with great big fresh naan, rotis and dhals and fragrant basmati rice. This is my idea of sheer gastronomic bliss, followed by my favourite *rasmalai* pudding which is a sort of fragrant ball of rose water and cardamom scented cream in milky syrup. Graham likes *gulab jamuns* of which I have written previously; fresh and in warm syrup they too are truly delectable plus his adored *jalebis*. A fresh piece of pineapple can finish such a meal cleanly.

The morning had been well spent meeting various people and then meeting our driver Prasad. I always use International Travel House cars and drivers for their reliability and high standard of English and smart appearance and willingness to be helpful. He looked after us beautifully and I was able to try out my rusty Hindi/Urdu on him which was good for me though probably painful for the other person;

however in about two or three days usually my vocabulary increases and phrases and verbs fall naturally into place. In the south of India I knew I would not have much opportunity to practise as the south is famous for its many other languages, none of which I speak. I asked him to take us on a drive round the city to familiarise myself with the old place and show Graham what I had been talking about for so long. This was time well spent and that is how I realised about the city's cleanliness – every roundabout or traffic island was well maintained let alone the kerbs and pavements. I immediately saw something that haunted me; in the middle of a smallish roundabout there was a woman cutting the grass with hand shears and alongside her, playing and just sitting, were her family of tiny children. They looked so vulnerable and I wanted to stop and scoop them up and take them to what we would consider a safe children's playground – but – this is India, with the traffic snarling around these little ones dutifully sat and watched whilst their mother worked. In every journey I make within India there is always something particular that haunts me, now I know that after this journey that image of that resigned, working, simple woman and her tiny children sitting good as gold, stays in my memory. All I can say is: find a way to give responsibly, it will not eradicate that troubling memory but it will help someone.

Hyderabad is known by its symbol the Charminar, of which I will write more in due course. Rocks however were in my abiding memory and now this long neglected feature is beginning to be associated with the city – its ancient rocks! These rocks are part of the Indian Peninsular Gneissic Complex spread over a large area covering parts of the states of Andhra Pradesh, Karnataka and Madhya Pradesh. The rocks sprang from the earth's molten crust as a result of its rotation many millennia ago. The rocks are older than the Grand Canyon of the United States, older than even the Himalayas. It is estimated that they are about 2,500 million years old.

I had this very clear memory of a city covered in the most wonderful rocks, or boulders as I came to think of them. Huge areas of them and indeed the house in which we stayed in 1958 had a lovely garden dominated by rocky formations, one of which made a very natural swimming pool, which really took my imagination. Sadly greedy commercialism has resulted in the indiscriminate quarrying of the beautiful rocks around Hyderabad and Golconda, but thankfully the Society to Save Rocks was formed in 1996 and they, together with a more enlightened local government, have realised how vital they are to the local ecology and beauty of their area. Most of the big rock formations have names like 'the three wise men', 'piercing the sky' and 'looking for prey'. In the 1990s some distinguished visitors to Hyderabad apparently preferred these natural forms of art to the man-made structures to which they had been invited; I think because of these sorts of candid comments the powers that be looked again and appreciated their natural inheritance. In a way they are even more precious than fauna and flora because they can be encouraged to grow again, whereas these massive and hard-looking rocks once destroyed will never grow back. They are indeed a part of a vanishing wilderness, and Henry Thoreau rightly warned more than a century ago "...in Wilderness is the preservation of the world".

There is truly so much to see in and around Hyderabad; there was no way that we could attempt all of this in our short stay but Graham loved the place and I have no doubt that we will return on a more leisurely visit. When I am back in India after an interval one of the first things I like to do, indeed need to do, is walk among the people, hear the language, smile and interact. This is easily achieved of course but with a short visit everything had to be distilled into small precious moments. We loved the road, Tankbund Road, along the edge of the lake. We had Prasad stop the car so we could walk and enjoy the evening air and look at all the new statues to India's famous men. The lake itself is very pleasant with a statue of Buddha which is 17 metres high, which is reputedly the second largest in the world – I do not know, it seems to me that Sri Lanka too has very big statues but I was not about to argue about this. We had visited the Birla Mandir (temple) earlier in the day and enjoyed that but one is not allowed to photograph inside it, however the view from the peak on which it is built – some of the rocks – gave a wonderful view of the whole area. The mandir was built in sculpted white marble, a temple of Lord Venkateshwara, which is a replica of an even more important one at Tirumala. In the evening we visited a Craft Fair in the Indira Park alongside the lake; that was both fun and interesting and so nice to interact with all the various stall holders from all over India. We bought a few small things to show willing but mostly just enjoyed seeing all the wonderful items from the length and breadth of India. When I look at the photographs I took at the fair yet again I realise how vibrantly colourful everything in India is, certainly at handicraft level of art and objets d'art. The pottery would brighten up any kitchen and the wooden toys are delightful. We bought some wooden tops for our grandsons. The furniture was amazing – intricately carved and in fact comfortable but not in a style that would really fit in here in the West, those items would look wonderful set out on cool marble floors with high ceilings and arches. I particularly like the items made out of hand made paper which are so individual, and the painting or intricate drawings on the paper have a special quality. Of course there was brassware and hand blocked fabrics and carpets and dhurries in wonderful colours.

A place worth visiting for the first time visitor is Shilaparamam, an ethnic arts and crafts village right next to Cyber Towers in Hi-tech City. The model village is spread over 30 acres and hosts a number of bazaars annually to encourage talented rural artisans from all over India. This venture has received the national Tourism Award for the best eco-friendly project in the country – a prize awarded by the Government of India. It is quite fun to stroll round it in the cool of the evening with all the bright lights and activity.

Hyderabad is however especially famous for Kondapalli toys carved out of wood. Kondapalli is a village near Vijayawada, also in Andhra Pradesh which is about 170 miles from Hyderabad. We know very little about the origins of this toy making; some of the artisans trace their origins back to Arya Kshatriyas of Rajasthan who migrated to the south in the 16th century. The toys are charming though relatively rough; they depict everyday life as well as ceremonial pieces and are very light being made from *punki* wood. The wood of a young tree is called *tella ponikki*, while the wood from a mature tree is called *nalla ponikki*. The toys are exclusively carved from the young wood. My childhood memory was very clear about them and though none had survived down the years I was determined to find some and buy them for our grandsons. We did find the most wonderful choice in a government craft shop called Lepakshi. Graham and I were so entranced that we bought so many it became a problem as to how to carry them and indeed we had to send them back to Scotland by post. Sadly some became damaged as they really are quite fragile but Graham will work on those that are worth saving and the rest are charming. Piers and William will receive them in due course as they are too small just now to treat them with respect. Now, you will be glad to know, that indiscriminate felling of the trees is not allowed and the toys are only carved from wood grown in managed plantations. The spirit of these toys is embodied in their depictions: characters and aspects of rural life with figures representing villages, armies, deities and animals are there in their hundreds from which to choose.

The Charminar must be the iconic image of Hyderabad; it was built by Mahammed Quli Qutub Shah in 1591 and it stands right in the midst of what constitutes the 'Old City' today, encompassing 45 prayer spaces and a mosque. Built in the Indo-Saracenic style the four elegant *minars* rise to a height of 180 feet with 146 steps taking one to the top. Char is the Urdu/Hindi word for the figure four. Charminar is also the name given to a brand of cigarette for which ITC is famous. They apparently roughly resemble Gauloises in taste and are also pretty addictive so I am informed. They are cheap and meant for any and every man to be able to enjoy. Cigarette smoking is an emotive subject but in India millions of people still smoke and I do not see that culture changing at all quickly – it is truly the opium of the masses.

We went and visited the Charminar briefly because in the middle of the day it is a nightmare trying to walk to it in the centre of swirling traffic, but at least Graham was able to see it and at night it is suitably floodlit; I consider it ranks with the Taj Mahal and the Eiffel Tower as an emblem. The bazaars around the Charminar are much the same as they were from my memory, and probably for the last several centuries! Laad Bazaar offers all the exotica of India with gorgeous glass or lacquer bangles, silver filigree work and Bidri curios. The latter is a special form of fine silver inlay in gunmetal which looks very handsome and stands the test of time, and many objects have an elegance about them that is modern and appealing to western tastes.

The Nizams had a legendary collection of jewellery. The Government of India purchased the collection in 1995 from the Nizam Jewellery Trust formed by the last Nizam, Mir Osman Ali Khan way back in 1952. The collection is exhibited in both Delhi and Hyderabad and is calculated to have a worth of Rs 1500 crore, which by my reckoning at a value of Rs70 to the British pound is approximately £21.5 million. It is just amazing with the most wonderful sarpeches, necklaces, belts and buckles, pairs of bracelets and bangles, earrings, armlets, toe rings, finger rings, pocket watches and other items like cuff links. The diamonds were mined at Golconda, very near to Hyderabad, but Colombian emeralds predominate and the Burmese rubies and spinels and pearls from Basra and the Gulf of Mannar off the east coast of India are amazing. Most outstanding among this collection is the Imperial diamond, now known as the Jacob diamond, weighing 184.75 carats, which is a fabulous weight for any single gemstone. Twenty-two emerald pieces form yet another set of jewellery and as for the pearls, beloved all of the Nizams, well they are of such a weight and size to be truly amazing. I have seen some of this collection, not in Hyderabad but on loan at the British Museum in 2001.

In my view the real gem in Hyderabad's sumptuous crown of antiquities is Golconda Fort. The name originates from the Telegu words *Golla konda* meaning 'Shepherd Hill'. Originally a mud fort, it passed from the Kakatiyas of Warangal to the Bahmani dynasty and later to the Qutub Shahis, who held it from 1518 to 1687 AD. The fort is famous for its acoustics, palaces and ingenious water supply and drainage system, which ensured water reached some of the highest points in the fort. A unique sound and light show narrates the saga of Golconda and this particular *son et lumière* is considered one of the

Golconda Fort

best in India. The fort that had originally been built in 1143 was passed on to the Mughals under Aurangzeb in 1687. I saw it first as a child and was awed by its size. It has massive battlements and the fort rises to a height of 400 feet and provided security for an entire kingdom. Within its walls there were palaces six floors high and courtyards with fountains and small tanks or artificial lakes. As a child I was enchanted with the experience of clapping my hands at the entrance of the inner fort, it could be heard at the top of the fort thus providing instantaneous communication.

Now I hear that a golf course is being constructed within so that enthusiastic golfers can play in a unique setting of an ancient historic fort. I could see that appealing to our golfing friends who tour the world finding new courses and environments in which to enjoy their game – we are not golfers sadly but I do value the social side of the game.

I cannot leave the subject of Golconda without referring to the famous Kohinoor diamond. Golconda was a renowned market for precious gems and the area specialised in the cutting and polishing of diamonds. As far back at 1645 Tavernier, a French jeweller, wrote that he had witnessed seeing 60,000 artisans at work. The Kohinoor is one of the legendary diamonds mined at Kallur in the Golconda sultanate. It has a weight of 108.93 carats and somehow became the possession

19

of Ranjit Singh, a Sikh warrior, who was vanquished by the British. His successor gave it to Queen Victoria. In 1937 it was mounted in the crown with which HM Queen Elizabeth, the consort of King George VI, was crowned. Indian MPs clamour from time to time for its return to India, but I actually hope it remains where it is for us all to enjoy on a visit to HM Tower of London.

The Qutub Shahi Tombs, lying a kilometre to the north of Golconda, are a combination of Persian, Pathan and Hindu styles of architecture. They were planned and built during the reign of each Qutub Shahi King; trellised balconies, overlapping arches, arched corridors and rich ornamental parapets make the monument spectacular. Apparently these tombs are unique in that the entire dynasty is buried there: that seldom happens in history.

Frankly there is just so much to see in Hyderabad – the Mecca Masjid, the Paigah Tombs, the Legislative Assembly building which became the Legislative Assembly of Andhra Pradesh when the state was formed in 1956, Osmania University and the Salarjung Museum and Andhra Pradesh State Museum. We visited the latter two and found them immensely interesting. Sometimes the exhibits are rather odd and this gives the experience something special. The Salarjung Museum is in fact a horde of treasure named after Salar Jung III and apparently is the largest single-man collection of artefacts in the world. It is still rather naively mounted and has yet to reach the sophistication of museum exhibitions in the West but nevertheless very interesting. I actually derive as much pleasure from observing the local people going round their own heritage. They are always curious and politely shy and love to engage in a conversation.

It is interesting to note that again Hyderabad has been chosen for a US presidential visit; in 2000 President Clinton visited Hyderabad and now George W Bush is due to spend a few hours in the city at the end of his visit to India. "I think it is the right city in India to visit...it is the most happening place in India...I am sure his visit will help the city to emerge on the international map...the beauty about Hyderabad is that it is a city of all religions; all of us live peacefully." These are some of the views expressed locally.

Chapter Three

The Pearl City and Ancient Andhra Pradesh

The pearl trade prospered in Hyderabad for centuries under the royal patronage of the Qutub Shahi kings and the Asaf Jahis. The Nizams of the State of Hyderabad loved pearls and in the old days not only did the Nizams wear ropes of pearls studded with diamonds as part of their regalia but they used crushed pearls as beauty aids. The princesses were covered in pearls and were weighed against them on their birthdays. Under their patronage pearl merchants from all over India flocked to Hyderabad. It is alleged that Osman Ali, the richest of the Nizams, stored pearls and diamonds in sacks in basement chambers of his palaces.

Originally the pearls were sourced in Basra (with which we are all too familiar with the current Iraq War). The Persian Gulf was a great source for pearls and this is highlighted in the history of the United Arab Emirates and Dubai. However the advent of oil led to the surrounding sea becoming polluted and this trade has dwindled. Nowadays the pearls are sourced in Japan and of course natural pearls are hugely expensive, whereas cultured pearls are, depending on the quality, quite reasonable. The markets are filled with scores of pearl shops from which to choose and the big hotels also have pearl shops in their arcades. I bought some very nice items as gifts and also for myself from a government emporium. If I had the joy of an unlimited piggy bank the choice was truly amazing, but as it is I have bought sizes of pearls that in this country would sell for large sums of money. I have not yet met the girl or woman who is not delighted with a gift of some form in pearls!

Nirmal is another local speciality. Funnily enough nearly fifty years ago the Nirmal work was full of lovely sophisticated objects from which to choose. Since then it has narrowed to rather lurid pictures on the beautifully lacquered wood. Bowls, plaques and flat pictures in beautiful Nirmal workmanship were wonderful gifts and immensely dramatic and stylish. Somehow that is something that has diminished and frankly I don't consider that the average international traveller would really want to buy a modern piece.

Hyderabad has some rather interesting modern choices, most of which do nothing for me, but I feel I must mention them. It has the world's largest 3D IMAX theatre;, the world's largest snow theme park;, the Birla Science Museum and Planetarium, and some film studios.

Something that is interesting and a little bit different is the Obelisk to Michel Joachim Marie Raymond who died in March 1798. He had become a legendary figure by the time of his death at only 42. Raymond was a French adventurer who became a military commander and the Nizam's confidant. He came to be revered by Hindus and was known as 'Musa Ram' and as 'Musa Rahim' by the Muslims. When Pondicherry fell to the British in 1778, the young Frenchman became a soldier of fortune; he journeyed to Mysore and joined the service of Hyder Ali, the 'Tiger Chief'. When Ali died in 1785 he joined the French Corps under Basalat Jung, the Nizam's brother, and then he entered the service of Nizam Ali Khan, the second Nizam of Hyderabad. Honestly there is so much to see in and around Hyderabad but I am going to stop with the next suggestion: the Shahi Khilwat Hkana was one of the royal buildings constructed during the reign of Nawab Nizam Mir Osman Ali Khan. The Nizam VII renovated the building in 1911 and inaugurated the new structure in 1913. All the Mughal and British durbars were held in this palace. It is quite close to the Charminar.

Falaknuma Palace was considered the most opulent of the Nizams' many palaces; it was built in 1872 and has a European façade but an Indo-Saracenic set of domes and cupolas in which the zenana or women's quarters were housed. Like at Gwalior and other palatial homes a huge amount of money was spent on it with Florentine craftsmen from Italy and tapestries from France and marble also imported from Italy. King George V stayed at Falaknuma but after the death of the sixth Nizam at the palace in 1911 – probably from alcohol poisoning – it was rarely used. I believe that there is a plan to convert the building into a luxurious hotel which would be lovely; heritage hotels have a special quality about them I think. This palace was in fact the royal guest house for the Nizams' guests so when it evolves as a modern hotel it will still be serving its purpose but in a twenty-first century manner.

I had a clear memory of the Secunderabad Club as a beautiful country club with a lovely outdoor pool in which I swam those long years ago. We visited it in the twin city of Secunderabad, which used to be like a garden suburb city of Hyderabad. The way the area has grown Hyderabad and Secunderabad are now totally entwined but the club is there and obviously very popular and well maintained. The old outdoor pool has a twin and it too looked very inviting and I suppose if I had asked to go and look up the register of members we would have found my parents' names. It was comforting that the place was full of people and popular, it would have been sad to see something so good in decay.

Hyderabad is well known for its cuisine. At the Kakatiya we had decided to eat at the Dum Pukht. Dum Pukht is a restaurant that has been established in the top ITC hotels because it is dedicated to a 200 year old culinary tradition of slow cooking food, in sealed 'deghs'. The fragrance of the meal becomes very enticing and though one can be seated at conventional tables it is also quite fun to sit at the low tables on a sort of very short-legged bolstered chair as would have been the way centuries ago in the houses of nobles. We had dined in the Dum Pukht on our first night and thoroughly enjoyed the whole experience. I had dined in the similar restaurant in The Maurya in Delhi and totally loved it. This is the sort of meal with which to have a good Indian wine. Maharashtra is the wine land of India and we enjoyed a very good red, and I might add the Indian equivalent of 'champagne' is also very pleasing. Hyderabad is perhaps most associated with *biryani* which is a fragrant rice dish with many different ingredients. I love rice, particularly Basmati rice and lamb, or chicken or vegetable biryanis are delectable served with a meat or vegetable curry or dhal and raita. Irani *chai* is the popular drink that most Hyderabadi men consume in the multitude of cafes. Often the buying of a chai is simply an excuse to have another cigarette, but these are the meeting houses of Hyderabad; however I would not think of sitting down in one of these; life is still old fashioned here and these are really men only places, like the old pubs in Scotland fifty years ago!

Lunch is a pleasant affair at Dakshin, the restaurant which has brought together the evolved cuisines of the four southern states – Andhra Pradesh, Karnataka, Tamil Nadu and Kerala. It was most beautifully served on banana leaves and thalis and the food was mouth watering. We could have eaten at a hundred different places but as our time was limited we chose to stay with the hotel's choice and were not disappointed. We both knew there was a long journey ahead of us and plenty of opportunity in which to be adventurous with food, but just at the beginning of such an adventure it is sometimes wise to be more circumspect and eat where there is guaranteed quality, ambience and hygiene.

Machilipatnam is a town about 211 miles east of Hyderabad. It was one of the first European settlements on India's eastern coast – it means the City of Fish – *machli* – is fish in Hindi. It was a thriving port and textile centre in the 17th and 18th centuries and became the headquarters of the English East India Company on the Coromandel Coast; the French and the Dutch too briefly achieved a foothold here. The local cemetery is full of Dutch obelisks. I am mentioning it because in 1883 the town was hit by a giant tidal wave – a tsunami – except no-one outside Japan knew that word then. 30,000 people perished and the wave was a result of the enormous eruption of Mount Krakatoa, the volcano thousands of miles away in Indonesia. That eruption of Krakatoa was felt at Lisbon and indeed up the River Thames in London. The tsunami of 2004 would appear to have been on a par with that dreadful natural disaster. The region was famous in the 18th century for its *kalamkari* fabric which became known to us in Europe as chintz. The Tree of Life design and motif was the famous design of Machilipatnam and that endures to this day with its variations on the theme. After the devastation of the 1883 tsunami the port became unimportant though the textile production continues to thrive. I was in India post-tsunami and felt that I should research any previous tidal waves. I had not really expected to find one of the same magnitude just 120 years before. In 2004 hundreds yet again lost their lives in this place; the Anglican Church of Canada talks of "A colossal loss of life, the victims especially being little children who were residents of orphanages run by NGOs (non-governmental organisations) and church organisations close to the sea shore…the information received is that a whole lorry load of little children, almost 100 in number were picked up dead strewn on the sands of the sea shore…".

I wrote earlier of the fact that my father was located at Guntur. This was a very ordinary sort of medium size Indian town with nothing special or remarkable about it. However modern day Andhra Pradesh has developed the various ancient monuments and the natural beauty spots surrounding it. Twenty miles to the north of Guntur on the right bank of the river Krishna is Amaravati; this was a great international centre of Buddhism for nearly 1600 years from the third century BC. Now there is very little for a visitor to actually see but that is really because of the vandalism and negligence of various authorities including the British. In 1958 archaeologists were still discovering valuable information at Amaravati and I was too young to understand the significance of it all but we did visit it.

Dhanyakataka was the full name of Amaravati; it rose to glory as the fortified eastern capital of the later Satavahana monarchs. It became one of the greatest seats of Buddhism in early times and it is acknowledged that Buddhist teaching and thinking flowed from here to Burma, Thailand, the Indonesian archipelago, Sri Lanka and Afghanistan. The ancient metropolis, which extended three-and-a half miles in length, is now reduced to the dusty little village of

Dharanikota. The amazing fortifications of this once noble city lie in ruins of massive embankments of earth and broken bricks. It is now known that Dhanyakataka became the focus of Buddhist culture. The Maha Stupa at Amaravati was the most stupendous monument of ancient India and the greatest architectural achievement of Buddhism. Through archaeology it has been discovered that the Romans and other empires did a flourishing trade with this region. The mouth of the Krishna River was navigable quite far inland. Ptolemy, the famous Alexandrian geographer, mathematician and astronomer, speaks of a people called the Andhras; the trade on the East Coast and the various ports, one of which Maisolia – Machilipatnam as it is now known, was renowned for its cotton garments. The ancient market town of this region specified in the inscriptions is Dhanyakataka in 250 BC.

Buddhist art and architecture appears to have reached its zenith at this spot and those of us who have visited the ancient capitals of Sri Lanka can see how much they were influenced by Amaravati at Anuradhapura and Sigirya. There must have been a large flourishing literate Buddhist kingdom here which influenced places that are now world famous such as Borobudur in Javanese Indonesia. In Sri Lanka, Anuradhapura was their first great stupa which is being carefully renovated. How sad that so little is left of this wonderful civilisation, but there is a great deal of fine sculpture on display at the Archaeological Museum next to the Maha Chaitya and in museums across India as well as in the British Museum. Unlike the stupa at Sanchi of which I wrote in my second book, India: The Tiger's Roar, where the Buddha is represented through symbols such as the Bodhi Tree or footprints, the Amaravati sculptures depict him in stylised human form. The museum has large standing Buddha images, some of which are more than seven feet high. It is suggested that the carving of these was influenced by Roman classical art.

Nagarjunakonda is another place in the Guntur district that has wonderful relics of a Buddhist settlement. Once there must have been large monasteries and stupas, wide roads and public baths and it was a flourishing town in the era of the Ikshvaku kings. In the early 1960s, when the huge Nagarjuna Sagar Dam was being constructed across the Krishna River, a number of these ancient Buddhist settlements were threatened with submersion. It is worth mentioning that the Nagarjuna Sagar Dam is reckoned to be the largest masonry dam in the world with a height of 124 metres, and apparently the artificial lake that resulted is the world's largest man-made lake. I do recall when it was being built that India was very proud of her engineering. Thankfully however, the Archaeological Survey of India salvaged and reconstructed the various priceless ruins and rebuilt them on the top of the hill where the citadel once stood. Now the dam waters surround this hill top and it resembles an island and can be visited by launch from the banks of the new lake.

The Buddhist Trail is very popular with travellers from the Far East and I encountered large coach loads of these people when we visited Sanchi in Madhya Pradesh. I think India has only awakened to the potential for the Buddhist pilgrimage trail within the last few years. I suppose a country in which millions of its own people regularly go on pilgrimage to the various Hindu shrines let alone those of any other belief, is blasé about this form of tourism. It is worth remembering for westerners that the very first tourists in Europe were pilgrims who put themselves through the danger and excitement of pilgrimages to Canterbury and other religious centres in Britain but also as far away as Rome, northern Spain and Jerusalem. The very idea of all that walking, and jolting along on horseback, or in carts, with indifferent, perhaps dangerous, inns on the road, plus the real possibility of robbery and murder, makes me feel weak. Medieval Christians must indeed have had a sure faith to sustain them on those journeys.

The Rig Veda, which is dated to at least 1,200 years before Christ, reveals information on the Andhras, a tribal people. Pliny, the Roman author, who must have drawn on the knowledge of Megasthanes the Greek ambassador at the court of Chandragupta Maurya, wrote of a powerful race near the eastern coast of India between the great rivers – Godavari and the Krishna – with lands that encompassed 30 towns defended by walls and towers. Andhradesa as it was known had a huge army of 100,000 infantry, 2,000 cavalry and 1,000 elephants and was second only in power and dominance to Pataliputra the kingdom of Chandragupta himself. Buddha apparently actually brought his new religion to this region and that is why modern day Buddhist pilgrims have such a reverence for this particular pilgrim trail.

All I can say is that having lived for a short time in that area and crossed those mighty and sacred rivers and now as a mature adult revisited the area nearly half a century later, I am once again comforted by the fact that whatever faith one follows, a land and its people over the ages endures and evolves and now in flourishing Andhra Pradesh modern Indians can take comfort from their ancient heritage but look forward to the economic future which is full of promise.

There are so many temple trails and pilgrimage sites in Andhra Pradesh but truly one of the greatest is Tirupati. This is a place 364 miles south of Hyderabad but is considered to eclipse St Peter's Basilica in Roma, Mecca and Jerusalem in the number of pilgrims who visit it. I did not go there, but you may recall I wrote earlier of the temple dedicated to Lord Venkateshwara called the Birla Mandir in Hyderabad which we did visit. That is a small replica of this great temple that draws Hindu pilgrims from all over India. Tirumala Devasthanam, or the abode of Lord Ventakteshwara, is considered to rival Varanasi in its importance to Hindus; it is about 4 km from Tirupati railway station and there is even a small airport with connecting flights from Hyderabad. The ancient myth is that Lord Vishnu, one of the Hindu *trimurthi* or triumvirate of Brahma, Vishnu and Shiva decided to come and live here for the benefit of humanity. The actual sacred spot on the top of the hill is known as Tirumala. The seven hills of Tirupati are considered to resemble the seven hoods of the serpent Adisesha on whom Lord Vishnu sleeps. It is one of the very few temples to allow non-Hindus into the Sanctum Sanctorum. On an average day more than 25,000 people visit the shrine and more than 15,000 pilgrims tonsure their heads everyday. Pilgrims mostly stay free of charge in huge dormitories that surround the temple and of course there are a whole range of hotels for most budgets.

The logistics of running such a shrine are immense as all devotees are given *laddus* a very rich form of Indian sweet as *prasadam*, a sort of devotional reward. The daily production of laddus amounts to 125,000: utilising 100 bags of sugar; 275 tins of clarified butter which weigh 15 kgs each; 90 bags of Bengal gram dhal weighing 50 kgs each; 90 10 kgs tins of cashew nuts; 200 kgs of cardamoms and 30 15 kgs boxes of raisins. 225 temple employees produce the sweet daily between 03.00 hours and 22.00 hours. Other forms of sweets are also made including Graham's favourite jalebis!

The temple earns crores of rupees, which is equivalent to many millions of pounds annually from the sale of human hair. There are 1,200 barbers on a monthly salary who keep the tonsure centre running 24 hours! On the subject of the sale of the hair it is interesting that the US, the UK, Indonesia and Malaysia are the chief importers. Tirupati Temple entered the Guinness Book of World Records for the largest donation of hair in 1999 – 6,500,000 donations – and now the temple authorities are planning to market the hair to the various wig manufacturers worldwide. Male and female hair is kept separately in 14 steel containers and about 208,000 kilograms of human hair earned the temple authorities Rs19 crore. It is believed that as hair usually enhances a human's appearance the sacrifice of cutting it off enhances the individual's potential for being granted his or her wish.

I am glad to be able to write about a temple which is essentially dedicated to Vishnu, as in the rest of south India most of the temples are dedicated to Shiva. Vishnu is the preserver and a benevolent aspect of God whereas Shiva is the destroyer. Here at Tirumala, Vishnu is worshipped as Venkateshwara the God who fulfils desires. Lakshmi the Goddess of wealth is his consort. I wrote of Vishnu and Lakshmi in my second book, India: The Tiger's Roar, when describing the annual festivals of Dussera followed by Diwali. Vishnu has ten avatars or incarnations. It is believed that he descends to earth periodically to redress the balance between good and evil. The Kondapalli craftsmen make wonderful little wooden carved images of his ten avatars, but the tenth it is believed is yet to come; Buddha is considered by Hindus to be his ninth incarnation, so you can see how the two faiths can intertwine.

Andhra Pradesh is the home of a living, apparently wise, saintly man called Satya Sai Baba who preaches religious tolerance, universal love and service to others. He has a following of thousands, both internationally and within India, but is also the subject of considerable controversy. I have no intention of writing about him but feel that in a chapter about Andhra's ancient spiritual and pilgrim sites I must mention a place that is the destination for so many modern pilgrims and people seeking peace, enlightenment or spiritual comfort. Puttaparthi is where the current Sai Baba has established his ashram.

Chapter Four

Dinkie the Mouse Deer

As a child on that holiday long years ago I loved staying at the beach. Perhaps because I had such happy memories of the fun at the company's beach house at Puri I had thought it might be very similar, but it was entirely different.

Chirala was a small village on the coast of Andhra Pradesh at the end of a very long and dusty drive. The beach house was made out of coconut matting creating a whole series of rooms and bedrooms and bathrooms with a big veranda. The plinth of the house was raised and made out of cement. It was a simple retreat with electricity only available intermittently. Anyone going there for a week's holiday had to take or make their own amusement and this we did. The house was set in the midst of a small clearing in the sea pines or casuarina trees with a very short walk of about ten metres to the beach. The beach was immense and at that time without any development whatsoever. Unlike Puri in the state of Orissa there appeared to be no fishing population on the beach, or even a beach village as I was to encounter in Kerala. No, there was nothing but us...and the crabs. We would go swimming cautiously, because the breakers were big and we didn't have the expertise of the fishermen to advise us. Sharks appeared not to have been any sort of threat but the beach had its challenges and my swimming was limited to the very shallow water. The real treat of the day however was to walk up and then down the beach with literally thousands of little red crabs walking ahead of one. It was at first very disconcerting, and I am not sure that had I been entirely on my own that I would have done it more than once, but with the parents I felt safe. When I say thousands I really am not exaggerating; it seemed that as one walked the pressure and rhythm of our walking made every single crab emerge out of its sandy burrow and walk along or scamper ahead of us. I wish we had had a camera because it really was worthy of a David Attenborough film shoot. The beach was really long and white fringed with green palm trees and sea pines and the crabs were

Author on her mother's lap at about the age she first travelled on an elephant

bright red so in my mind's eye there still exists this picture of us slowly advancing with a sea of red crustaceans with their pop-up eyes walking ahead of us and the blue ocean on one side. When we stopped they stopped, when we moved they moved. Then one day a friend of my father's came to lunch and we invited him to join us and see this phenomenon; he seemed very cautious and then said that on the homeward walk, were they to be inclined, we would be completely overrun by the army of red crabs and how would we cope? I was appalled, until he had suggested the idea it had not occurred and we did not think we were on the verge of being victims in a horror film.

I really do not know if Chirala, which is also recognised for weaving some of the world's best sarees, has been swallowed up in development and it really was too far to drive and find out on this visit – besides sometimes these happy memories are best left alone, but it was a happy family time with lots of reading and playing scrabble and simple card games and learning to shoot accurately with an air pistol at swinging targets of empty tin cans, and of course good food and plenty of lovely fresh fish, cooked for us by the family cook who had accompanied us. From time to time in our children's growing up years we had similar holidays up here in Scotland on the beautiful west coast. Sadly here however the weather can be horrible and sitting indoors and reading or watching television is almost compulsory for a lot of the time, but yet those holidays, on reflection, were very happy family times and we all made the most of the lovely dry and sunny days when we would wind sail on the lochs or have simple picnics with a fire and fry potatoes and sausages and drink plenty of cheap red wine. Mackerel were here in plenty off the Scottish coast in those days in the early 1980s and we would fish and relax in a boat on the sea loch and just drink in the scenery, then land on a small island only inhabited by a few sheep and collect lovely artistic stones or pieces of slate; the long silences in the boat were only interrupted by the occasional excitement of sighting a dolphin or a seal. The latter usually signalled poor fishing, but then we were not there really to catch fish but to use it as an excuse to be out in the beautiful environment that is the Scottish Highlands; happy days that I hope will be replicated for our grandchildren in the years to come.

Before arriving out from England for this holiday my father had told me in detail of the latest addition to our family, a Mouse Deer. Dinkie, as he was named, stood about a foot tall and was perfectly formed. My father had been in some country place and a man approached him and took out of his top pocket a minute baby fawn. He had offered it to Daddy who realised that the tiny creature would not have much of a future unless he took it, so he offered to buy it. He then took little Dinkie and slipped him into his own shirt pocket and brought him home. The tiny animal needed a lot of attention having been parted from his mother so early in life and father wondered how to feed it. This was resolved by Kesri, our wonderful sweeper who was an Untouchable, or in today's modern infinitely more acceptable terms, a member of the Dalit caste. I had always had a great affection for Kesri who was gifted with animals and in other ways too. He was a bit of a musician and was very good at modelling little figures in minute detail. He also cooked rather well and made delicious rotis, which I ate, though clearly at that time in the 1950s this would have not been encouraged by the rest of the household. Kesri decided that the only way to feed this little scrap of an animal was to teach him to suck on a cloth steeped in a dish of milk. Dinkie picked up the idea very easily and loved his milk, and then he was fed a sort of gruel as well to help him grow and then lots of fruit. He absolutely adored loquats, seedless grapes and other sweet small fruit and some leaves that Kesri knew would not harm him. We taught him to come and stand by our chairs at the dining table and fed him all his favourites. Dinkie lived his entire life inside because it was thought that large predatory birds would soon find him in the garden; moreover we owned a Siamese cat called Tigger and had he and Tigger had a confrontation we considered that the cat would have come off worse as Dinkie's little hooves were incredibly sharp and could do the most awful damage. Tigger lived outside with a bed on the veranda.

Dinkie loved to be petted and stroked and would sit at one's feet quietly in the sitting room. There was no way one could lift him up and give him a cuddle, he was still a wild animal, but just in a benevolent captivity for his own good. He also had his own little wooden house in a dressing room. Kesri and father had taught him to be house-trained.

He never made a mess anywhere once he was introduced to his own sand tray! When later on that year my parents made the huge long train journey up to Saharanpur in Uttar Pradesh to the north of Delhi, a journey that lasted in those days for more than two days, Dinkie travelled in their first class compartment and was allowed loose until they reached their destination. The little deer just sat quietly and accepted all that was happening around him. He particularly loved sitting in front of the open fire at night. Northern India becomes really cold in the winter and every night he would settle down to sleep in front of the glowing embers, and if you watched quietly he was sometimes so overcome that he gentled keeled over and was totally off his guard. I took particular pleasure when a new friend or stranger visited in watching their reactions. What they seemed to assume was just a stuffed deer would suddenly stick his long tongue out and wash his ears, or if he felt really energetic he would start to jink about and show off in front of us. It was a source of huge amusement to us to watch the various faces change from caution to sheer disbelief.

The Nagarjunasagar – Srisailam Sanctuary is in the Project Tiger scheme and the closest wildlife park to Guntur. It is really a dry, deciduous, mixed riverine forest rather than dense jungle and the River Krishna cuts through the Nallamalai hills forming deep gorges and valleys. Apparently tiger, panther (leopard), sloth bear, wild dog, jackal, wolf, fox, ratel, the Indian giant squirrel, tree shrew, chital, black buck, sambar, nilgai and wild boar inhabit this forest. I am confident that every animal except the tiger is present, though it is claimed that tiger still exist in this reserve – I do hope the authorities are right. As I have written in my second book, the tiger is under immense threat from population pressure and poaching and the sheer negligence and corruption of government departments. In April 2005 the Prime Minister Dr Manmohan Singh assumed personal control of tiger conservation. He took the chair of both the influential Tiger Steering Committee and Project Tiger, whose powers he significantly increased. I was appalled, along with all other people who care about tiger conservation at the ensuing revelations of poaching. When it was discovered that the very people who are entrusted with conservation and patrol had been found to be in league with poachers there was a sense of angry déjà vu as this had all occurred previously in the early 1980s. Fortunately the Indian Government appeared to feel a genuine embarrassment, and the fact that Indira Gandhi had set up Project Tiger probably influenced Sonia Gandhi her daughter-in-law, who currently wields huge power and influence to try and make amends. The trouble is that the sense of complacency that is beginning to envelop India at the moment because of the economic upsurge in her fortunes as a country, seems to act as a collective sedative. The world will not forgive India as a nation if the tiger is allowed to be poached out of extinction. Sadly the other huge emerging economic super power is the country guilty of exploiting the secret evil market of tiger parts. Chinese people appear to still think that the various body parts of a tiger will either cure all their ills or act as an aphrodisiac. Moreover their burgeoning bourgeoisie want to compete with each other by wearing exotic animal skins, regardless of the cruelty and waste of the lives and vital numbers of precious endangered species. The Chinese appear to be a very cruel race and allow such barbaric practises as skinning live animals and eating cats and dogs. They have cruel autocratic ideas about their people so I suppose it is no wonder they have no veneration whatsoever for their wildlife, or that of any other country.

There are seventeen wildlife sanctuaries in Andhra Pradesh and so if wildlife and peace and quiet is what you are after there is plenty from which to choose; indeed some of the sanctuaries are quite close to Hyderabad, and it has the largest zoo in India. Not everyone likes zoos, and indeed some Indian zoos are now pretty frightful, but Graham and I feel that good zoos do a great deal of good and inform people and allow them to become familiar with endangered species; that has the obvious beneficial effect of conveying the importance of conservation and it is the only way that the average little person becomes acquainted with huge exotic animals and begins to value them, other than as fictitious characters in a children's book. When writing this I think

Author making friends with the elephants in Kolkata

Author trying out sitting on an elephant, aged 7 years

immediately of that wonderful book The Life of Pi by Yann Martel. I loved that curious book which was all about a wonderful family who owned a zoo in Pondicherry and thought they would move lock, stock and barrel to Canada. Sadly the ship on which they are travelling is shipwrecked and only one son and various animals survive, which finally becomes one son and one tiger. I mention it simply because apart from being a very good read it highlights the importance and value of the tiger. Certainly the Edinburgh Zoo is well regarded and has a lovely array of tigers and other wonderful creatures. Piers and William, our grandsons, love an outing to the zoo.

In 1960 I was again out in India on a long summer holiday and by this time we lived in Kolkata or Calcutta as it then was named. We had gone for a wonderful beach holiday yet again to Puri in Orissa, but it was monsoon time and the railway line between Puri and Calcutta was washed away whilst we were down in Puri. The only way for us to return was to make a rail journey from Puri down to Visakhapatnam or 'Vizag' as it is known, and then change trains to travel inland to Nagpur, from which we then returned to Calcutta. The whole detour took three days but at least I had the opportunity of seeing Vizag. This flourishing sea port is India's second largest port next to Mumbai. It was then however rather a model town and appeared attractive. Much is said about how the modern city of Vizag is growing but it is well to remember that it was originally an ancient fishing port named after Visakha, the Hindu God of valour and once was part of the empire of Ashoka the Mauryan emperor. Through the centuries it was ruled by passing empires like the Pallavas, Cholas and Gangas. In the fifteenth century it became part of the Vijayanagar Empire for which Hampi, in Karnataka is very famous. In fact there are shrines dedicated to Christian, Hindu and Muslim saints and I recall the picturesque lighthouse with a beam that can be seen for 64 km or 40 miles. It somehow reminds me of lighthouses in France or Britain.

Andhra is very fortunate to have this tourists' paradise with lovely beaches and lush valleys. The traveller can find both beach sunshine and hillside cool. The cool hillsides around Araku provide the ideal climate for coffee growing. Tribal life is very well represented with nineteen tribes in the area. The real gem however is a place called Bheemunipatnam, twenty-five kilometres away. This is the second oldest municipality in the country and was a flourishing Dutch settlement and port. The beach at 'Bhimli' as it is still called is excellent with safe shallow bathing and there is a Dutch cemetery with old obelisks, the sort that one comes across all over India in neglected European cemeteries. Apparently as it is the headquarters of the Eastern Naval Command the Indian Navy conceived the idea of sprinkling the neighbouring hillsides with seeds of various indigenous trees by helicopter; the idea was successful and thousands of saplings have survived and are growing and turning the hillsides green. Buddhism flourished here centuries ago and helped to spread the faith to the Far East, but the God Vishnu is favoured in this part of the country and Vaishnavism still thrives with various temples dedicated to Lord Vishnu in his various avatars.

I had heard many many years later that my grandmother Aline who was French had relatives here and used to like to visit them annually. I cannot really find much out about the French elements of this developing city but it would make good sense as the French had positioned themselves all along the eastern coast of India. We planned to visit Pondicherry, one of the Union Territories that was French and is separate from Tamil Nadu, further south.

About 90 kilometres from Vizag en route to Araku there are the Borra Caves which are a million years old. The great attraction within the caves is the Shivalingam and an idol of a cow. This means a great deal to the local tribes people but the caves themselves are interesting and well presented by the tourism authorities. The Aruku valley is populated by numerous hill tribes who seem to flourish here and are very colourful; they appear not to be threatened in any way as sadly has been the case in central India with the progress of the Narmada Dam project on the sacred Narmada River. It warms the heart to see tribes people still happy and flourishing in what appears to be a time capsule, and I just hope that may continue. Chattisgarh, the state that was formed from the eastern side of Madhya Pradesh in 2000, which is to the north of Andhra Pradesh, has a large number of tribal people also; naturally they are all special but I feel that unless governments are very determined modern progress will erode their way of life, particularly when minerals or ore are found in large amounts on their ancestral lands and big commercial interests become greedy.

Northern Andhra Pradesh was in ancient times known as Telengana; the language Telegu originates here and is one of the major languages of Andhra Pradesh. This part of the country had been in the Chalukyan Empire but then it became an independent kingdom under the Kakatiya ruler in the eleventh century, who was himself a vassal of the Chalukyans. The goddess Kakati or Durga is the family deity for the Kakatiyas and they ruled for almost three hundred years till Prince Ulugh Khan, who became Mohammad-bin-Tughlaq of the Delhi Sultanate conquered the kingdom in 1323. The capital became Warangal and the Kakatiya period was called the brightest period of Telegu history. It is a wonderful old place and worth visiting. Marco Polo, the Italian adventurer and traveller, spoke of this city in his diaries and there is also fine Jain architecture, many temples and mosques and most famously of all the Thousand Pillar Temple. This temple was dedicated to Lord Shiva in 1163 AD. The temple that allegedly Marco Polo called 'the brightest star in the galaxy of temples' is however Ramappa temple situated in the village of Palampet about 70 kilometres away. It is built out of unique bricks that are so light they float. Again this whole area is full of pilgrim destinations.

Kripa had warned me that I could very easily be 'all templed out' as she charmingly described it and indeed by the end of this very long but enjoyable journey I think it would be safe to say that Graham and I did not need to visit another temple for quite some time. That however in no way is trying to undervalue all these wonderful places. Indeed every time we visited an historic temple I was filled with awe for the commitment and dedication of the temple builders, rather as with our own medieval cathedrals throughout Britain, France and Italy.

It was now however time to leave Andhra Pradesh and I knew that our time had been just too short to do the whole beautiful place justice. What I particularly valued on this occasion was the melding of all the different faiths and cultures and yet the great respect for each one of them. There are indeed also some cathedrals to the Christian faith in and around Hyderabad; I have not mentioned them because further down in the south, which has a thriving Christian community, we did visit Christian churches and I will write about those instead.

Dinkie the mouse deer sitting at the author's feet

Prasad had been a most helpful driver in all our wanderings and we liked talking to him. His life has the prestige of being an International Travel House Driver, with smart white uniform and nice modern car. However, he too has quite a hard life, about which he was not complaining but just explaining. As with us in the UK people commute to work in India and this was the way for him, which meant rising very very early in the morning, travelling to work and ensuring his uniform looked fine and fresh. We did not keep him late at night but presumably had we done so thoughtlessly he would then have had to make his way home, and start the whole procedure the next day. That is work for millions of people the world over but when someone's life touches one's own it is always thought provoking. When we have a driver we always try to take into consideration that if we are hot and tired he may be too, despite being Indian and used to the climate. Drivers are not expected to enter luxury hotels but when one is out and about it is always good to ensure that bottled drinks are bought for all three of you; or a tea or coffee stop is taken along with one's own 'comfort stops'. With Prasad what was fun was that he liked to come into the shops with us and was helpful in that respect. He was delighted about my memories of the Kondapalli toys because they are so much part of the local culture.

We departed from Hyderabad on a Jet Airways flight. Jet Airways is one of the best companies within India and the airline is beautifully run and very punctual. Moreover the food is good and well presented. I have flown both Business Class and Economy with them and received very good service. Graham and I enjoy domestic flights in India because it is a way of quietly inspecting the middle class population going about its business. India is thriving and its people are travelling on business as well as leisure. The mobile phone of course is the most amazing piece of technology for the masses. It is so easy to own a mobile phone and when one thinks of all the bureaucracy that it entailed to have a land line in India one can see how the mobile or 'cell' phone is king.

I recall being in Venice in 1997 on a gondola crossing the Grand Canal; a man was standing upright talking on a mobile phone which was very amusing with all the attendant gestures. Graham and I had to sit down as we found it quite unstable but he was oblivious and chattering away nineteen to the dozen in Italian. Of course he might have just been telling his girlfriend what he wanted for supper that evening! In India now it is a similar sight. Not gondolas of course, but

Elephants on the roadside, 1956

the Indian equivalent of every form of human transport has its gaggle of Indians chattering away on their phones. I like the memory I have of a young Indian boy talking away in a rather insouciant fashion on a mobile while directing his bullocks on a bullock cart. I waved at him, just out of friendliness and he waved back in a startled fashion and flashed me a great big smile.

To quote the Chairman of ITC Yogi Deveshwar: "If India has to grow fast, 60 per cent of the country's private consumption that comes from villages has to grow fast..." This huge influential company has started an initiative called *e-choupal*. Choupal is the Hindi word for village square where elders meet to discuss matters of importance. The all important letter in the word is 'e'. It stands for a computer with an internet connection for farmers to gather around and interact with, not just among themselves, but with people anywhere in the country, and even beyond. ITC has installed a computer with solar-charged batteries for power and a VSAT Internet connection in selected villages. Because of the solar power the computer does not face the usual energy challenges associated with India! A local farmer called a Sanchalak (conductor) operates the computer on behalf of ITC, but exclusively for the farmers. His position is one of respect and trust and now the job is very sought after. The e-choupal offers farmers and the village community five distinct services. Information: daily weather forecast, price of various crops, emails to farmers and ITC officials, and news are all in the local language and free of cost. Knowledge: farming methods specific to each crop and region, soil testing, expert advice – mostly sourced from agricultural faculties at universities is all free. Purchase: farmers can buy seeds, fertilisers, pesticides and a host of other products and services ranging from cycles and tractors to insurance policies. Over 35 companies have become partners in the e-choupal to sell their products through the network. Sales: farmers can sell their crops to the ITC centres or the local market, after checking the prices on the internet. Development: various non-governmental organisations working for cattle breeding improvements and water retention, and women's self help groups are also reaching villages through e-choupal. In some states farmers can even access their land records online, sitting in their village. Soon it is hoped that e-choupal will bring access to health and education services. To give you an idea, by 2005 there were 5,050 choupals, 29,500 villages and 3.1 million farmers benefiting from this idea. The target is to reach 100,000 villages and 10 million farmers by 2010.

Obviously to a westerner this is all very heartening; I feel however that education, health and an awareness by the simple hardworking people of their place in the greater scheme of things is even more important. Self respect and pride in achievement, plus education and good health have an exponential effect on peoples wherever they are in the world.

ITC is one of several companies including Tata – the huge conglomerate, Godrej, Mahindra, Bharti, Pepsi, Shriram and Reliance who are all developing the rural business side of India. It seems to me that this is the only way the 'rural poor' will be lifted out of poverty and allowed to have aspirations which realistically can be achieved. This will revolutionise the way food is produced within India and indeed change the lives of 600 million villagers and, most important of all, e-choupal is a scheme whereby villagers are enriched without anybody – least of all the government – subsidising them.

Chapter Five

Chennai and old Madras

We flew into Chennai on a warm evening, but because it gets dark so early in the evening in India there was nothing really that I could see and recall. We arrived at the Chola Sheraton hotel where we both received another very warm welcome. The management had very generously given us a most beautiful full suite with sitting room, with dining table and desk, and a huge comfortable bedroom, dressing room and luxury bathroom. All good hotels greet one with some form of soft, cool drink and usually a wet towel with which to freshen the face and hands.

On the last occasion I had been here it was the end of my holiday in 1958 and I was feeling wretched at the prospect of flying home alone to the UK for the first time. Both my parents would now be in India, whereas for my first year at boarding school my mother had very gamely stayed in England and was able to visit me as often as permitted and been able to provide happy school holidays. Now I knew I would be on my own and with the prospect of seeing them again at Christmas. When one is only eleven years old this whole idea was pretty challenging; lots of children of expatriate British people experienced the very same thing – it was just part of one's childhood but lonely and frightening nevertheless. Often in the years to come I helped another small child to cope with the sadness flying back after a holiday in India. On one occasion I had two little twin boys both asleep half in my lap, one on either side of me. I was fortunate in that my parents did their best to bring me out on holiday nearly every time, which must have been a drain on their financial pocket – air fares were not a competitive item in those days! So, my memories of Madras, as it was to me, were not really happy ones, though that was not the fault of Madras!

The Chola Sheraton's bar was a delight and there was a small band playing the sort of music we both love which made for a relaxing evening. The hotel has an excellent Chinese restaurant called Shanghai but we decided on the Peshawari as we love that cuisine. The hotel gardens are not large but hold a decent sized pool and there is a health club as well.

On a return visit I stayed at Le Royal Meridien, another five star hotel. This too is a superb hotel very well placed for the airport. It has a wonderful circular, open foyer and lounge which gives a gracious and spacious air to the place; it too has very good restaurants and a wonderful health club. The hotel executive office services were also most helpful to me. On this visit I was on my own and therefore eating alone and observing my fellow guests. Tamil Nadu is striving and achieving its aim to be another power house of economic force for India. It was interesting to observe the amount of businessmen from the Far East doing business here and the various flight crews of the world's major airlines who used Le Royal Meridien because of the convenience; I also found it intriguing being alone how much strangers eyed one up! We are all capable of conjecturing about others but it seems, however middle-aged, a lone woman attracts rather more attention; I found it so irritating that I decided to have a room service supper on occasions.

The next morning we were informed that our government guide and car and driver had arrived in preparation for our trip around Tamil Nadu to see its various attractions and its world famous temples. Chennai is India's fourth largest city but is chiefly known by its old name of Madras, and as the first foothold of the British East India Company. I was interested to see how this would work out; usually any travel that we undertake is all organised by me but this time I was in the hands of the local tourist commissioner's organisation. The government official introduced himself and then the guide called Nandu and the driver called Aniva. They were friendly but shy and the situation became comic. Graham's face when he spotted the little car in which the four of us were to travel was an absolute picture. Normally we hire a medium size vehicle or preferably a jeep or 4 x 4 and either way it has to have air conditioning. Well, this little car seemed to be the size of the old VW Polo which I had owned years ago and was destined to take the four of us hundreds of miles (or kilometres) around Tamil Nadu, thankfully with air conditioning. None of us were tiny people! There ensued a typical Indian sort of dilemma. How was our luggage to be secured in this tiny car along with the small amount of luggage that was owned by the guide and driver? This challenge was undertaken by not only Nandu and Aniva but the hotel's commissionaire and all their efforts were ridiculous. In the end some of the luggage had to be tied onto the roof. Graham finally stepped in and organised it much more efficiently, but as it was poor

Nandu had to have his case under his feet. Then we finally said our farewells and got in the car. In no time we realised that the backseat was obviously the favourite resting place of a bunch of jumbo sized mosquitoes, which did not bring cheer to our hearts; it was with some misgiving that we set off as a couple, but looking at the cup half full is my motto and in no time at all once Nadu and Aniva had overcome their initial shyness we all got along famously and they very soon understood our real pleasure at being on this journey and the depth of our interest in what we were being shown.

Nandu diffidently suggested that we might like to drive round some of the major tourist attractions of Chennai en route to our first destination. This was a good idea as Graham would not be with me on my return visit and would have missed seeing Chennai, all be it in a very superficial way on this sunny Sunday morning.

In southern India there are very few people who speak Hindi, whereas in Hyderabad Urdu/Hindi is spoken as well as Telegu and of course English; in the south it is not and there are the four major languages none of which I speak. In Tamil Nadu obviously the language is Tamil, so from that point of view I would be heavily reliant on the guide. Naturally English is spoken by all the educated people as it has been a second official language of India, but I missed the easy communication that I have in the rest of the country.

Chennai remains proud of its past and was the first to be settled by Europeans, occupied at different times by the Portuguese, the French, the Dutch and finally the British. Madras is the shortened name for the fishing village of Madraspatnam and was the first settlement of the East India Company which was founded in 1639 on land given by the Raja of Chandragiri, who was the last Vijaynagar ruler of Hampi. Hampi is in modern day Karnataka and is famous as the seat of a great empire and truly one of India's great abandoned old cities like Orchha, Mandu, and Fatehpur Sikri.

Chennai is the largest city in South India. I was glad to see that the various fine buildings built in times past are well maintained and in use, either as they were intended or in some other equally worthwhile way.

It was relatively quiet and peaceful by mid-morning on a Sunday and therefore a good time to be driving around sightseeing. We drove to the Marina Beach. I had swum in Madras all those years ago but more recently all of us worldwide had seen the Tamil Nadu beaches on television news showing the horror after the tsunami. I felt I wanted to go there first. Marina Beach is a good, long, flat beach stretching for eight miles (13 km). This beach connects Fort St George with San Thome Basilica. It was once described as one of the most beautiful marine promenades in the world and indeed today still provides a most welcome area for Chennai's citizens to relax, take the air, walk and socialise. Actually that Sunday morning it was quite nice and empty. At the Fort St George end there is a fine Victory War memorial to the dead in two world wars, and the Indo-Saracenic Presidency College, which is the nucleus of Madras University, is probably the most eye-catching building. My government guide, I don't think, would have wanted me to see anything unfavourable, so I didn't push it but on my second visit with Ranjit Jacob, Kripa's father, I was able to get close to the fisher folk. This was not an attractive area at all and I was overcome by the smell of rotting fish and the general poverty of the locality. I couldn't help but feel that there was a general lack of any concern, and a feeling that these people are at the bottom of the social class or caste system and have to bear the blows and tragedies of their lives long after everyone else stopped and was momentarily horrified by a natural disaster.

Fort St George is now the seat of government for Tamil Nadu; the first building to be seen on entering the Fort is the Secretariat and behind it lie the Legislative Council Chambers. These two buildings are very impressive and nicely maintained and are thought to be among the oldest British buildings in India built between 1694 and 1732. Governor Elihu Yale was the first man to hoist the Union Jack in 1687 on the flagstaff erected here, and now of course it flies the Indian tricolour. Yale began his career as a clerk with the East India Company and later founded Yale University in the USA with some of the wealth he made during his lifetime. This fort was Britain's first bastion in India and remained the East India Company's principal settlement till 1774 when Calcutta, now Kolkata, was declared the seat of government. Reputedly the oldest Anglican Church in Asia stands to the south of the Legislature building; St Mary's Church with all its memorials and tombstones and silver gives a fascinating insight to the early British occupation. Both Elihu Yale and Robert Clive were married in this church and the three daughters of Job Charnock, the founder of Calcutta, were baptized here. Indeed Arthur Wellesley, who later became famous as the Duke of Wellington, lived in the Fort, as had Robert Clive.

So much has been written about Robert Clive that I am not going to add much, except to say that he was one of the most flamboyant personalities of that period of history; he was only nineteen when he began his career as a clerk, then he became a soldier very very successfully, after which he was given the stewardship of Fort St George and later became Governor of Bengal. He amassed a huge fortune which led to his undoing because he was charged and put on trial for corruption. He committed suicide in 1774.

I particularly enjoyed visiting the various churches in Chennai with Ranjit Jacob, Kripa's father, on my second visit. We started with San Thome Basilica at Mylapore. To an outsider like myself there is no difference in Chennai and Mylapore, but I realise that would be like saying to a citizen of Edinburgh that Leith is the same thing as Edinburgh, whereas in fact they are two different towns that have now become one with development and population growth. Nevertheless they have completely different origins. Mylapore was the site of the great Pallava Dynasty's port in the 7th and 8th centuries. It has Chennai's most important Hindu temple called the Kapaleshvara Temple, but this temple, though of immense value to worshipping Hindus perhaps, has no huge significance to other visitors. This building is about 350 years old and is the successor to an 8th century Pallava temple with the characteristic gopuram (tower) in Dravidian style and welcomes all visitors. Mylapore worshippers find the shrine of Shiva's consort Parvati beneath the *punnai* tree very appealing. Legend has it that Shiva observed Parvati admiring a beautiful peacock and became so jealous that he turned her into a peacock, or maybe peahen would be more accurate! Eventually he forgave his wife and restored the goddess to her original form at Mylapore. 'Mayilapore' means the place of the peacock. There are some fine sculptures and the temple is obviously dedicated to Lord Shiva.

The San Thome Basilica is what most people associate with Mylapore. Tradition has it that Thomas, one of Jesus's disciples, the one who had doubted his resurrection but had finally been convinced of his divinity, came to India. Just before his ascension Jesus spoke to all the disciples and said, "Go out all over the world, and preach the Gospel to the whole of creation..." and Thomas, who by now was utterly convinced that Jesus was 'His Lord and God', went eastwards to India. Is this a fact or a wonderful fiction?

Did Saint Thomas really go to the India we know today? Well there are many written documents referring to his work in India. An expression used was, "India and all its own countries" – perhaps this was a way of referring to a huge sub-continent with all its kingdoms and provinces? India was well known to many writers and geographers and historians of the ancient world. There was commerce between India and Persia, Chaldea, Palestine, Asia Minor and even Italy, as indeed I have shown in the brief history of the Andhra people of what is now known as Andhra Pradesh. Northern India was particularly known to the Greek world since the invasion of Alexander. After the rediscovery of the monsoon winds even South India became well known to the west. The trade in teak, ebony, sandalwood and other things was flourishing. The Red Sea route linked India with Arabia, Judea and Egypt. Cargoes of gold, ivory, silver and precious stones were conveyed to the west and the proof is in the many discoveries of Roman coins, such as at Machilipatinam, in Andhra Pradesh.

One of the early reference books for the life and mission of Saint Thomas is called 'The Acts of Saint Thomas' which is dated to the early 3rd century. It is understood to be an apocryphal work; but serious scholars seem to favour the historical foundation for the main statements in the text. Apocryphal or legendary writings take their origins from historical events, which in the course of the development of the work get mixed up and confused amid the exaggerated even fantastic details and narrative embellishments. Yet in the Acts there is a statement that, "When the Apostles had been for a time in Jerusalem they divided the countries among them in order that each one might preach in the region which fell to him; and *India* fell to the lot of Judas Thomas." India was actually mentioned.

Subsequently in the writings of the various venerated men of the Christian Church such as Saint Ephrem in the 4th century, Saint Gregory, Saint Ambrose, Saint Jerome and even The Venerable Bede (famous in early English history), "The Apostles of Christ…received their allotted charges in distinct parts of the world. Peter receives Rome; Andrew Achaia; James Spain; Thomas India." So, it was in 52AD that Thomas is believed to have arrived in India and he spent the next twelve years along the Malabar Coast, spreading the Gospel and converting the local population. He gradually moved east from what we now know as Kerala and settled in Mylapore. Mylapore had a variety of similar names in ancient writings but the various scholars consider that they all amount to the same place. He spent the last years of his life living in a cave on a hill called Little Mount, from where he would walk to the beach, resting and preaching. He was stabbed we think in 72AD and fled to Little Mount. It is believed that he was grievously wounded by a Hindu Brahmin's lance and fled first to the cave; but it has been suggested he actually left the cave and made his way to St Thomas's Mount where he was put to death. St Thomas's Mount is about three kilometres away from the cave; inside the cave is the opening through which Thomas retreated leaving behind a still visible imprint of his hand near the entrance. At the end of the cave is the Masonry Cross before which the saint is said to have prayed. St Thomas's Mount is about 100 metres above sea level and was once a forested hillock, but now it is really a place of granite boulders and has a flight of one hundred and thirty five steps to the summit which are said to have been built by an Armenian Catholic. By 1523 the Portuguese following the saint's trail established a settlement of San Thome and to their lasting credit they did everything they could to revive Christianity in this area and they immediately set about clearing the ruins and built a sanctuary. Subsequently this summit was used as a gun emplacement in the Anglo-French wars but the Bishop of Mylapore objected and the military authorities promptly removed it.

The site of his martyrdom has exerted a supernatural influence on the pious from far and near. The sanctity of the site attracted many settlements of Persian and Armenian Christians down the centuries. The Syrians and Nestorians then followed. Marco Polo also visited the site in the 13th century.

The body of Thomas was carried to the little church he had built at San Thome. This subsequently was built over with a larger church in the 10th century by a group of Nestorian Christians from Persia. The present minor Basilica was built in 1898 and I find it very reminiscent of the gothic architecture of English churches. Nearby is the Luz Church which was built by a Franciscan monk in 1516 and is thus the oldest Catholic Church in Chennai.

The late Pope John Paul II visited San Thome when he went to India. I visited San Thome the day after the Pope had died and it was filled with hundreds of devout Christians who had come to pay homage to the deceased pontiff. I found it a peaceful, well maintained, big church and it has a beautiful stained glass window portraying the story of Saint Thomas. I also visited the crypt where there is a casket ontaining a small bone from the saint's hand and the weapon that killed him.

I am going to explore the story of Saint Thomas in more detail when we reach Kerala so I will just say that I did find it profoundly moving to think that a man's saintly commitment and devotion may have driven him to come to India where it is devoutly believed by many he was finally martyred. Watching silent masses grieving for the death of the old and weary Pope, who had himself been so challenged with his infirmities, I found the visit quite affecting. Later on that evening I saw the Basilica of San Thome featured on the international news when talking about the late Pope. The Christian population of India is just under 19 million people.

I really enjoyed my visit to St Andrew's Kirk which was consecrated in 1821. This church was designed by Major Thomas de Havilland and Colonel James Caldwell of the Madras Engineers, and built at a cost of £20,000. People say it was inspired by St Martin-in-the-Fields in London, but I would argue with that supposition. In Edinburgh there is a church in George Street called the Kirk of St Andrew and St George which might have been the template for this one in Chennai, and indeed there is the other St Andrew's Kirk in Kolkata, in which my parents were married in February 1941, three days before my late father went off to Malaya to see action in World War II. The Kolkata St Andrew's appears to be very similar and I have worshipped in that church many times. The architecture of this St Andrew's is a marvel. The dome has a framework of brick supported by an annular arch and is filled in by pottery cones; its blue interior is formed by crushed sea shells mixed with lapis lazuli. The steeple is fifty metres high (164 ft), four metres taller than its apparent inspiration St Martin-in-the-Fields. Because of the sandy soil on which it is built and because the area is prone to flooding during the monsoon, the church's foundations are actually a series of wells sunk to depths ranging from four metres to fifteen metres below ground level. This example of engineering ingenuity is based on local practice in the area. The wells are constructed either of specially made curved bricks, or pottery cylinders. These are placed so as to ensure maximum compaction of the soil, allowing the water to rise within them and thus protecting the main structure. The pews are made out of mahogany and there is a fine pulpit. From 1839 the pews were let out to prominent citizens, which of course was so typical of Victorian snobbery and also a feature of churches in Scotland at that time; all men are equal in the eyes of God is the trite saying which it appears large sections of the Christian church happily ignore. The stained glass window at the altar end is beautiful. Sixteen fluted Corinthian columns support the dome which gives a most wonderful feeling of balance and elegance. The entrance to the church is a double colonnade of twelve polished Ionic columns. The organ was installed in 1883 and built in Yorkshire in England.

The grounds of the church are still quite spacious and I was surprised to see that it had been left alone – in most expanding cities that sort of land is highly prized and someone sells it off to developers. We talked to the church administrative staff who were very friendly and showed us records dating back to its origins. I liked walking about and taking photographs of the memorials to old Scottish names. One that took my fancy was the beautiful marble memorial to Major General Sir Robert Henry Dick of Tullymet. He was one of the heroes of the Peninsular War and Waterloo and had commanded the 42nd Royal Highlanders. He had subsequently held the chief military command of Madras and this memorial was raised in grateful admiration by the public of The Presidency of Madras. He had died on the field of Sobraon in February 1846. Another was to the Reverend Robert Kerr Hamilton, born in Glasgow in June 1810. Kerr is a family name of the Dobbies. Graham's great grandfather had been a minister and served both in Edinburgh and at the Lansdowne Kirk in Glasgow. This Robert Kerr Hamilton obviously had served the church in Madras but died in Edinburgh in 1865. I like the inscription on the plaque:

'All flesh is as grass, and all the glory of man as the flower of grass; the grass withereth, and the flower thereof falleth away; but the word of the Lord endureth for ever'.

Ranjit and I also visited St George's Cathedral, the centre of the Anglican faith in Chennai. It too is in very good condition and was being prepared for a wedding that evening; the whole building was decorated with arches of fresh flowers which was lovely. I gathered that the bridal couple belonged to high society in Chennai and there was the usual Indian 'messing about' of officials and people who were there to arrange proceedings and make it all run smoothly. I am always amused by this in India because invariably there are at least four or five people who are just standing about doing absolutely nothing, which means they were redundant to the preparation anyway!

Chennai is really a conglomeration of overgrown villages, with no real single centre but the area around St George's Cathedral is probably what I remember with the old Taj Connemara hotel nearby which was I think the only suitable place in town in which to stay fifty years ago. Now this bustling energetic city with its appalling traffic has any amount of good hotels in which to stay.

Having spoken of the various Christian churches it is only fair that I should mention the famous Theosophical Society situated in the city's Adyar neighbourhood, which is on the banks of the Adyar River. Colonel Henry S Olcott, a veteran of the American Civil War met a Russian aristocrat and clairvoyant called Madame Helena Petrovna Blavatsky in Vermont in the USA, at the farm of a Christian Scientist, Mary Baker Eddy. Together they launched a movement to 'foster the spirit of universal brotherhood', aiming to create a Utopian society in which people of all castes, creeds and colour could live in harmony. The movement founded in 1875 attracted great intellectuals, among them Dr Annie Besant, president of the Indian National Congress in 1917, she became the Society's president in 1907. In fact the idea of forming a national political party was first mooted at the Society's headquarters in the 1890s at Adyar, under the famous 400 year old banyan tree which still exists in the gardens of the Theosophical Society. The Adyar Library founded by Olcot in 1886 is one of the finest libraries in all India. It houses a collection of 165,000 books and 20,000 palm-leaf and parchment manuscripts. The surrounding gardens have shrines dedicated to various faiths. The fine old building is called Huddlestone Gardens, and was built in 1776 by a John Huddlestone; it is now the world headquarters of the Society. This is a peaceful, worthwhile place to visit; the great tree was partially destroyed by a storm in 1989 but the branches are held up by posts

– it has been witness to so many of the Society's meetings and spiritual discussions.

I really enjoyed our visit to the Indo-Saracenic Government Museum, which is a labyrinthine building but full of wonderful antiquities, including artefacts from Amaravati. These were brought here by Colonel Colin Mackenzie. The 2nd century stupa panel from Amaravati is particularly memorable.

I found the Bronze Gallery with its 700 bronzes very impressive. Fortunately we were gently pursued by a man called Wilfred Daniel, an official guide. He and I did a deal with which he was very happy. Wilfred then proceeded to explain a great deal about the wonderful bronzes that are exhibited in the gallery. I was fortunate in finding a copy of a reprint of the definitive work by F H Graveley and T N Ramachandran entitled Catalogue of the South Indian Hindu Metal Images in the Madras government Museum. This is such a long title that you might be feeling sleepy just reading it, but believe me unless one has such a reference and/or a very good guide much of the beauty and sophistry of the bronze work is lost on us mere westerners! Hindu Iconography is a large and complex subject. The authors have given a brief summary of the chief characteristics of the principal images through which one could more easily understand the Hindu pantheon of gods and goddesses. The *mudras* or poses of hand and fingers, which form an important part of the symbolism in Hindu images, are so delicate and graceful – each one is drawn and explained and my head is spinning with all the detail. This book helps to translate the symbolic gestures which are shown to have been devised in a strict iconographic guideline. There is a meaning for every gesture, stance, weapon and adornment; Shiva, the Cosmic Dancer known as Lord Nataraja, and his wife Parvati are favourite subjects for the bronzes. Nataraja, the figure of the cosmic dancer symbolizes nature's cycle of evolution, and there are fine temples dedicated to this form of the deity, some of which we were fortunate enough to visit. I am also reminded of the Christian hymn which is often sung for children's activities which starts, "I am the Lord of the Dance...", which is a very catchy tune.

I most heartily recommend a visit to the gallery; I was in the fortunate position of seeing it at the end of my visit to Tamil Nadu when I had already feasted my eyes on exquisite bronze statues at Thanjuvar. I intend to explain how they are made with the Lost Wax method when I come to that part of our journey. If however you are not able to visit all those places this gallery is a microcosm of what Tamil Nadu has to offer in the way of sculptures in metal i.e. bronzes. William Daniel was excellent and a nice chap to meet – it was quite obvious that he wanted a photograph taken of him so Ranjit obliged and took one of us both. He then showed us a strange tree in the precincts of the museum which is called the Cannon Ball tree which is unique I would say. Beautiful flowers fade and form amazing fruits that are as hard as cannon balls.

The most beautiful of all the museum and gallery buildings is however the National Art Gallery which was designed and built by Henry Irwin, one of the city's most celebrated architects. I love its mellow pink neo-Mughal stone exterior and it is reminiscent of the great doorway at Fatehpur Sikri. It too houses some very fine Chola Bronzes. Nearby there is also a Contemporary Art Gallery which focuses on South Indian artists.

Chennai has a lot to offer the first time visitor and I have not even mentioned shopping as yet. Like any other great Indian city there is plenty to tempt the tourist be it at the beginning or the end of a visit to Tamil Nadu.

Chapter Six

The Road to Mamallapuram

Driving out of Chennai going towards Mamallapuram I began to feel that good feeling of anticipation; I was soon going to see something that had long intrigued me – the famous Shore Temple at Mamallapuram. This temple is a World Heritage Site and the subject of some conjecture over the years: was there always only one temple or were there more centuries ago?

It is a pleasant road going south, the land is very flat but with lush palm trees and fields and on the left a distant view of the sea. Very soon we came upon new settlements of huts made out palm leaves and also of corrugated tin – these were obviously, by the configuration, settlements for people whose homes had been destroyed by the tsunami. These huts seemed to be in the middle of nowhere but at least far from the seashore, though we thought the corrugated tin shanties would become dreadfully hot in the full heat of the summer to come. I considered them rather isolated and far from a town to be really convenient for displaced people.

In 1996 at Dakshina Chitra, along this road, a heritage village was opened to the public to show people what life would have been like in the four southern states of India in centuries past. This was the first heritage village to be established in India and it is a really good idea for all travellers to see and enjoy but I would think amazingly helpful in educating Indian children about their very valuable heritage and the importance of maintaining crafts and their respective cultures. Original houses from the southern states have been relocated, brick by brick, in this lovely setting. The cultural village is a microcosm of the traditions of architecture with authentic and ancient traditions of craftsmanship, the performing arts and cuisine of these regions. Here within ten acres of grounds there are guided tours, exhibitions, workshops for children and adults, demonstrations of folk theatre and themed food festivals; there are also exchange programmes for scholars and professionals.

The entrance is through a majestic old carved wooden doorway from Chettinad. The Chettinad House is large enough to accommodate four generations of a family and is constructed on the basis of Vastushastra. This means that the front and the back door of the house are directly opposite each other so that the good spirits can enter from the front door and the evil spirits can retreat from the back door. The Tamil Nadu section has a weaver's house and an exhibition of other crafts. By crossing a little bridge one comes into the Keralan section and here is a superb Keralan house built out of wood. The kitchen has a well attached and there are other pointers to the matrilineal system of society in Kerala with emphasis placed on the woman.

Karnataka is represented and the Andhra Pradesh house is one from the Andhra coast, the design of which is said to have remained unchanged since the Neolithic period. To make the visit more worthwhile the lady in charge of each representative house has been trained to teach visitors simple handicrafts using natural materials. One can learn basket making, block printing, palm leaf parrot construction and other things that would certainly take a small child's fancy. I would have loved to have had our grandsons with us.

Dakshina Chitra is a splendid idea and indeed it is a magical experience to have one's kai joshyam (palm reading) while one is seated on an 18th century thinnai (platform) or be told your fortune through killi joshyam (that is a parrot picking up tarot cards)! The guide map is delightful and vivid and makes it easy to find one's way through the lanes. There is a south Indian restaurant, a craft shop, a craft bazaar, a library, a conference room and an open air theatre which all help to make this Chitra (picture) of Dakshin (south) a very good experience.

The fact that this is situated on the road to the Shore Temple is ideal because visitors to Chennai who do not have the time to venture further into Tamil Nadu, for whatever reason, would at least, through visiting Dakshina Chitra, understand a little more about the charm and different cultures of South India.

Further along the road there is the Madras Crocodile Bank which is the largest breeding site for crocodiles in India. In the 1970s the crocodiles of India faced extinction in the wild due to indiscriminate hunting for their skins. This crocodile conservation project was started in 1976 and now has thousands of crocodiles, turtles, tortoises, water monitor lizards, green iguanas, king cobras, common cobras and pythons which are all housed in natural enclosures. The world has twenty-three species of crocodile of which fourteen are here, with the three Indian species included. The Mugger or Marsh crocodile which was once found in all lowland water areas; the Gharial – with the longest jaw with a sort of pot at the tip of its snout (ghara in Hindi means pot from which it gets its name); and the largest of reptiles the Saltwater crocodiles found in the Andaman and Nicobar Islands, the Sunderbans in West Bengal and in coastal Orissa. Many other species have been donated by foreign zoos and crocodile farms and includes Morlet's crocodile from Mexico, the Spectacled Caimen from South America, the Nile and the Dwarf crocodiles from Africa, the Siamese crocodile of which less than 100 survive in the world, and the American Alligator.

We had visited a crocodile farm years and years ago in South Africa, but this is a much more impressive undertaking and well worth a visit. The whole area is nicely landscaped with a good collection of forest trees and plants which are well maintained and it is home to more than seventy species of resident and migratory birds. Equally important, the Crocodile Bank also houses India's only venom extraction centre, run by the Irula tribe, whose primary occupation is snake catching!

As we reached Mamallapuram the sun was high in the sky which was a perfect blue. The temperature though hot for us just out from Scotland was pleasant. This is a most pleasant little village. Graham and I instantly loved it and indeed though our long journey showed us place upon place of amazing interest I think we both rate this first encounter with one of Tamil Nadu's great treasures very highly. Mamallapuram is now a UNESCO World Heritage site but it once was

Goats playing on top of the rock face at Mamallpuram

the great port city for the 7th century Pallava king Narsimha Varman I, also known as Mamalla the 'Great Wrestler'.

Mahabalipuram is the other popular name for Mamallapuram, and the one that springs to my mind initially; it means city of Bali, whom Lord Vishnu chastised for his pride, and of whom there is a relief in one of the excavated temples. This village was already a centre of pilgrimage when in the seventh century Mamalla decided to make it his sea port, and thus was the point from which so many Indian colonists, who included sages and artists migrated to south-east Asia. The national chronicle of Sri Lanka, the 'Mahavamsa' testifies to this fact.

The European name for Mamallapuram, since the first western visitor wrote of it in the sixteenth century is the 'Seven Pagodas'. The myth continues that perhaps there is a larger city sunken under the sea. This story was further embellished in a poem called 'The Curse of Kehama' published in 1810 by a man called Robert Southey. After the 2004 tsunami the myth and legend once again gripped people's imaginations and in fact thankfully, though the tsunami's towering waters did come half way up the height of the Shore Temple, no real damage was done and mercifully only twelve people died from the village of Meyyurkuppam just up the coast.

Since we have now reached the first temple in our temple trail it is worth explaining that invariably it was a king or his nobles who built temples or made additions to existing ones in later times, and the style of architecture adopted is named after the dynasty to which the king belonged. The first kings to build temples in the whole region of Tamil Nadu – which was bigger than the state which we now know – were the Pallavas. They were the parallel kingdom with the Pandyas, who like the Pallavas, built temples out of rock as well as new build constructions. The Cholas displaced both dynasties in the ninth century and probably built the most magnificent of all South India's many temples. Nandu explained a great deal to us as we went along.

It is heartening that the authorities maintain all these sites well and the atmosphere is one of seaside charm, sand, casuarinas trees, neem trees and grass. I would have hated it if the village had been allowed to encroach on these wonders, but the village exists in harmony with all this amazing architecture and carving. We first went and visited the Panch Rathas (five processional temple chariots). I was just enchanted with these huge monolithic creations. The Panch Rathas were named after the five Pandava brothers heroes of the *Mahabharata*. The Mahabharata is one of the two great epics of Indian culture and philosophy. It is the story of the rivalry between the five heroic Pandava brothers – Yudishthira, Bhima, Arjuna, Nakul and Sahdeva and a hundred members of the Kaurava clan. The story culminates in a great battle and various other fables and legends are woven into the main story. It is worth recalling that the Mahabharata is longer than the *Iliad* and the *Odyssey* of Greek mythology put together! The Bhagavad Gita is the sermon given by Lord Krishna to Arjuna when he supported him as his charioteer on the battlefield of Kurukshetra and is full of wisdom on the ethics and morality for daily life – this contains the essence of the Hindu religion and philosophy and is often referred to as 'The Gita'.

Graham and I were so intrigued by the detail of the carvings on the various rathas and just wandered around or sat and gazed. The neem trees provided lovely dappled shade and were in flower. I watched our fellow tourists who on that day all appeared to be Indians enjoying themselves. Sometimes that involves some macho posturing, presumably for western consumption, and indeed these young fellows do some silly things but the girls were lovely in their brightly coloured garments and I asked them to pose for a picture. What is the point of looking at all the beauties of ancient India if one does not recognise its future as well? The granite carvings comprise: Arjuna Ratha, Draupadi Ratha and Nandi – the bull. They stand as a sort of trio. Arjuna Ratha is a two-storeyed temple and has a graceful portrayal of Shiva leaning on his mount, the bull Nandi. The Nandi carved out of a single rock faces the ratha. Then the Draupadi Ratha is a stone replica of a thatched tribal shrine, it is the smallest in the group and is dedicated to the goddess Durga. The mount of Durga is a standing lion placed in front of the Draupadi Ratha. The Nakul Sahdeva Ratha which is named after the Pandava twins is unique for its architectural form of *gajaprishta* (back of an elephant). A beautifully sculpted elephant carved from a single stone stands next to it.

Bhima Ratha, a gigantic rectangular ratha with a barrel-vaulted roof which is unfinished, is named after Bhima the Pandava brother known for his strength. Dharmaraja Ratha is the most imposing of the rathas, three storeys high with an octagonal domed roof. Sculpted panels are carved on the upper storeys. There are beautifully intricate niche figures carved onto the sides of the temple – one in particular is special called Harihar, a composite form of Vishnu and Shiva, with the right side of the body carved with matted locks of hair depicting Shiva, and the left is Vishnu, with a smooth tapering cylindrical crown.

I enjoyed talking to Nandu whilst we enjoyed the whole Panch Rathas experience. He under gentle questioning told me about his family and daughter; she had graduated in a very good technical degree, quite which escapes my memory but her future would be assured. Still, in the ancient manner of India Nandu was going to set about arranging a marriage for her. It seems odd in this day and age that people should still wish to participate in this age-old tradition, but if it works for the majority and is in step with their philosophy then who am I to argue with it; western norms now are of rushed marriages, quickie divorces and lots of living together. The latter leads to even quicker separations it seems, judging by what I have heard from our own sons, who are both happily married. The children of these unions reap all the forlorn heart-braking consequences of these break-ups. So maybe the ancient cultures of the Middle East and East have a very good point – but I am pretty sure their way also leads to quite a bit of heartbreak and lifelong unhappiness. I enjoyed listening to a proud father recounting his daughter's various achievements and reflected that India was certainly getting that right – educating the girls in middle class families.

We decided that a rest was indicated and lunch beckoned. Nandu informed us that we would be staying at the Sterling Mamallapuram property, which is in walking distance of the Shore Temple. This we would visit after lunch when the sun had lost its ferocity.

The Sterling Resort was thoroughly charming. We were immediately given a very warm welcome and with an action which to us was unique. The young man asked us to sit down and have a welcome cool drink and damp fragrant towel for our hands, but then proceeded to massage our feet with ayurvedic massage. I loved it, and so did Graham; it certainly is refreshing and gave one time to look around

Stone masons carving Hindu deities at Mamallapuram

and absorb the surroundings. This resort is in large grounds that lead down to the shore and the famous temple. Indeed, the watchman told me how on the day of tsunami he was at his place at the gate to the actual public beach when the waves rushed in; he fled and climbed a rather short but stout tree which he indicated to me. Fortunately it was early in the morning and the usual small crowds had net yet congregated in the Shore Temples' precincts, they certainly would have drowned. Apparently the story goes that a small boy shouted a warning and those who were around fled to safety. I do not know if this is true but undoubtedly it will become the myth surrounding this wonderful place. The Sterling Resort has placed a most wonderful branch of driftwood on their Reception area; the water had just lapped the building and when it receded the driftwood had been left. They have now placed it as a reminder of what can happen.

Lunch was delicious and vegetarian. We invited Nandu to eat with us, which he did but it was quite obvious that he would probably have preferred to be left to his own devices because he was very shy. The resort has a fine swimming pool and people are housed in individual cottages or semi-detached cottages. Ours faced the sea and was very simple but comfortable – there were no added luxuries and it reminded me of holidays in India during my childhood. Alongside the main building of the resort is a village tank (artificial pond) which was attractive and on the other side of that village life carried on as it had done for centuries. I arranged to have a full ayurvedic massage later on in the evening to soothe away all the aches and pains of the flight and car travel of the last few days.

After a quick stretch out on our beds (the little car rather necessitated this!) we again set out for the Shore Temple. By this time the moon was also to be seen in the blue sky, and I couldn't help but think of that fateful full moon. The sun had lost its strength and the whole atmosphere in which to view the famous temple was perfect. The precincts were of course slightly damaged by the tsunami but overall everything was well, one could just see the tide mark on the *vimanas* of the temple itself. Now the authorities have put a fence around the precinct to help preserve it; in former times it just stood there with the sea close by which must have been so dramatic and perfect visually. I subsequently suggested to Shaktikanta Das, Commissioner of Tourism for Tamil Nadu that though I understood the need for a fence it should be much more aesthetically pleasing. India is quite capable of devising something elegant and durable out of stone or clever masonry. There were very few tourists that afternoon, mostly Indians, and we so enjoyed the tranquillity of the experience and took our time. Looking out on a calm ocean on the Bay of Bengal it was difficult to imagine the horror of a forty foot tidal wave and the strength and force of such a wave and the nightmare of its speed. I thought of how we had been at a resort quite near Trincomalee in Sri Lanka in early January of 2004. Our comfortable beach side suite was about fifty metres from the actual sea shore and would have been engulfed – Nilaveli must have been destroyed – it was a pleasant simple place rather in the same fashion as the Sterling Resort; my first thought was of the shell man selling lovely shells from whom we had bought one; I do hope he survived.

Walking and sitting amongst the temples stones I thought of Lord Vishnu to whom this temple was dedicated; he is the preserver of life. Around the precinct is a stone wall with rows of seated Nandi bulls; there are two Shiva shrines that were added by Narsimha Varman II. All this has stood for thirteen centuries and will long outlive us mere mortals; that always gives me a comforting feeling – humans do not possess the great courage that would be required for true immortality. Till decades ago the temple was partially buried by sand and as has been demonstrated the temple is vulnerable to the sea but yet it survives in its beauty and intricacy.

By now the sun was low in the sky and we moved into the village to view the bas reliefs. There really is no word to describe these other than stunning. Bhagiratha's Penance, also known more widely as Arjuna's Penance (current thinking is that the figure is Arjuna not Bhagiratha) is a depiction from the Mahabharatha also represented in both mural relief in Lepakshi which is a famous place in south Andhra Pradesh, which was too far away for us to visit. The inspiration for this bas relief apparently came from a man called Bharavi a dramatist living in Kanchipuram in the seventh century.

The surface is 29 metres by 13 metres consisting of two large boulders with a fissure in between. In the fissure that looks like a carved gutter there are a serpent god and a serpent goddess in the act of worship. The two sides of the boulders are literally covered in hundreds of images carved out of the stone.

The story being shown us is of an ascetic performing severe penance, standing on one leg. Near him is Lord Shiva, with his attendants. Immediately below them there is a small shrine with a relief of Lord Vishnu inside with alongside many sages seated in meditation. The fissure indicates a river and in Pallava times it is thought that actual water flowed down the carved guttering or cleavage from the hill behind, where there is indication of what might have been a water tank. The story is connected to the one of Arjuna obtaining a weapon to use in the impending war against the Kauravas.

Interestingly there is a similar relief in the Isurumuniya in Anuradhapura the ancient Buddhist capital of Sri Lanka which we had

The beautiful shore temple at Mamallapuram

visited in January 2004. On the northern face of this bas relief are the most beautiful huge sculpted elephants; these elephants are considered to be among the very best in the whole range of Indian sculpture. When it is pointed out one also sees the cat which is pretending to perform penance, and its prey some rats, and then besides all this there is the lion, the tiger, the boar. Above there are a number of semi-divine figures flying around.

I just loved the elephant carvings and one other in particular of a cow being milked with the calf standing by in the Krishna Mandapa, where there is also another huge bas relief showing the god lifting Mount Govardhan to protect the people from torrential rains. There are also stories from the Panchatantra, the Indian version of Aesop's Fables also carved in this rock. Every year from mid January to mid February there is a Festival of Dance held against the backdrop of the bas reliefs. Indian Classical Dance has different forms such as Bharatanatyam, Kuchipudi, Odissi and Kathakali. I was, when we reached Kerala, to have the opportunity of watching wonderful Kuchipudi dancing which originates in Andhra Pradesh actually, but here in Mamallapuram with this backdrop it must be stunning at the time of the feast of Pongal in mid January – a very good time to visit the whole of South India.

A little to the side is Krishna's Butter Ball, which is a natural boulder of immense size seeming to be precariously balanced on a slope. In fact on closer inspection it is not that round at the rear so one can understand how it has withstood the attempts of various kings to unseat it. In the late evening sunshine we watched as all the young children slid down the rock face under Krishna's Butter Ball – just simple fun. One of the sights that I particularly enjoyed was of kids – the young progeny of goats – walking about on the rock face at the top of Arjuna's Penance and with their sure-footed way scampering around and sitting down in the setting sun which highlighted them against the blue sky.

After looking at all these wonders we then wandered through the village lanes and inspected the workshops of the famous Mamallapuram sculptors. Throughout the world if a Hindu temple requires a new deity it will more than likely be ordered from these stone carvers and sculptors. Their work is amazing and full of detail, and they are mostly still working in a monolithic way, just as the famous rathas had been carved thirteen centuries ago! We walked from workshop to workshop looking at animals, birds, humans, frogs, hogs, Lord Buddha, flowers, herons and gods. We wanted a heron for our garden but we realised that the cost of the work, which was not excessive, coupled with the costs of shipping would make it the most expensive carved heron in the modern world. However, joking apart, apparently there is a huge market in Europe for these things and the Germans in particular are very good customers. The workshops just quote immediately what it would cost and are quite up to the minute about these things. One of these days I might indulge myself and ask them to carve me a seated Lord Buddha. Since even the tiniest carving is very heavy it is obviously not something one can just buy and tuck under one's arm to take on a plane.

We returned to the hotel, by this time rather weary because hours in the sunshine walking about can be dehydrating, but a cool drink immediately had a good effect and I went off to have the full ayurvedic head, face and body massage and gram bath. I will talk about the whole science of Ayurveda, but perhaps not at this moment. The young woman who attended to me was a sweet girl called, I think, Shinu. She was very shy but very thorough in her massage and gram wash and bath afterwards. I found a quick empathy with her and she also took endless trouble that Sunday evening to contact the local ayurvedic physician, who was off duty, to ask him on my behalf about how to treat something. The massage rooms were very basic at this resort whereas at other more sophisticated places of which I will write they are more in tune with the western eye. However, I have had massage in a small hut on the side of the road in Sri Lanka with the lorries roaring by and the local elephants visible through the back door patiently waiting for customers to ride them! The quality of the massage is all important and Shinu did a marvellous job and had this sweet essence about her personality – we couldn't really communicate you see as I don't speak Tamil and she has no English; that is a rare situation for me in India. Finally after the gram wash, that has to follow a really good massage using fragrant oils one comes out with a smooth polished skin and a feeling of total relaxation. I had been gone for some time so Graham was very relieved to see me again and we settled down to a cool drink and contemplation of supper.

The Chef came out to meet us along with the management and we decided to go with his recommendations all of which were delicious and involved some seafood. The gulab jamuns at the end were fresh and hot which made for a very happy Graham!

By this time it was late and dark but though I was really tired I had promised the management I would go on their bullock cart ride. The bullocks had been brought in with their owner and were waiting patiently for us to use the cart. Usually one would make this trip at sunset but because I had gone to my massage it had to be fitted in after supper. Frankly after the relaxation of a wonderful massage and a good meal I was not looking forward to be jolted about in the dubious delight of a bullock cart ride, but I am so glad that we did it!

The Activities Manager accompanied us and there were some cushions with which to protect oneself and the wheels were not the old normal version in wood but had rubber inflated tyres. The bullocks had the normal huge horns and are powerful beasts. One enters from the rear of the cart and I took two cushions to help protect me. The peace and quiet of a simple most ancient form of transport in the silence of the village night was incredible. Indian villages settle down to sleep much earlier than we do in the West and so all the shops were shut and the streets had minimal lighting; there was however enough lighting to see through open front doors and windows and catch a glimpse of a community settling down for the night. Graham and I reminisced how we had actually walked back late in the dark in Jaisalmer and experienced very much the same feeling. The various animals were all sitting and settling quietly tethered at the respective homes and looking up there was the moon. The bullocks' owner took us on a circular drive. When we came to the bas relief of Arjuna's Penance we could see it in the light of one street lamp, and something special happened.

The shadows and silhouettes of the covered bullock cart with the two bullocks and their massive curved horns, and indeed our own heads, all showed in this clear shadow upon the bas relief; somehow it was very moving. Us, in the twenty-first century in a most ancient form of transport throwing a shadow on this ancient rock carving with its still

The famous bas relief of elephants at Mamallapuram

perfect depictions of god and man and animals – with the elephants being my favourite.

Up above, oblivious of us were about fourteen goats all asleep on their rocky places of rest, very safe from most predators. We tried to photograph the scene but of course the flash dispensed the shadow. I just loved the silence, the shadow, the symbolism for me of us in a thrusting modern India sitting in a bullock cart that was around in Harrappan times. Modern roads from Chennai to Trichy are making such a difference to travel but guess what, the odd bullock cart is also on the modern road! Plus buses that appear to be on the wrong side – for short distances – something to do with reaching villages on the other side of the road. Whether the road engineers had not thought out sufficient intersections or what I do not know, but I do know it is most disconcerting to have a bus bearing down on one instead of it driving along on the other side of the new motorway.

We thanked the bullocks' owner and went to bed. I like to be up early and walk about a place and watch the sun rise. The beach is nice and clean with hotel benches but bathing did not seem to be a good idea and I thought that perhaps people just paddle in the spent waves. An old blind gentleman played the flute which was lovely and a pure sound; he does this for the management early in the morning and as the sun goes down. The Sterling Resorts put great emphasis on conservation and eco-friendly management. They have their own desalination plant and generator also.

There are some statues in the grounds going down to the shore; I had walked down to again contemplate the great temple. This is when I met the watchman who described vividly to me how he had escaped. One statue is of a man sitting astride the world depicting presumably man's domination, but the world yet again demonstrated its awesome power and man had to run for his life. We said our farewells to the management and set off the long way round for Pondicherry.

The new interstate highway apparently had no check gate yet for a permit inspection to drive from Tamil Nadu into Pondicherry, which is a Union Territory, so we had to go the long way round on the old roads which added hours to our trip, and was a perfect example of stupidity that is often evident in government ventures in India. We could see the new road which was even more irritating!

Chapter Seven

Pondicherry

When we had set off from Mamallapuram the usual army of mosquitoes swarmed up in the back seat, but Aniva stopped at a flower stall before we left the village and purchased some freshly strung jasmine necklaces, which he then hung from his rear view mirror, and he also gave us one at the back. This helped a great deal and was a beautiful way of coping with the mosquitoes.

After what seemed an age we arrived at Pondicherry. I shall explain briefly about its origins and history. Pondicherry is a Union Territory of India. It was formerly ruled by the French. It consists of four non-contiguous enclaves. Now the name has undergone a name change to Puduchery I am told. The name 'puduchery' means 'new village' in Tamil. The French spelt it 'Poudichery' which is the closest French approximation to the Tamil pronunciation; however the hand written 'u' was mistaken for an 'n' and the misspelling prevailed. In early writings dated to 2nd century AD a place named Poduke was mentioned and Roman pottery was found at Arikamedu in 1937. There is a theory that in ancient times a Sanskrit university had been established in the area and that the great Sage Agastya established his Ashram here, after which the place was known as Agastiswaram.

The history of the 4th century AD tells us that was when the Pondicherry area belonged to the Pallava Kindom of Kanchipuram. In the ensuing centuries Pondicherry was occupied by different dynasties of the south; in the 10th century the Cholas of Thanjavur ruled, and then were superseded by the Pandya Kingdom in the 13th century. The Sultanate of Madurai was established and subsequently the Vijayanagar Empire took control of almost the entire south of India and lasted till 1638, when the Sultan of Bijapur became powerful.

Cardinal Richelieu, the Machiavellian, larger than life, character of French 17th century history founded the French East India Company in 1642. Previously French ships had set out for the East in the reign of Francis I but had not been heard of again. The Company was then reformed under a man called Jean-Baptist Colbert in 1664 who sent an expedition to Madagascar. In 1667 another expedition was sent out to the Indian Ocean which reached Surat on the west coast of India in 1668 and established the first French outpost in India. The Dutch however who had reached India first were intent on driving out the French who had to fight for their new found possessions and in 1674 the French acquired Valikondapuram from the Sultan of Bijapur and thus the foundation of Pondicherry was laid. By 1720 the French had lost their earlier territorial gains to the British but on 4th February 1673, a French officer called Bellanger took up residence in the Danish Lodge, at what is now Pondicherry, and the French period of Pondicherry began.

People referred to 'French India' which became a general name for the former French possessions in India. These included Pondicherry, Karikal and Yanaon on the Coromandel Coast, Mahe on the Malabar Coast and Chandernagore in Bengal. Machilipatnam, of which I spoke in Andhra Pradesh, had also belonged to the French for some time. My own French ancestors had lands in Pondicherry and Chandernagore as well as indigo estates in West Bengal or Bihar. I would have loved to go and do some detailed research about my French forbears but there was not sufficient time and I know how frustrating that sort of activity is – particularly in India.

French is still spoken amongst the older residents of Pondicherry and there is a definite difference to be seen on entering the area; freshly painted white classical entry posts and little gazebo-like structures are used along the main road into the enclave. It is a thriving town and has a colonial feel to it in some ways. We had in fact met an Indian couple from Pondicherry at a wedding in the south west of France some years back. The man runs the only French-speaking newspaper in India. We in fact had to speak to them in French because they did not speak Hindi or English. I found that quite a strange situation.

The grid-like streets were laid out in the 18th century and it expanded to become a large and rich town. Indeed its most famous governor, Joseph Francois Dupleix, began to cherish the ambition of a French Empire in India. This was not achieved because the British were equally determined to have supremacy and Robert Clive was primarily responsible for dashing the hopes of the French colonists. The independence of India in 1947 led to the union of France's Indian possessions with former British India. In 1948 an agreement between France and India allowed for an election in France's Indian possessions to choose their political future. The actual union of French India with the Indian Union did not take place until 1962, although the bureaucracy had been united with India's on 1st November 1954. Pondicherry still has a large number of Tamil residents with French passports, whose ancestors were in French Government service and who chose to remain French at the time of Independence.

Pondicherry is a Union Territory which means it is not a separate State. It has its own government but falls directly under the Central Government in New Delhi. Though a Union territory also has an elected chief minister and cabinet members, laws and legislative regulations made in these areas must get approval or be ratified by the central government. The Indian, i.e. Union, Government is represented by the Lieutenant Governor, who resides at the Raj Nivas, which was the former palace of the French Governor.

The other Union Territories are: Andaman and Nicobar Islands, Chandinagore, Dadra and Nagar Haveli, Daman and Diu and the Lakshadweep Islands.

We drove along the Marine Drive and stopped and inspected various memorials and observed where the tsunami had created breaches in the sea wall. The elegant Gandhi Memorial is very fine and I also looked at the War Memorial to two world wars which was gated and locked but nicely done and, of course, all in French. The *Douanière* is still so named as it would have been in decades past i.e. The Customs House. Frankly I thought the whole place was a bit underwhelming, despite my French antecedents. The central park could be better maintained. We stopped and walked around because there was a silent demonstration for women's rights making a peaceful protest under the shade of the trees. The French colonial architecture is quite different and rather charming and the wide streets give a languid air to the centre of town, but we were very disappointed with the Botanic Gardens. They are beautifully sited and could be wonderful but the maintenance was very poor; this was such a contrast to the beautiful world famous botanical gardens in Kandy in Sri Lanka which we had thoroughly enjoyed.

The Pondicherry Museum is however worth a visit and has interesting artefacts from the French colonial period. There is a pousse-pousse on show which was an early version of a rickshaw. There are also some lovely Pallava and Chola bronzes and artefacts excavated from Arikamedu, the ancient port which I mentioned had had trade links with the Romans.

We enjoyed the visit to the Aurobindo Ashram, which is Pondicherry's best known landmark. This probably dominates the life of this town. Founded by Sri Aurobindo in 1926, the Ashram is a peaceful retreat with tree-shaded courtyards and lovely annual flowers in the garden. The flower-festooned *Samadhi* (memorial) of Sri Aurobindo who died in 1950, and The Mother lies under a frangipani tree in the main courtyard. There was a huge interest in this as with a religious shrine and the courtyard was filled with people of all ages and a school party.

The interior of the house is kept to show how this distinguished and determined old man had lived. I always enjoy that sort of experience and there was a very peaceful air throughout the whole property.

Sri Aurobindo Ghose was a Bengali poet-philosopher, a patriot before his time who joined the struggle to free India in the 1900s. To escape from the British who had imprisoned him at Alipore, a suburb of Calcutta, he fled to Pondicherry, which was of course French; here he became drawn to yoga and spiritualism and his life became entirely devoted to achievement through spirituality. Gandhi and he were friends and he was visited here by Gandhi in the years of the freedom struggle. His disciple Mirra Alfassa, was later known as 'The Mother'; she was French and the daughter of a banker who emigrated to France from Egypt. Mirra was born in 1878 and grew up to be very talented, both as a musician and writer and also an accomplished painter who exhibited in Paris. As a teenager she had some spiritual experiences which led to her becoming a psychic and very deep thinker and at the age of thirty-six she came to Pondicherry and met Aurobindo in March 1914. She recognised that he was the 'spiritual master' for which she was searching. She had to leave to return to France at the beginning of the First World War but she returned to Pondicherry in 1920 and resumed her work with Aurobindo. At the time of Mirra rejoining Aurobindo a small group of disciples had gathered around him, and her coming led to a significant increase in numbers and eventually this informal grouping took shape as an ashram or spiritual community.

The Mother, as she became known, took on the full material and spiritual charge of the Sri Aurobindo Ashram in November 1926. Under her guidance, which extended over nearly fifty years, the Ashram has grown into a many-faceted community which at present consists of about 1,500 people. The Mother also founded the Sri Aurobindo International Centre of Education in 1951 and the international township Auroville in 1968. That however is not part of Pondicherry. She died at the age of 95 in 1973. Once confined to a few buildings in one corner of Pondicherry, the Ashram's growth has caused it to expand physically in all directions. Today Ashramites live and work in more than 400 buildings spread throughout the town.

In popular imagination ashrams are connected with hermitages or religious orders, but in fact 'an ashram is not an association or a religious body or monastery'. The Sri Aurobindo Ashram has nothing to do with asceticism or retreat from the world. The character of this unique institution may be summed up in these words from one of his letters:

"The way of Yoga followed here has a purpose different from others – for its aim is not only to rise out of the ordinary ignorant world-consciousness into the divine consciousness, but to bring the supramental power of that divine consciousness down into the ignorance of mind, life and body, to transform them, to manifest the Divine here and create a divine life in Matter."

In ashrams where liberation from worldly existence (*moksha*) is the sole object, there is a tendency for members to withdraw from outward life – to become ascetics. But in accordance with the comprehensive goal of Sri Aurobindo's teaching, members of his Ashram, "are not *sannyasis*... It is an inner freedom and equanimity and not an outward renunciation that is required...What is being done here is a work – a work which will be founded on yogic consciousness and Yoga Shakti (the divine power), and can have no other foundation. Meanwhile every member here is expected to do some work in the Ashram as a part of this spiritual preparation".

I have written in some detail to explain the Sri Aurobindo Ashram because it is a special place with worthwhile values; subsequently a new town called Auroville, or the City of Dawn, which is eight kilometres from Pondicherry was estabished. This was the brainchild of The Mother and was designed by the French architect Roger Anger in 1968. It was conceived as a sort of utopian paradise and planned as a futuristic international city. I became aware of it when in my early twenties and was fascinated by the whole concept, and was full of youthful optimism for its ideals. At the height of the Viet Nam War the idea that a city could be born where people would live in peace and goodwill in an international commune devoid of caste, class or religion, with forty settlements with names like Grace, Serenity and Certitude seemed wonderful to our generation, sickened by what was happening in what had been another French colony. The Matri Mandir was built to reflect The Mother's spiritual beliefs; it is in the centre of a sixty-two acre site and has a spherical marble chamber with a crystal placed inside reflecting the sun's rays. The concentrated light acts as a focal point to aid meditation. The mandir is not yet complete through lack of funds.

Graham and I needed lunch and a rest and we went to a rather ordinary looking hotel that Nandu suggested. The food however was very good and nicely served in a rather odd little restaurant but what intrigued us of course was the patisserie shop on the hotel's forecourt, which might have come straight from France. We had seen shops like this and carts by the wayside in Viet Nam, but delicate French pastries and choux patisserie are not that usual in India.

There appears to be a natural attraction between the people of India and France; the average French man or woman is much more knowledgeable about India than for example the average American, who is often very ignorant, to the point that he or she does not know where India is situated geographically. They may now have a more accurate idea because George W Bush is due to pay a state visit at the very beginning of March 2006. For a long time in France there was an intense interest in India. The French philosopher Pierre Sonnerat wrote:

> "Ancient India gave to the world its religions and philosophies. Egypt and Greece owe India their wisdom, and it is known that Pythagoras went to India to study under Brahmins, who were the most enlightened of human beings."

Curiously, as I write in February 2006, the French President is paying a state visit to India, but for some reason this is not being treated with the attention it should deserve. Both countries have tested nuclear weapons individually and incurred the world's displeasure, and of course that means largely that of the United States. Now India is confident of shopping for weapons and equipment in the United States; but that could always be vulnerable to the whims of the incumbent American regime – the latter has a history of expediency in its dealings with all of us, be we western or eastern nations.

Perhaps France too has to learn some humility; most French officials go to Delhi, Mumbai or Bangalore for a few days and think they have seen and understood everything. India is a complex country and it is not as easy to do business there, but it is the future of Asia, a democratic, pro-western, liberal nation, which is a bastion of freedom in an Asia threatened by Islamic fundamentalism and the shadow of Chinese hegemony.

Refreshed and reinvigorated we set off from Pondicherry. I wanted just to touch on Cuddalore; this town in Tamil Nadu had received a full onslaught of the tsunami and I felt duty bound to go and see for myself. Cuddalore lost 6,000 boats to the tsunami and in Nagapattinam more than 10,000 boats were completely wrecked and 800 partially damaged. When we visited about 29,000 fishermen were without work in the two districts. The thorny question of compensation and the acceptable amount for a fishing boat i.e. a catamaran as opposed to the mechanised fibre-reinforced plastic boats was the cause of much resentment. The figures were considered to be much too little, so the local community worked together and discouraged fishermen from accepting aid, forcing the Government to improve the grant for each catamaran very substantially. The village elders said that if men were to resume fishing they might negate their rights for compensation, which would have been terrible, but equally if people did not make a start then the whole economy was in stasis. It appeared to me that some double standards were operating between what was financially handed out in Karaikal, which falls under the Union Territory of Pondicherry and is adjacent to Nagapattinam and Cuddalore, and the latter two areas. By the time I visited they had received full compensation in Karaikal. Far away in Kannyakumari, the very tip of India, which we were to visit, was even more shabbily treated with no compensation for boats and nets. In Nagapattinam more than 86,000 people were provided with shelter in 82 relief camps and the non-governmental organisations or NGOs and various big companies were providing fans and bicycles to victims. There were some real success stories too; the District Collector of Cuddalore Gagandeep Singh Bedi helped restore electricity in all the villages within two days of the calamity. Without waiting for government orders he spent money on immediate needs like drinking water and temporary shelters. He instigated the building of children's parks to help restore normality to the children. In Cuddalore 21 children were orphaned and 137 lost one of their parents. Victims of the tsunami have themselves done wonderful things to help their community; one man offered his house to be turned into an orphanage after he lost three children in the tragedy.

Three months after the tsunami had destroyed the livelihoods of thousands of fishermen and turned their lives upside down, as if that was not enough, the usual local politics and petty haggling was preventing a return to anything like normality. In the months since the tsunami struck teenage girls the length of Tamil Nadu's battered coast have been forced into early marriages. Some are married off by parents terrified of their honour being compromised in the crowded relief camps; some because their parents can no longer afford to look after them, and widowed men come asking for the young sixteen year olds. The tsunami killed four women for every man. The men were stronger swimmers, and the women were slowed as they tried to rescue their children. Most of the coastal villages now have a dangerous gender imbalance. I don't think the government actually helped by offering a wedding package worth Rs40, 000 (£500) to every bride from the stricken area. This policy was intended to help the normal eighteen year old brides but parents of under age girls saw it as an opportunity to cash in, particularly if they had lost their livelihood, and the rules were very easy to circumvent.

I talked of female exploitation in my second book, India: The Tiger's Roar. Well in this circumstance of a huge natural disaster there was plenty of opportunity for unscrupulous behaviour and exploitation. Young men preyed upon the young teenage girls and started entering their camp shelters which put enormous pressure on them or their parents. Apparently village elders also saw an opportunity to exploit the situation by hastily agreeing to a marriage where the parents were dead and then pocketing the money. In relief camps there have been horrible tales of sexual assault which have led to the suicides of the young women victimised.

In southern India 934 villages were affected by the tsunami. More than two million people's lives were changed in one way or another. Twelve thousand people died and 541 children were orphaned. Seven hundred schools were lost. Men who had lost their wives thought very little of taking their girl children to an orphanage and then remarrying. In Indian society, orphans even when they become adults have a low standing, so when they reach eighteen there will be virtually no support for these orphans. UNICEF workers say that they will be thought of as 'tainted'. The children are full of rage and grief and desolation; this would be a huge problem with which to cope in western society, but in India somehow it becomes that much uglier with little sense of responsibility being shown by the remaining parent or families of these children. I am aware of the poverty of these people but the foreign relief money pouring into the small communities coupled with the government compensation, though desperately needed, complicated the structure of people's lives.

As I write in February 2006, 65,000 people in this part of India still live in shelters. More than 500 children exist without parents. The tsunami may have changed village life for ever in this coastal region; there is now competitiveness and division. The full moon that I love so dearly spells potential disaster for so many and they move inland and stay with relatives at that time of the month.

For those reading this book and for me and my family there are so many choices and alternatives in life; for people who only know poverty and the daily grind of a dangerous job and its few rewards life is totally different. I am not in a position to be judgemental, though any form of female exploitation I do condemn.

The Coromandel Coast, which is the name given to the east coast of India from the Godavari Delta in Andhra Pradesh in the north to Point Calimere in the south, received its name from Cholamandalam – meaning the Realm of the Cholas. Tranquebar was a Danish settlement in the 17th century and is now known as Tarangambadi, which is a lot more difficult for westerners to pronounce! It has a fort, churches and a beautiful brick gateway. Nagapattinam, of which I have written about with regard to the tsunami destruction is an old Chola port and was a major Buddhist centre till the 13th century, it was later occupied by the Portuguese, the Dutch and finally the British. Sixty kilometres south of Pondicherry is Chidambaram – sacred Chidambaram where Lord Shiva is believed to have performed his cosmic dance. The famous Nataraja

Temple, built by the Cholas in the 9th century to honour the Lord of the Dance, has an unusual gold-plated roof but in a unique shape of four quarters; there is the huge Shivaganga man-made lake and four highly coloured gopuras. Religious traditions in this temple are carried out by a group of hereditary priests whose ancestors came to Chidambaram 3,000 years ago.

Tamil Nadu also has a sort of backwater of canals at Pichavaram which is sixteen kilometres east of Chidambaram. Mangrove swamps and 1,700 islands and 4,000 canals can be explored in rowboats but I was looking forward to the Kerala Backwaters experience later on in our journey.

Rameswaram is one of the most sacred towns of India. It is well known for its temple corridor, the longest of its kind with 1,212 pillars; the corridor surrounds the core of the temple on all four sides. The complex has an amazing number of artificial ponds (*tirthas*) in which to perform ritual ablutions. It is believed that a bathe in the Agni Tirtha, in front of the temple removes all sins. It is situated on the sacred island of Rameswaram which protrudes into the Gulf of Mannar, the narrow channel of water separating Tamil Nadu from Sri Lanka. A pilgrimage to Rameswaram is among the important injunctions laid on the Hindu from the beginning of time and therefore the Rameswaram pilgrimage has passed into folklore – particularly in Tamil Nadu. Through the centuries many kings came to give thanks and erected columns to celebrate their respective victories. The temple has grown over the centuries into its present huge dimensions and stands on the eastern shore of the island, which is shaped like a conch, similar to the one Lord Vishnu bears in one of his hands. A magnificent railway bridge, built at the beginning of the 20th century, connects the island with the mainland. It is believed that Rama gave the Linga, dedicated to Lord Shiva to the temple having returned from slaying Ravana in what is now Sri Lanka. After killing Ravana he offered his devotions to Lord Shiva to expiate the sin incurred in destroying the demon. Everything in and near Rameswaram is traditionally connected with incidents in the 'Ramayana'. This temple was built by the Cholas but also expanded during the Nayaka period in the 16th and 18th centuries.

This is a temple we were not able to visit on this occasion but I wanted to mention it as the story is such a fine one and its importance is well known. I have heard that there is going to be some hotel development in the region and careful opening up of the beaches; we were told the snorkelling and diving around here will be wonderful when all that is complete. Graham and I hope to visit once that is accomplished and I am confident development in the hands of that particular hotel group known to me will be responsible.

Chapter Eight

Gangaikondacholapuram

Whilst we had been driving around Nandu had been telling us about the various treasures we were about to enjoy. He had a way of saying the above word so fast that neither of us could decipher what he was saying. Eventually, without being rude I was able to ask him to say it very slowly, in the end he had to write it down for us. I shall explain.

We knew that we were to visit the world famous temple at Thanjavur and I had done my research about it. However, before we reached Thanjavur we would see other amazing temples, one of which is *Gangaikondacholapuram*. Tamil Nadu now has at least five World Heritage Sites, of which the above temple is a relatively new one. Mamallapuram had been the first one that we had enjoyed. I will explain about the beautiful Thanjavur temple as we reach it but to describe this one I have to describe the chronology. The ruler of this area was Rajaraja, one of the great Chola dynasty, who had come to the throne in 985 AD. His son Rajendra I subsequently, within a quarter of a century of the erection of the Thanjavur temple, built another almost equally wonderful. Rajendra I, the son and successor of Rajaraja, was an equally successful monarch and conqueror like his father, and like all the Cholas immensely pious. The greatest feat of arms in Tamil history is his military campaign as far as the banks of the Ganga (the Ganges) in the far north; so rightly he became known as the 'Gangaikonda Chola', an honorific of which he was very proud.

He built a new capital near the northern banks of the Kolladam at a place called Gangaikondacholapuram and he laid it out according to the ancient Hindu town planning manuals. He built a huge superb temple called the *Gangaikondacholaisvaram*. He had sufficient filial respect towards his late father not to try and outdo him in temple building but he organised a spectacular event. He instructed that all the vanquished rulers he had defeated from the north should come and empty a pot of Ganga water in a big lake he had dug nearby. This lake he referred to as his 'liquid pillar of victory'. Apart from a victorious flourish it was a very wise thing to do for this arid region, and Rajendra did many other good things for his people; sadly however the lake has dried up in the intervening centuries.

The temple however survives though now the town is small and unremarkable. We were hot and tired by the time we arrived in the mid afternoon. It was for us just perfect. The sun had lost its strength but gave the temple environs a beautiful light. It is a well kept area within the temple with smooth green lawns and a few temple trees (frangipani) and the air of tranquillity was just what we needed after lots of driving in a tiny car. I thought the approach to the temple could be improved and simple gravel parking area organised with a sense of having arrived at a World Heritage Site, but maybe this is yet to come. There were no tourists around and Nandu explained the history and significance of everything to us.

There were lots of young people sitting around in groups; it was explained that they were college students who had come to the end of the academic year and would now soon be saying farewell to each other and thus were having a sort of informal get together. Nandu returned to the subject of his own family whilst he and I just sat and visually drank in the magnificence of this great place. He has two daughters of twenty-three and twenty-one, the first of whom studied

Dining outside at Swamimallai

maths then computing and has now completed an MBA – it is for her that he will arrange a marriage of which I wrote earlier. The younger daughter has yet to finish her electronic engineering degree. Graham and I so enjoyed this conversation; it might have been us talking about our two sons Hamish and Stewart a decade ago and taking pride in their achievements. Here is an ordinary Chennai family with two successful girl children reaching academic sophistication which leads to great hope for the future of India; the old adage, "The hand that rocks the cradle..." will come to the fore in time.

This sort of historic site in India does not yet have any periphery attractions like a coffee shop or souvenir shop or indeed toilets! No matter, we actually enjoy it in its simplicity and when we are alone except for a few Indians it is such a special experience. If one is thirsty the bottled water we always travel with is very welcome but otherwise nothing takes away from the initial awe of the place.

The temple has been carefully renovated but its *gopura* (tall, tapering structure over the gateway) had been dismantled and I think some of the outer walls had also been used to build a dam on the river nearby; however that has been rectified by the Archaeological Survey of India. The temple consists of the sanctum, an ardhamandapa and a mukhamandapa. Mandapas are columned halls which sometimes take on vast proportions such as at Madurai and Rameswaram; they are

Gangaikondacholapuram temple's statues in Tamil Nadu

usually flat roofed and when built in front of one another are referred to as the ardha and mukha mandapas. There is also a very fine huge Nandi bull and a huge sacred Lion rather in the style of a *chindit* lion.

Because this temple is not in use and is just a historic monument it does not receive crowds of visitors or pilgrims, which from a selfish traveller's point of view is a definite plus. I like the well ordered garden with paths and lush green lawns around it, which in the heat was very pleasant. The vimana tower is fifty-five metres high, just three metres smaller than Rajendra's father's temple tower at Thanjavur. This was a deliberate decision, it is considered, out of filial respect – the tower is nine storeys and people think of it as the feminine counterpart to the great temple of Thanjavur. The Linga in the sanctum is four metres high. There are five shrines and a famous well in the prakara. The lion is the superstructure over the well and is thought to have been built in the 19th century.

The sculptural glory of this temple lies in the niche images on the outer walls of the sanctum. There are fifty of them, three of which are considered among the greatest achievements of the Hindu sculptor down the centuries. Two are of Lord Nataraja and of Goddess Saraswathi. The third is of Lord Shiva placing a garland around the head of a devotee: probably a symbol depicting approval from the God of Rajendra's achievements. There are some superb bronzes in this temple and an outstanding one is of Lord Subramania. Some of the images still worshipped in the local villages are thought to have come from the Chalukya and Eastern Ganga lands in the north a thousand years ago.

We finally went on our way knowing that in the following few days we would see equally wonderful feats of architecture and artefacts. Thankfully we did not have far to drive and arrived at Swamimalai as the sun was setting.

The Sterling Swamimalai Resort is the big sister to the one we had stayed at Mamallapuram; it is enchanting in so many ways. Nandu and the driver took us to the reception area and then took their leave. The staff at Swamimalai were very welcoming and we went through the same ritual as previously, i.e. a foot massage and fragrant damp towel with a glass of cool fruit juice. All were very welcome by this time in the late afternoon!

The resort is built within a large coconut grove around the typical landlord's house that had been built in 1896. It had been the home of Sri Shankaracharya, the late Hindu sage and is typical of a house belonging to a prosperous Tamil Nadu village elder; the hotel group has renovated it most carefully and built neighbouring buildings in sympathy with its original design. The resort is eco-friendly with individual cottages and complexes built in the same theme which one reaches on footpaths made to resemble typical village streets. There are terracotta statues of Tamil frontier gods at the end of the streets. These deities are believed to be the protectors of the village. Hotel guests can also experience bullock cart rides here. We had been given a most charming house, which was obviously considered one of the most luxurious, but yet totally simple. I loved it. As an exotic touch our en-suite bathing facilities had the addition of a lotus bath – which in fact is a bath probably made out of concrete but painted to resemble terracotta in the shape of a lotus flower with plumbing to one side. The water had been prepared with blossoms floating on the surface and scented towels to hand. The room in fact was like a very elegant open hut thus giving privacy but still light and fresh; our more conventional bathroom had a good hot shower in it along with a basin and WC. Our house was close to what is considered the 'village square' traditionally called 'oor maiyyam'. The square, which is a misnomer really as it is a huge circle of brick paving, is used for yoga in the mornings and other communal activities. Just outside our house with its charming veranda is a huge white image of Lord Murugan, the second son of Lord Shiva and brother to Lord Ganesh. Surrounding the brick circle are lush green lawns and shrubs and little pools of lotus or fish. Everywhere one walked something charming was revealed and the trees and coconut palms and vegetation gave it such a lush feel. The swimming pool had been designed to resemble a village tank of water, so is square with a wall behind with gods on top watching over you as you swim. It is floodlit at night which looks very inviting.

We retired to the lotus pool and had a sort of laze in it and contemplated the day's activities. We had driven an awful long way and seen a great deal; it gets to the stage that nothing more will sink into the brain, but I had been informed that a distinguished group of Carnatic Musicians had been instructed to play for us and so that was something that would have to be accomplished before we finally relaxed.

The managers and administrative staff at the resort were all friendly and eager to chat about my origins and why I had been invited to make this trip; it is amazing that when one starts chatting India becomes a small place and inevitably you find you have mutual friends or at least acquaintances. The courtyard in which the musicians were to play is utterly charming and a perfect venue for such a concert. Imagine if you will a courtyard with pillared verandas on three sides. The fourth is actually a wall on which has been moulded a beautiful head and shoulders of Lord Nataraja, the Cosmic Dancer. The whole wall is taken up with this depiction and thus provides a most wonderful backdrop. In the middle of the veranda opposite were positioned two little thrones painted in gold with the backrests being two reclining lions. This seat is at the edge of the veranda so one has one's feet resting on a little plinth and is sitting on the veranda's edge leaning against the lions. It was surprisingly comfortable really!

The Carnatic Musicians who played for us were friendly and glad of our obvious appreciation. They played two violins, a tabla, a rounded pot as a drum and a real drum. This is the classical music of South India and we probably heard some of the most talented musicians playing that evening. Though based on the general concept of *raga* (melody) and *tala* (rhythm) it uses different percussion and musical instruments and develops the melody in a more structured manner. Some of the greatest Carnatic music was composed between 1750 and 1850. The violin which is similar to the western instrument is played in a seated position i.e. cross-legged on the ground. The *ghatam*, is a clay pot which can produce fabulous rhythms in the hands of an expert. That night the player was a young boy who was truly amazing and delighted with our response. The *veena*, which resembles the more widely seen *sitar*, is a beautiful hand crafted string instrument that has to rest on the ground. The *nadasvaram* is a wind instrument which is a must for auspicious occasions and the *thavil* is the drum which is

Statue of Lord Murugan at Swamimallai in Tamil Nadu

Swamimallai's courtyard with the dancing Shiva head

essential for the more complex rhythmic improvisations to accompany the melody. The flute is ever constant in Indian music.

Music festivals are held in the large cities where concerts take place in quite small auditoriums called *sabhas*. The vocalists are very famous throughout India, indeed one wonderful old lady singer called M S Suba Lakshmi had recently died; she was a legend in her time throughout India, although most particularly in the south. The vocal sounds of Carnatic music are unique, by themselves perhaps not particularly musical but in conjunction with the instruments quite electrifying – a sort of system of vocal clucks and clicks and tongueing! I was enchanted with this concert and asked them for a CD to purchase, but they did not have any, though they still had some tapes. I urged them to make the leap to CDs. Sona Rupa of Leicester in the UK are the leading exponents of Indian music in Britain and make the most wonderful CDs of which we have several. In fact a day does not start without us waking up to one or other of their calming evocative discs. The Mattanis, father and son, who own Sona Rupa have been most generous and allowed me to use their music on the DVD I have made to promote India.

Supper was very welcome that evening and we were thoughtfully served in the main dining room with a wonderful thali (round brass or metal tray) meal. None of the courses looked big enough, but when one has had several they all add up to an elegant sufficiency; the waiter explained what each was made from. I particularly remember the herb soup which was unique.

The next morning I had 'bed tea' at just after six – I like to be up and walking around before anyone else stirs; the sun had not yet risen but the birds have sung a dawn chorus and the geese and turkeys and ducks were making their welcome noises and strutting around. The resort has a nicely built cow stall for their dairy herd and there are also deer in an enclosure which are let out to roam around the grounds. All the sounds were of livestock and early morning village life, without the blaring of horns or other noisy interruptions.

The rangoli lady follows the girl who throws water on the ground and sweeps it in front of every entrance. The rangoli artist then very expertly with two fingers quickly draws a free hand pattern out of a white chalky liquid – no two are ever the same – and fresh flowers are placed to adorn the deity. Breakfast was very good and I asked for my usual tomato omelette and fruit. The Ayurvedic Physicians' courtyard was lovely. It comprises consulting rooms, separate loos, massage rooms, a medical store and a lovely well in the centre with terracotta peacocks in decoration. Visitors come from many countries to experience the ayurvedic treatments of Swamimalai; it was quite obvious that they have a significant following from the Far East who come for a week or ten days and follow a regime of treatment to help with a broad spectrum of ailments and aches and pains along with serious chronic conditions. I was told of one guest who had suffered for many years with pain that meant he hardly slept. After a full week's treatment and massage he was so much better, that though he had to return to Malaysia he came back as soon as possible to have fifteen days after which he felt a totally different man. Lack of sleep must indeed be one of the most debilitating afflictions and I certainly felt able to ask the young lady physician about one or two things. She was helpful and I bought a few items, all of which I would like to replicate, but sadly Indian web sites promise much and never actually respond – nor it seems are they vigilant about updating them!

We left with great regret that our time with them had been so short. We went on to visit the Swamimalai temple, but in a cursory fashion as it is a 'working temple' and though of huge significance to the worshippers not really so easy to go round. The temple here is one of the six sacred shrines devoted to Lord Murugan, the son of Lord Shiva who legend has it propounded the meaning of 'Om', the sacred mantra to his father, and thus assumed the title Swaminatha (Lord of Lords).

We were more interested in the Image Makers of Swamimalai, who work in the famous 'Lost Wax' form of moulding and carving. Today on Raja Street in Swamimalai there are many image makers who have lived and worked there for generations. The *sthapathy* or sculptor first sends up a silent prayer before starting his work. The ancient treatise called Shilpa Shastra has set down in writing the fixed rules and guidelines to which he must adhere. He can be working in a courtyard or small room in his workshop, but this work has been going on since time immemorial. The sculptor is a serene individual with enormous talent, he works in a very dextrous fashion quietly moulding a wax figure in his hand of Nataraja or some other deity; an apprentice holds a head of beeswax close by and he pinches off as much wax as is required for the figure. This wonderful art has been fashioned since the Pallava and then the Chola dynasty ruled in the 9th century and the descendants of those first sculptors are working there to this day. I found this a most marvellous thought; so little in life has a constant, but here in South India there are men working away producing images of deities that are precisely similar to those first worked over one thousand years ago! It was explained to us that many craftsmen were brought from villages to the north of this region, men who had worked in both stone and metal, but because the Chola kings were looking for fine craftsmen to embellish their temple building they were brought to Swamimalai, where the special sand that was found on the river banks was exactly the right consistency to pack over the wax figures. If the sand was just a bit too coarse it would not work, as the bronze would be pitted.

In a very small way I was already familiar with the lost wax method of casting, but in nothing less than gold. In the 1960s we had a close family friend who was a most gifted jeweller and craftsman and lived in Kinross here in Scotland. He would often work in wax to create a model which when melted and drained would be replaced with molten gold. However, sometimes, he carved or fashioned something out of dried cuttle fish and poured molten gold in the mould, which then, once allowed to cool, he would fashion into a ring or a brooch or pieces for a necklace. He made my gold wedding ring and engagement ring in that fashion; a craft learned at Goldsmiths' College in London, following in the footsteps of Italian craftsmen through the ages, particularly from Milan. I once or twice helped him to pour the molten gold which was so beautiful and exciting. He made a brooch for my mother inspired by a dried sea horse, which was placed in wax and then baked to shrivel up and create the mould for a gold one – quite enchanting. I have a gold brooch made in the same way using heather to create the design – it is of course unique.

We watched the men fascinated. The wax figure was finished and sent over for preparatory work. Fine, wet sand was packed firmly over the figure and steel wires were used strategically to band round it. Over

Temple in renovation at Darasuram

this a mixture of wet sand and clay is packed to a thickness of four inches and this bulky parcel has one drainage opening from which the hot wax would drain out. It is again tied with wire to prevent it from splitting open during the metal pouring stage. Left out in the blazing sun, the wet mud dries out completely both inside and out. It is now ready for the critical stage. The bulky parcel is then heated on a gentle fire for the wax to melt, as the wax melts, it pours out through the mouth and is collected in a container. This is where it gets its name of the lost wax technique. A fire is kindled with the help of an industrial blower to a temperature of 1,500 degrees. Into this a crucible containing the *panchaloka* or five metals namely brass, copper lead, silver and gold are placed. I don't think many statues these days are made with the inclusion of silver and gold. Meanwhile the cooled wax-less clay is buried in the earth with the mouth protruding. When the metals have turned into a molten liquid the crucible is lifted out with heavy tongs. Now the sculptor is once again there to supervise closely; he carefully pours the liquid metal in one steady continuous motion till it overflows resembling volcanic lava – an angry red overflow. When the molten metal has cooled down completely, the baked clay is broken apart with a hammer to reveal the icon that resembles the wax image that is now nonexistent. The icon is brought into the central courtyard where the smoothing, filing and finishing take place. The embellishments are now

Women stone carriers

worked on. Finally, the eyes of the image are 'opened' with a time honoured ritual; the eyes are sealed with a mixture of honey and ghee (clarified butter) and then ritually opened by a priest using a needle made of gold, and then it is ready for presentation. All the time the work is being done on the face of the image the craftsman is calm and peaceful – this is essential. According to their beliefs tranquillity of mind is most important as every mood will be reflected on the face of the icon. He works on his figures with deep reverence and is happiest when the idols are installed in temples.

Had I been able to communicate with the workmen it would have been nice to explain my attempts in molten gold exactly forty years ago in a far away land.

The magic of India is that one can be walking down a street perhaps becoming irritated by the crush of people who surround one and immediately start begging, and then one is transported back a thousand years by watching craftsmen at their work, which they consider quite normal and yet we in the West find outstanding.

I needed to make an important telephone call and so stopped in a tiny little STD kiosk and made my call, which was clear, efficient and so cheap. So often I phone home to Scotland and speak to my mother and when the shopkeeper presents the bill it is the equivalent of a couple of pounds. State of the art modern telecommunications and timeless artistry all housed in the same street – indeed that is India!

Nandu wanted to show us yet another beautiful ancient temple, but this one still has the deity and is considered a 'living' temple. Darasuram temple just a little way from Swamimalai is really called the *Airavatesvara* temple. The word Darasuram is a corruption from the original name of 'Rajarajapuram' and was part of the subsidiary Chola capital called Pazhayarai. This temple was built in the reign of Rajaraja II in the 12th century which was the high meridian of Chola power. It too has been declared a World Heritage Site and is being carefully renovated at the moment. Someone once called this "a sculptor's dream re-lived in stone"; this temple is smaller than both Gangaikondacholapuram and the great temple at Thanjavur, which we were yet to see. The temple environs are nice with grass and trees and that same feeling of tranquillity. Because this is a living temple we had to take off our shoes and sprint on the stones because of the hot sun. The renovation is painstaking and slow and being supervised by the Archaeological Survey of India. The work however is being done much as it must have been done to build it originally with manpower heaving the great stones. Local women heave the stones onto their heads and walk from A to B; they are paid about Rs70-80 per day, which is just over one pound daily, the men receive Rs100.

The front mandapa in this temple is in the form of a chariot which makes it special and there are some superb, huge, bronze images still sited in niches. The priest came out and blessed both Graham and me and then put the tilak on our respective foreheads, and we gave money to the temple. We thought the women toiling away would enjoy having their photographs taken and since this was done on the digital camera we could show them, which made them giggle and thank us shyly.

Nandu then asked us if we would like to visit a home in which silk and cotton is woven into sari lengths. We loved the idea and were delighted with all we saw. The little house would fit into our double garage but was clean and neat. At the front door on the doorstep was a spinning wheel of the sort associated with Gandhiji. Inside there was the tiniest of kitchens and a minute hallway and then living room, in which a motorbike took pride of place. Hanging from the ceiling, from a heavy metal hook, was a looped sari in which the latest member of the family was sound asleep. The sari made a natural cot and that is the custom in these parts. Up some narrow stairs was a room in which two girls were weaving on two looms. The girls were eighteen and twenty-four and I think bonded to the family, or certainly employed by the family. We watched the weaving process and asked the girls about their work. They looked happy and healthy but it must be quite endless and depressing though thankfully in bright clean surroundings, quite different from the mill workers of Britain in the nineteenth century.

We asked to be shown the finished articles and looked through wonderful saris and shawls. I bought a shawl for Rs1,000, which I may do something with, but really I bought it out of courtesy for the household, having shown us their way of life. The middle man makes most of the profit in this business, which seems the norm sadly; it takes four days to set up the complexity of the design for the weaving as the sari borders have intricate patterns and a further two days of weaving.

Chapter Nine

Thanjavur and its Glories

The drive to Thanjavur was not a long one for which I was thankful. However the car started to give some trouble and it became obvious that the air conditioning had ceased. Graham very firmly told Nandu that he wanted that repaired as soon as possible and it was – over the lunch break!

Thanjavur has a great deal to offer and I was sorry that our visit was so short. Had we been visiting in a private capacity I would recommend two nights to really enjoy all that there is to see. We stayed at Hotel Sangam and were received with great warmth and hospitality. The group owns a hotel at Trichy – the full name of which is Tiruchirapalli but nobody ever refers to the city by its full name!

Because of the car requiring repair we had time to spare and it was very welcome. The hotel suite was immensely comfortable with a welcoming basket of fruit and the management very kindly had our laundry done very quickly so as to be ready by the evening. I was quite glad to be able to stretch out on a very comfortable bed and look out in anticipation on the great temple we would later see and catch up on the world news on the television and read some local papers in English. In the middle of the day it was really far too hot to be sightseeing. The hotel provided very good food with attention to detail and in no time the maitre d' had decided we would be given all sorts of extra delicacies of South Indian cuisine. They quickly latched on to the fact that we enjoy papaya and other fresh fruit and this was beautifully prepared for us; the chef then wandered out to see if we were enjoying our lunch and appreciated our obvious enjoyment. There was an excellent pool in a walled garden in which to cool off.

Thanjavur lies in the fertile valley of the River Kaveri. The Kaveri is one of the nine sacred rivers of India and this is the rice bowl of Tamil Nadu. For a thousand years this town has dominated the region and been a headquarters for three great dynasties; the first, as I explained earlier, was the Cholas from the 9th to the 13th centuries, the second was the Nayakas between 1535 and 1676 and finally the Marathas from 1676 to 1855. The Brihadishvara Temple built by Rajaraja Chola I was completed in 1010 and was the symbol of the power and might of the Cholas; built out of granite it is considered the finest example of Chola architecture and is now a UNESCO World Heritage Site. This great temple is dedicated to Lord Shiva. This temple although under the jurisdiction of the Archaeological Survey of India has recently reopened for worship.

I could see the temple looking golden in the sunlight but we were first to go to the Rajaraja Museum and Art Gallery, until the sun had lost its heat. Of all the cities in this region of what is now Tamil Nadu, Thanjavur the capital from 846-1279 AD has been the treasure house of art for centuries. Even now modern day Indians in Tamil Nadu, who are largely Tamils, consider the Imperial Cholas gave life to the conception of a land of heroism and culture. The Chola kings after establishing their kingdom and making it stable and strong turned to religion to provide a bulwark against Jainism and Buddhism which they saw as a threat to their own Hinduism. Hinduism is not a proselytising religion, nor indeed is Buddhism or Jainism but these rulers obviously felt it their duty to uphold Hinduism and perhaps promote it through the making of these wonderful bronze sculptures that could then be paraded on holy days, ensuring a very visible presence of their beliefs.

The Chola Empire which lasted for about four hundred years was followed by the Nayaks who were vassals of the great Vijaynagar Empire centred on Hampi in Karnataka. These people spoke Telegu, the language of which I wrote in the chapters on Hyderabad and Andhra Pradesh; their rule lasted less than two centuries to be followed by the Marathas but most of the palace complex and the art gallery building were constructed by the Nayak kings during the 16th and 17th centuries.

The Thanjavur Art Gallery was established in the palace in 1951 allegedly because of a rather trivial incident. In a suburb of Thanjavur an archaeologist from Calcutta (Kolkata) spotted an icon in the image of Brahma standing neglected on the riverside. In fact it was the image of Vageeswara Shiva and he wanted to remove it to the Calcutta Museum. The local people however were adamant that they did not want their local heritage removed and it was agreed that pieces found scattered and lying about, which sadly was the way in newly independent India, would be preserved in the palace corridors. Thus was this great treasure trove born and is now respected worldwide as one of the most important collections of bronze and stone idols in the world.

I thoroughly enjoyed visiting the museum and it was all explained to us by the curator but I so wish that the authorities would look again

Thanjavur's Temple Elephant

at the museum in terms of current ideas and décor and maintenance; it longs to be renovated and made up to date. What was acceptable in 1951 is desperately old fashioned and dull now; were this immensely beautiful work to be shown in a major city it would be wonderfully exhibited, whereas now it is still to be seen in dusty rooms and showcases. One of the groups that I loved is the celestial marriage of Lord Shiva and Parvati – it is a unique example of a complete group showing Lord Vishnu giving away his sister Parvati in wedlock to Lord Shiva; these bronzes were sculpted in the 11th century and the detail is exquisite.

The Royal Palace has a pyramidal temple-like tower with seven storeys which served as an observation tower for the ruling Nayaks out with the actual palace complex; it is interesting but in no way can it rival beautiful palaces in the north. However, if the authorities were to really work with conservationists and designers, this whole complex could become very worthwhile as an attraction. The splendid Maratha Durbar Hall built buy Shahji II in 1684 has elaborately painted and decorated pillars, walls and ceilings. A wooden canopy studded with glittering glass pieces and supported by wooden pillars stands above a green granite slab on which the Maratha throne once stood.

Thanjavur painting became a distinctive School of Painting during the rule of the Marathas, patronised by Serfoji II. The themes are mostly religious and the stylized ornamental depiction in vibrant colours is often studied with semi-precious stones. To a western observer it has no special appeal but I quite understand its value to believers in the Hindu faith and one can make comparison with early Christian art.

Graham and I particularly valued our visit to the Saraswati Mahal Library. This strange old building crammed to the ceiling in some places with manuscripts and as old fashioned as it is possible to be, is one of the most important medieval libraries in the world. Indeed, The Encyclopaedia Britannica in its survey of world libraries mentions this as 'the most remarkable library in the whole of India'. Frankly it seemed almost by chance that we visited it. Our guide knew of it and the local representative of the tourism ministry met us at the library but it was quite obvious that this was in an intellectual realm above Nandu's perceptions. When we arrived it was explained who we were and why we were visiting and this led to the director being called, who then hastily disappeared for some reason and then reappeared and took over our visit and inspection. How glad we are that he did because he then took us to his desk in a huge high ceiling office and proceeded to show us wonder after ancient wonder until our eyes were popping.

Whilst explaining about the library and its treasures the director kept bringing out the most beautiful fragile and rare written works that are not ever seen by the general public.

The Maratha rulers who captured Thanjavur in 1675 became active patrons of the culture of Thanjavur and developed the Royal Palace Library till 1855. The royal family actively used the library. Maharaja Serfoji II, 1798-1832, was an eminent scholar and when young he studied under the influence of a Danish missionary priest who was his father's friend and guide. He learnt to speak English, French and Italian and had a knowledge of Latin. This was the motivation for him to really enrich the royal library.

When he went on pilgrimage to Benares, now known as Varanasi, he employed many Brahmin Pandits to collect, buy and copy a huge number of works from all the renowned centres of Sanskrit learning in the north of India. This library very sensibly has been named after him.

I could not help looking round as we listened and looked at all before us. That room was extraordinary in its size and height with huge cupboards of wonderful wood which lined the walls and also made corridors through which we could move about. It was the sort of atmosphere in which an equivalent of a Dickens' story could be filmed, antiquated with fans lazily circulating the air and wide open doors to the outside. Indeed I needed to use the loo and was shown to a series of latrines outside which were totally rudimentary and pretty awful really; I worried about all the people who might have used them and then come inside and touched all the wonderful manuscripts! At one stage I thought I had returned to the India of my infancy...and yet?

The manuscript cupboards are cleaned twice a year and are kept fresh with insect repellent like napthalene balls and indigenously prepared organic insect repellent mixture comprising bark of cinnamon, cloves and camphor. The palm leaves are periodically cleaned and smeared with citronella oil which gives flexibility to leaves and it acts as a natural insect repellent (don't we know that in Scotland where it is very efficacious on the Scottish Midge). If the script of the manuscript becomes illegible then the soot from an oil burning lamp is mixed with citronella oil and used to help improve legibility. Teak wood reapers are fixed on both sides of the palm leaf manuscripts to safeguard them from damage.

13,062 Sanskrit manuscripts have been recorded in microfilm form with the joint venture of Indira Gandhi National Centre for Arts in Delhi. Currently they are microfilming all the foreign language books in what was the personal collection of King Serfoji; so far 1,600 books have been microfilmed. The library now has computer technology, since the late 1990s, and it is proposed to digitalise all the palm leaf and paper manuscripts.

Again, you see the dichotomy of India: on the one hand complete old fashioned premises which look slightly decayed and dusty and on the other the bright new technology of our times.

I would like to tell you some more about this library. Ancient squares of beautifully patterned materials are used to protect the manuscripts in a sort of book or file form. The material squares have now become a reference for the designs of 400 years ago. The director had worked in his young days in both the Victoria and Albert Museum in London and at the Scottish National Library in Edinburgh.

The illuminated manuscripts look so like the illustrated medieval manuscripts of Europe, the various wonderful Books of Hours, or psalters and early bibles; I last saw such beauty in the Strahov Library in Prague but in either western or Cyrillic scripts, but on that occasion we were not really allowed near them. Here I was looking at items on a desk.

The palm manuscripts were what took our fancy. I will attempt to describe them and how they were made. The palm slats cut from the leaves are strung together and are taken from the inner palm sections of a particular form of palm leaf – it is a leaf with which we are all familiar in tropical places. The scribe used a stylus of wood or bone, which was steadied through a notch in the left thumbnail of the writer.

The great temple at Thanjavur, Tamil Nadu

When demonstrated to us it was quite easy to see how efficient this would be. The ink used was a mixture of vegetable juice and soot. The palm leaves would have been soaked in turmeric mixture to prevent fungus growing and they would have been protected from light, damp and humidity in the cupboards and with lemon grass spray acting as an insect repellent.

We actually saw a complete Hindi text of the Mahabharata engraved on palm leaves, but also on parchment. This was an experience that on reflection one realises has been a very privileged one and for which we were both very grateful. I have no photography of this as you could imagine but it is all imprinted on my visual memory.

This library has a small museum but really it requires serious funding to make it a lot more visible for interested people from all over the world and obviously Indians interested in their own wonderful heritage.

When we emerged from the shaded, indeed slightly gloomy, interior the sun was low in the sky and a pleasant breeze had come up. We drove to the Brihadishvara Temple which most scholars consider the grandest temple in all of South India. It is thought that only the Lingraja Temple in Bhubaneshwar in Orissa can compare with it.

Rajaraja I conquered much of South India, a great part of Sri Lanka and the islands off the west coast and then he built this great temple. Within twenty years he restored power to his dynasty after suffering initially a heavy defeat at the hands of the Rashtrakutas. The Cholas' patron deity was the Lord Nataraja, that is, the dancing Shiva of whom I spoke earlier who is venerated at the great temple of Chidambaram. Rajaraja received his inspiration to build this temple from worshipping at Chidambaram which was of course also a Chola creation. Many Chola kings had been crowned there.

Rajaraja had come to the throne in 985 AD at a time of difficulty and uncertainty; on the two hundred and seventy-fifth day of his twenty-sixth year as king he presented a finial covered with gold to be placed on the top of the vimana of the Thanjavur temple. That marked its completion and all this information is inscribed on one of the walls of the temple. The inscription is so long that it contains one hundred and seven paragraphs.

The huge temple stands within a small fort. As we see it now it is probably a renovation of the original fort and is dated to the 16th century. There is a moat on three sides of the temple. The glory of this temple is its vimana. Four Chola temples alone, among all the hundreds in Tamil Nadu, have towers over the shrine which are bigger than their gopuras. The common practice is to build the gopura to a greater height than the vimana. The Brihadishvara was the first to reverse that custom. As we have seen the Gangaikondacholapuram temple built by his son Rajendra I was built in similar fashion, and then followed Darasuram in the 13th century and Tribhuvanam which is quite close to Darasuram. The Thanjavur vimana is fifty-eight metres high and is in thirteen tiers.

Graham, Nandu and I went in as the sun was setting. There were masses of people as this is once again a living temple. As I entered the gate under the gopura I saw an elephant; as I approached her handler asked if I would like a blessing. Indeed I would and I stood and had the elephant gently bless me by touching my head and hair with her trunk and I could hear her snuffling; I put up my hand and patted her and stroked the trunk, she just patiently allowed me this contact and kept her trunk on my head. For me this was very auspicious; I have loved elephants since a tiny child and first rode on an elephant at the age of six weeks when my parents were going into the jungles near Bareilly in Uttar Pradesh. I have climbed up a trunk of an elephant as a little girl and sat on her head, and have had a tiny baby elephant smack me on the bottom from behind, and feeding elephants was a favourite pastime as a small girl in Kolkata Zoo.

The Nandi bull in the temple forecourt is a very fine one and is comparable to the one at Lepakshi in Andhra Pradesh and the Chamundi Hill Nandi in Mysore in Karnataka. It is over 3.7 metres high, 6 metres long and 2.5 metres broad. It is a monolith weighing about twenty-five tonnes. There is no local stone so all the stone required for these huge buildings was brought over long distances. Another legend says that this Nandi stone was actually brought from the river bed of the Narmada River, another of India's great sacred rivers and one of which I am very fond and visited in my second book India: The Tiger's Roar.

Rajaraja, his queens and nobles gave a large number of metal images to the temple. There are inscribed references to nearly seventy, but very few of these survive today. Some of them were cast in gold. Rajaraja also gave extensive land to the temple, some of which apparently was in Sri Lanka. The Daniell brothers and others of their contemporaries – the British artists – drew this temple in the late 18th and early 19th centuries.

I could go on and on about all the wonderful artwork and carvings on this temple but it would be boring; on the western wall however there is a huge panel of Lord Shiva as Dakshinamurthi with two saints who are riding on an elephant and a horse respectively. Also on this wall there is a carving of a stately personality with three ladies and their attendants carrying staves of office. This obviously was a depiction of Rajaraja I and three of his queens.

What I enjoy at this time of day is to sit and contemplate and watch the sun set and be aware of all the people around me and know that through a thousand years other people in other times have done exactly what I am now doing. That I find immensely comforting – the land and its people, and now foreign peoples, but then I am not exactly foreign as India is the land of my birth.

We did not wish to enter the holy areas of the temple but were amused by the 'sound system' which at first we thought was authentic drumming; then we realised it was a cunning sound system that actually had the same effect!

Reluctantly, after giving the old cow elephant another affectionate stroke we departed, but to do something very 21st century – shopping. No, I was not after wonderful trinkets and mementoes but something

Author being blessed by an elephant

much more prosaic; a new hairdryer, some films, some fresh socks for Graham and a new wash bag since mine suddenly split. Nandu found us a strange little supermarket which we promptly found curious and worth going round. Actually everything we required was found in the place but not before a lot of people watched us with interest – most foreigners shop in the craft shops, not for socks and wash bags. I still have that hairdryer which I keep for my visits to India as the plug is correct for their electricity and I imagine that Graham is still wearing the very nice blue socks!

We returned to the Sangam Hotel, which I find easier to say than Hotel Sangam, tired and happy. Nandu took his leave and we went off to have a quick stretch out and then dine. The restaurant was full, much to our surprise. There were masses of westerners and I asked the maitre d' about them as we had not seen them earlier. He replied rather disparagingly that they were only dining in the hotel and preferred to stay at cheaper hotels. Since the Sangam worked out at approximately $65 for bed and breakfast for a large, comfortable, air conditioned suite I was intrigued that people come to India and do it on such a shoestring. These people I hasten to add were all our age, not backpackers. The hotel manager then enlarged on the theme and said that they are prepared to stay at very basic accommodation on these big tours from Spain and France and Germany but always come to eat in his hotel. Their accommodation in the other places would be very minimal and they always complain how awful Indian hotels are apparently but do not think of spending just a little more money to live and eat well. We both found this quite extraordinary – some of the people gorging on the food, the only way to describe it, were probably in their seventies.

The chef looked after us very well again, though it was a sort of buffet meal for everyone, he wanted to ensure that we had exactly what we wanted and it was a pleasant relaxing evening.

There is so much to see in the area that I really would advise a second night in the Sangam which would allow time to relax by the pool or take a walk through the town as well as see and enjoy all the ancient historic sights. The next morning we were treated to the most wonderful breakfast with the chef or his assistant making wonderful, huge, thin dosas and there were also home-made jams on the table; this was a good hotel.

Chapter Ten

Cashew Nuts and Chettinad

Leaving Thanjavur we found ourselves very quickly in a semi-arid landscape which reminded us both quite a bit of the journey we had done through Rajasthan in 1997, and of which I wrote in my first book India: The Peacock's Call. Dry, flat, with boulders and masses of thorn trees it was not very inviting; then we noticed a tree that was more like a massive green bush in that it was not the normal height of a tree but very broad. There were so many of these that it was obvious they must be an important local crop. Nandu said they were cashew nut trees and we became very interested. I had never given any thought to what sort of plant produced the cashew nut though I enjoy eating them enormously. Ground nuts or peanuts as the name suggests grow underground on the roots of a low bush but I am used to the lovely almond trees of Mallorca or northern Italy and walnut trees.

Nandu was looking for something and then told Aniva to stop. He had found a property with walls and a large garden gate behind which were some cashew trees. The ones in the open countryside were much more difficult to reach on foot down from the side of the road through thorn bushes. Nandu seemed quite confident that the owners of the house would not mind so we came in through the gate and looked at a fruiting cashew tree. It is quite amazing in that the fruit is quite large, about the size of a kiwi fruit, a bright yellow colour and quite leathery and hanging beneath it is the seed i.e. the nut, normally the seed of a fruit is within the fruit as with peaches, plums apricots.

As we drove along we noticed little groups of people working away on the sides of the road. Nandu explained that their job was to extract the cashew nut from its shell; they built a simple fire over which a dish rather like a wok was balanced. It had a small hole drilled in the bottom in the centre; the nuts would be fried in their thick shell, for want of a better term, and the resulting flammable oil that was generated from this cooking then dripped down through the hole into the fire, which was then self perpetuating. This made the shell easier to peel off and extract the cashew nut as we know it and the women then bagged up the freshly extracted nuts. This was actually happening on the side of the road – I don't mean twenty feet away, I mean on the side of the road and I kept well clear of the passing traffic! We bought a bag of cashews in courtesy but did not eat them though they smelled gorgeous. The lack of hygiene was all too obvious and we felt it would have been seeking trouble for our stomachs. At certain times of the year the markets are full of fresh cashews and I love them but I hope those are processed in a more efficient way.

We later learnt in Kerala that cashew nut oil can be reduced to a black tarry substance with which the coir ropes, used to bind the planks together for Kerala's Kettavellums (old spice boats), are made waterproof.

It was a really hot day, made worse by our arid surroundings and when we came across a fine old fort on a boulder strewn outcrop it was without much enthusiasm that I climbed to the top. It had not been a residential fort but was nevertheless substantial and from the top there was a fine view all around. I sat under the shade of a thorn tree to rest and just look out on the pond below and Graham and Nandu sprang about like mountain goats. I said it was a case of 'Mad dogs and Englishmen out in the midday sun...' and Graham laughed and tried to explain the origins of the song and about its famous composer to Nandu. He was obviously puzzled and politely laughed but you could see that his thought was why would a man be thought clever and talented when writing about the obvious. Indeed!

Looking down on the village scene with the dhobi washing village laundry and hanging it up to dry on the thorn bushes and the children and dogs playing it was a typical Indian village scene. When we came back to the car a wonderful Indian cock was strutting around in his gorgeous plumage looking just like an Indian Jungle Fowl with glossy deep green tail feathers; it is when I see things like that, which take me back over half a century to my childhood memories of similar experiences, that I feel comforted that some things are just the same – I mean the good, simple, healthy things like village children playing, dhobis doing laundry and village life.

We were on our way to Chettinad. Chettinad is home to the Nattukottai Chettiars, a prosperous business and banking community of South India. A unique feature of this region is its palatial mansions with their quite extraordinary architecture. The structure of a typical Chettiar home illustrates how human dwellings can be in harmony with nature – the technique used keeps the interiors cool in hot and humid summers. Chettiars are intrepid travellers who left their arid homelands in search of fortune in the countries of South East Asia, which became accessible to them through the consolidation of the British Rule in that part of the world. Chettinad and the seventy-six villages in and around Karaikudi the main town became the sacred haven to which they would one day return.

'Nattukottai' means a country fort. The ancestral homes of the Nattukottai Chettiars that are still standing in some of these villages are magnificent. Or indeed they would be once they are all renovated. The mansions extend the length of a street. Secreted behind high brick walls they are rather like town fortresses and concentrate the activities of each family inwards. The Chettiars made huge fortunes as traders and financiers and their riches were used to build these fantastic mansions. The gates bear the initials of successive generations of house owners, a veritable family tree. Stucco art was very popular with gods and heroes given equal prominence in the decoration. All homes have a 'mittam' an inner pillared courtyard.

The ancestral homes reflect their complex Chettiar social structure. They consist of vast public areas, where perhaps a hundred and more of the family members can dine together in the elaborate feasts that have made the Chettinad cuisine famous. These then lead into the private areas with more formal rooms which are succeeded by long courtyards surrounded by pillared verandas, with one more floor on top, where each of the different members of the family may nurture their own family unit – in small heavily guarded rooms that contain all their valuables.

We arrived at The Bangla; that is the Tamil Nadu pronunciation of 'The Bungalow', but in fact this strange assortment of buildings is a most charming home but definitely not ever a bungalow! It is run by Mrs Meenakshi Mayyappan, a distinguished old lady who is a senior member of a local Chettiar family; they renovated and restored this property as a heritage hotel for visitors to Chettinad and it has recently been classified as a heritage property by the Government of India.

Actual mansions were built out of brick and Burmese teak with pillars fashioned from individual teak trees – these are so elegant and if I was building a house in Tamil Nadu I would definitely attempt to buy some old pillars from dilapidated houses to adorn a new building. There is everything good that could be brought from all the lands to which the Chettiar businessmen went: they have incorporated teak pillars; huge carved lintels and sides of entrances to the main rooms; decorative tiles originally from Japan; hanging glass lamps and other fine objects. Indeed now there is a flourishing trade in antiques extracted from the dilapidated homes.

The Bangala however had been built in quite a different style and was the idea of her father-in-law; he was a prominent citizen and wanted a property in which he could entertain his British visitors such as the Governor of Madras State and other important people. A traditional Chettiar mansion would not be one that I would find relaxing. For a start, there is no real privacy or area in which to relax, plus the bathroom facilities are quite odd with everyone having to seek bathing and lavatory facilities somewhere at the very rear of the house. Outside each locked room in which the family unit kept its prized possessions there was a stout hook in the ceiling from which the infants would be put in the sari cradle – as I described at Darasuram. Everyone else seemed to sleep on the floor.

No, thankfully The Bangala is a style of house with which I was very familiar as it had been built in the 1930s and had the architecture of that decade, and so many properties in which I had lived as a child were very similar, so for me it had a feeling of 'home'.

Having arrived after a hot dusty morning's driving from Thanjavur it was a relief to finally stop at this dainty, white painted mansion set in a garden of green with bright flower blossoms. Along the front there is a charming tiled and sloping roofed veranda, fringed with a hanging wooden canopy with bamboo chiks at the window. 'Chik' is the word for reed or rattan blinds. The woodwork is painted in silver which was a Chettiar custom of old to make the wood last longer. Apparently a lot of the 'art deco' design of the house was influenced by Hollywood films and the Mayyappan family, like several others amongst the Chettiars, were also involved in the making and distribution of films in the south Indian film industry.

The house was once in a suburb of the town of Karaikudi, but now the town has caught up with the house and though there is a large village tank (pond) just outside it cannot be considered to be truly rural. Village buffaloes are brought in the morning for a wash, followed by their owners. The space immediately outside the Bangala's front gate is most often used by the local farmers to park their bullock carts on their way to the weekly 'shandy' or market. There are now twelve bedroom suites and we had a very spacious suite on the ground floor. The bathrooms have been renovated but without losing their charm.

The Chettinad cuisine is legendary and with good reason. After a welcome cool shower we went into lunch and were on our own. The house domestic staff looked after us wonderfully and lunch was served on banana leaves – as is customary in Tamil Nadu – truly it was delicious and we very soon felt totally satisfied. The whole ritual was so reminiscent of our own family's ways in my childhood that I had to pinch myself looking around; the only difference was that we did not eat on banana leaves, but our cuisine in my parents' house was equally good. I counted about twenty retainers in all. The evening meal was however very elegantly laid out with conventional plates. I liked poking my nose into the kitchen and pantry and felt that half a century had not passed; moreover all the condiments and jams and sauces were scrumptious and made in-house.

A young Chettiar lady accompanied us on our visit to all the local places of interest; she was friendly and knowledgeable and was taking time off from her duties as a wife and mother of two. Mrs Mayyappan was away in Trichy doing some business and sent us her best wishes and looked forward to meeting us that evening. The fact is in the heat of the day it is very difficult to go and sightsee. So we enjoyed a welcome stretch out on our beds before all five of us embarked in the little car! I was grateful for its air conditioning.

Chettinad art is a major draw for tourists to this area; it includes woodcarvings, woven saris, gold jewellery and handmade tiles. The most famous local craft is however the Chettinad basket which has bright intricate patterns woven into the object which is made out of date-palm leaves.

Our female guide took us to other nearby villages to inspect a couple of the mansions and then visit the royal palace. I found it all rather odd as these houses were totally empty at the time of our visit; sometimes there was a durwan (watchman) but otherwise we just walked around in large empty mansions. The basic design comprises a 'thinnai' which is the enclosed courtyard surrounded by family rooms. The walls it was explained are smooth and made of special plasters. This plaster is made to a special formula which consists of a finely ground mixture of powered shells, lime, jaggery and spices, including gallnut (myrobalan). It is thought that this special plastering technique helps to cool the house through the long hot summers. At the very back of the building the huge kitchen quarters are really an open courtyard, at one corner of which the special huge pots and pestles and mortars of the female members of the family are lined up. Each one belongs to a particular female family member.

Graham and I found the visit slightly odd because though one is very used to visiting old houses that are now museums, these are not actually that, just deserted for most of the year so rather soulless and I thought not that well maintained. I suppose for the custodians of the various properties it is a bit depressing cleaning as it were for nothing but in the Rajasthan area of Shekhavati where a similar situation exists the various houses had fallen into real neglect. The Marwaris of Shekhavati are similar to the Chettiars and have gone throughout India and made vast fortunes. When we visited Shekhavati we both were aghast at the state of dilapidation of some of the great havelis. That visit was in November 1997 so perhaps the various Marwari owners have seen the benefit and wisdom of renovating and maintaining their homes, not for themselves but for the tourist trail. Well the Chettiars will have to work harder at their inheritance. It became clear in conversation that there is so much wealth in the Chettiar families that this can be achieved quite easily but some do not see the benefit to themselves and certainly have not yet absorbed the idea that they are custodians of their heritage for the whole country.

Though I found it all interesting I nevertheless considered the empty houses depressing and felt that somehow, if they want this area to prosper through tourism, a new formula will have to be found. Here in Scotland people will come and look at old ruins but by and large the better the state of the building and the more inside the ancient peel tower or castle or mansion the more visitors it attracts. People like Catherine Maxwell Stewart of Traquair work very hard to make their ancient homes attractive and inviting. Indeed Traquair House here in Peeblesshire has positively grown in stature from the early days of its tourism attraction. Forty years ago Catherine's late father Peter was doing his best to entice people to go and visit Traquair; now under Catherine's determined commitment it has become a favourite visitor destination and indeed a centre for so many functions that are both public and private. The Chettiar mansions are I believe in demand by the film industry as locations for their various romances and great stories, but that and the infrequent western visitor will not keep them alive.

To each of the nine main villages in Chettinad a Pandya king had granted a temple in perpetuity. These nine temples became the 'family' temple of each of the cluster villages, and each cluster evolved as a subdivision of the Chettiars or what might be described as a fraternal clan. There is some similarity there with us in the Highlands of Scotland and the great clans and their clan lands. All nine temples have architectural interest and value, but we did not have time to see them all; the best known of the Nagarathar clan temples is Pillaiyarpatti which is about twelve kilometres from Karaikudi; this temple is dedicated to Lord Ganesha and attracts a large number of visitors from all parts of India and abroad. Here there is a huge bas-relief in a cave carved out of a hillock. This sculpture is dated to 5th century and I suppose is reminiscent of Mamallapuram. The rajagopuram tower over the eastern entrance rises to five storeys, and the temple is rich in stone and terracotta sculptures and has thirty bronzes dating from the 10th century. The Chettiars built temples in all the places to which they dispersed around South East Asia and South Africa.

I enjoyed a visit to the raja's palace at Kanadukathaan which is in good order and has some furnishing. One of the royal ladies had set up a museum in some of the upstairs rooms to show visitors the cultural artefacts of their way of life. All this would be greatly enhanced if the surrounding village was cleaned and maintained.

India will suffocate under a wealth of plastic detritus unless the government or state governments act decisively. Here locally in Scotland at last our regional council has implemented an eco-friendly cleansing and rubbish collection model. It was well overdue. In India the amount of plastic bottles for drinking water plus all the popular cool drinks is enormous and various hoteliers and heritage property owners candidly admitted they just do not know what to do with them. Quite a lot is recycled by being cleaned and given to local children to use for water bottles for school but in fact that is just passing the buck really. The problem will not be solved till governments put pressure on the manufacturers to make each plastic item eco-friendly and impose a levy on each item to help towards recycling and conservation.

Small hoteliers could very easily bag up the bottles and at least segregate them from their organic waste; rubbish that is ordered and bagged is instantly more acceptable and easier to dispose of and indeed collectable.

At Athangudi, a village about fifteen kilometres away from Karaikudi the cottage industry is tile making. This was so interesting and of course many of the local mansions have used the tiles in their interiors. Now quite large orders are received for tiles all over the country and I could see why. We watched the craftsmen go through the whole process. The tiles are made of cement but with beautiful traditional design on the one side. The craftsman paints the design in the wink of an eye on a glass template, on which he then throws fine sand and then the cement is poured in and the mould allowed to dry in the heat of the sun. Once dry the tile is carefully removed from the glass mould – the glass gives the tiles a shiny smooth surface. All the materials are sourced locally and it is still carried out as a cottage industry. The tiles are wonderfully colourful and when finished beautiful to the touch and they never become hot, which is essential in this very hot country. We saw some very old tiles and they still retained their marvellous colour. I hope that any modern building that may take place in the area to provide more tourist accommodation will use these tiles as a feature in their large public places. In my childhood many old mansions and mansion flats in Kolkata had mosaic floors made up of broken china, which were rather charming and that was then replaced with terrazzo, which is elegant but has a tendency to crack; however it is easy to clean and cool to the feet. These tiles would be a strong feature and therefore not to everyone's taste but would look marvellous in a hallway or on a veranda or dining room.

Chettinad had its own tiny royal railway station at which the raja could arrive in style but it now looks rather forlorn and is just a relic of a bygone grand era. Most wealthy Chettiars live in Chennai or Bangalore and conduct their business interests from these two great cities; it is sad to see an area in decay but with careful renovation it really could become a popular short break destination for Indians as well as a stop on the way for westerners following the Temple Trail.

Dinner that night was delicious and then Mrs Mayyappan arrived back and we had a pleasant conversation. It is heartening to see an old distinguished lady, who at her senior time in life could be just relaxing in a family home, taking such a brisk interest in running this establishment. I was amused that when I asked if we might have a tray of tea in the morning she seemed pleased and surprised and then directed her equivalent of a butler in the local language – but I understood enough to realise that she told him to make sure and put out the best china on a clean tray cloth on the best tray; I teased her about it and she laughed and admitted that it was good to have someone visit who appreciates these little niceties. Sure enough, at 06.30 hours the bearer came to our locked door and I was glad to have the tea, after which I walked around the garden in the sunrise and silence. Breakfast too was a positive feast and the cook went berserk making dosas and idlis when he realised that we liked them. Staying in big plush five star hotels is truly wonderful, but I always feel that staying in charming, well run, heritage properties such as The Bangala shows the visitor the true India. The lovely old photos on the walls and carefully grouped pictures all told the history of the place and we were sorry to leave after breakfast.

I think travellers could spend two nights there very easily and take their time enjoying everything there is to see and also relaxing in comfortable hospitable surroundings. We, on the other hand, had to make our way to Madurai, and this too was a place of which I had heard so much and was looking forward to seeing. Chettinad is an area that has only been part of a tourist route relatively recently. I looked it up in my old Lonely Planet Guides and the Rough Guide to India and it is not even mentioned, yet is an obvious little detour for people on the Temple Trail. I hope tourism helps the local people to prosper.

Chapter Eleven

Two Sacred Cities

Tamil Nadu, among the southern states of India, has the longest recorded history and its language, Tamil, is the oldest of the Dravidian tongues. Tamil Nadu's oldest temples trace their history from much earlier than the Christian era; its political history goes back to the mists and legends of time. There is a belief that the land we know as India extended well beyond the tip of India, now known as Kannyakumari, into a vast land mass known as Gondwanaland, which touched Australia to the east and Africa to the west. It was thought that Madurai was the capital of this land once the sea had engulfed the majority of the land mass to the south. The legend has it that a Pandya king called Mudhatirumaran stayed in a village called Manavur about eleven kilometres north of the present city of Madurai and that he shortly thereafter built a temple and laid out a town around it. This is the origin of the great Sri Minakshi Sundaresvara temple and the city of Madurai.

The more fanciful legend says that Lord Shiva appeared in a dream to the then king; the king was amazed to see drops of nectar 'madhu' falling down to earth from Lord Shiva's matted hair. The nectar or 'madhu' was so sweet that the place where it fell came to be known as 'Madhurapuri' which in time evolved into Madurai. Legend and traceable history are interwoven but it is known that the fame of Madurai stretches back over two thousand years. Madurai and the early capitals were not merely cities but seats of learning with literary academies. Madurai became an established seat of Tamil culture and writers and poets would congregate to read their work; the city appeared to have been the capital of the Pandyan empire without interruption for approximately a thousand years and it is a known fact that three successful conferences of Tamil scholars called 'Tamil Sangams' took place under the benevolent royal support. Sangam means meeting ground or joining. Tamil Sangam poetry, which has been ascribed to the first three centuries of the Christian era, bears witness to the fact that temples existed in some form for centuries before – probably constructed in perishable materials like bricks and wood. Before that there is the evidence of caverns and cave temples which were decorated by worshippers and ascetics. The monoliths of Mamallapuram carved in the seventh century preserve the styles in which their predecessors were made.

Though an inland city on the banks of the river Vaigai it was described as the Athens of the East by the Greek ambassador Megasthenes who visited it in 302 BC. The Romans also traded in silk, pearls and spices from Madurai and it was considered one of the most civilized cities in south Asia.

It was in the age of *Bhakti* or love of God in the seventh and eighth centuries that the idea of temple building in Tamil Nadu took form. The Hindu temple and Tamil literature had been a feature down the centuries from the days of the great Sangams where poems were submitted and adjudicated by scholars. In time the temple became the centre for communal life in a village or town, not just religious life but also cultural, economic and administrative and indeed, as with the medieval Christian belief in the West, when the church was the centre of the community nothing could happen without the priests. The saints and singers of the Hindu religion would go from temple to temple singing of the greatness of the particular lord enshrined in a respective temple. At one time there were sixty-three Saivaite (followers of Lord Shiva) and twelve Vaishnavaite (followers of Lord Vishnu) saints who were drawn from all castes and walks of life.

Warring dynasties were no obstruction to temple building; indeed the rival dynasties competed in artistic development and thus the temples flourished. I have described the great Pallava temple of Mamallapuram and in this chapter will talk of the others at Kanchipuram, which is also close to Chennai; then there were the four great Chola temples in Thanjavur, Gangaikondacholapuram in the eleventh, Darasuram in the twelfth and Tribhuvanam in the thirteenth centuries. I did not have an opportunity to visit the latter however.

Earlier whilst writing about Andhra Pradesh I wrote of Amaravati; the Pallavas it is thought were influenced by the Buddhist art of that age; the early Pandyas created some superb rock art. The Cholas as we have seen were the master builders; the Pandyas once again flourished and added to the temple art and architecture in places, the Vijayanagar kings contributed and the Nayakas continued with the tradition. Between them all they filled Tamil Nadu with temples, big and small, all of them objects of interest and beauty, be it in a small village or a town; the fountain of all this great religious art however is Madurai, the most traditional and typical Tamil city since the beginning of documented history and it too has a great temple.

Madurai first came into my thoughts at the age of eleven, when I took my first flight back to London alone; the aircraft was called the Rani of Madurai. Air India named their various aircraft after Ranis who were famous in Indian history. One other I particularly recall was the Rani of Jhansi, of whom I wrote in my second book. Madurai was famous of that much I soon became aware, but since it was not on the way to anywhere our family needed to be we never went there. Now I was at last going to visit this ancient famous city.

The drive from Chettinad is not long but we nearly had a serious mishap. Along the road we saw some really huge palm trees that looked totally different from any others we have ever seen. We asked Aniva to stop the car to have a closer look; Nandu got out of the car and was behind it when for some reason Aniva decided to reverse a little. The result was that poor Nandu nearly was run over and in fact fell down the bank. The whole incident was so foolish with potentially disastrous consequences but thankfully Nandu felt embarrassed rather than injured. We drove on through the boulder strewn landscape with rocky outcrops, rather like the ones in Andhra Pradesh – in fact this was very close to that sort of terrain.

The Sangam in Madurai was a recent purchase for the hotel group but very comfortable and spacious; we received a warm welcome with flower garlands and fruit juice and discovered our suite to be huge and comfortable with a full lounge area. The swimming pool at the rear of the property was filled with children who I think had just come on holiday for the Spring break. The dining room provided very good food and was elegant with a rill of water in the raised area. These Indian hotels at three star level are good and provide a welcome oasis from the heat outside and also the crowded streets and historic sites. The management were enormously helpful about putting me through to Delhi telephone numbers and also arranged for some of my work to be colour photocopied; the price was infinitesimal compared to prices here in Britain.

After lunch we ventured forth to visit the great Meenakshi Sundareswarar twin temple complex. The Meenakshi Temple houses one of the five traditional 'dance halls' where Lord Shiva in his form as Nataraja, the cosmic Dancer is said to have danced – it is known as the 'Silver Hall (Velli Ambalam). The temple complex is literally a small city – one of the largest of its kind in India and undoubtedly one of the oldest. The temple grew with the contribution of each dynasty and victorious monarchs adding their own embellishments in gratitude to the god and also I suspect to enhance their respective egos. The temple complex now extends over an area of 65,000 square metres, and though most of the temple as we see it today is the building accomplished in

The famous Meenakshi Temple at Madurai in Tamil Nadu

the 16th and 17th centuries, its origins go back to two thousand years ago.

Modern Madurai encompasses the temple and the streets around are hugely crowded and seething with people; however the massive twelve gopuras tower over one and the highly coloured stucco mythological figures entwined and covering the towers are repaired and painted and ritually reconsecrated every twelve years. I have written about gopuras at other temples but at Madurai they are in another league. The four pyramidal gates rise to a height of more than fifty metres and these towering gateways indicate the entrance to the temple complex at the four cardinal points, while lesser gopuras lead to the sanctums of the main deities. We could see the main gopuras from a distance as we approached Madurai.

The temple is entered from the eastern side through the Ashta Shakti Mandapa or the Hall of eight Goddesses. We had to leave our shoes at the entrance and walk bare feet and it was still very hot. The throng of devotees was nearly overwhelming – any day of the week approximately 15,000 visit the temple which increases to 25,000 on a Friday (which is sacred to the Goddess Meenakshi). There are fifty priests employed here and the whole business of running a temple and making it accessible needs huge organisation, rather like at Tirupati in Andhra Pradesh, of which I wrote. We were disapproving of western tourists who had brought very small children with them; the sheer throng and noise and heat and possible health hazard seemed a very unwise potential threat to the safety and good health of their infants. This sort of experience either is very enjoyable to a person or a bit daunting; I tend to belong to the latter category. I have never really enjoyed visiting anywhere that is overwhelmed with human bodies shuffling along. I much prefer visiting temples that are either no longer living temples or where the pilgrim numbers are far fewer.

The seven-storeyed Chitra Gopura is the tallest tower in the complex, and next to it is the Potramarai Kulam or Golden Lotus Tank with steps leading down to the water. To the west of this tank is the Meenakshi Shrine, one of two main shrines comprising two concentric corridors and halls and galleries. Every night Sundareshvara's image is brought to the goddess's bed from his own Sundareshvara Shrine which stands to the north. The Thousand Pillared Hall with 985 beautifully decorated columns constructed in the 16th century is very impressive. Each pillar features high, ornate, bold sculptures that look life-like. Viewed from any angle these pillars appear to be in a straight line; a set of pillars, carved in stone produce the seven notes of Carnatic music.

Suddenly we found ourselves in a sort of strange action. Several half-dressed men were attempting to lift on to their shoulders the silver statue of a bull; it was heavily carved and quite a fine piece of art but they managed to make a drama out of chaos which was quite amusing to watch and photograph. I then found the temple elephant which pleased me and was very happy to receive yet another blessing from her. All this action was taking place within the temple, not in a courtyard. Overall it was a worthwhile experience but I know Graham and I enjoyed our other temple visits much more.

Nandu then wanted us to visit the Thirumalai Nayaka Palace which is really quite close to the temple. This once grand palace was built in 1636 and once totally renovated will be extremely impressive. It has rather odd massive proportions as a building and obviously has been in decay. There is a bit of an Islamic influence and it had been partially restored by Lord Napier, governor of Madras between 1866 and 1872. Once again the authorities have to grasp the nettle of litter. No historic building on this earth will look impressive if the surroundings are strewn with litter and garbage. I cannot think why the Indian authorities do not immediately do something about this; there are so many people requiring jobs, surely the municipality could employ sweepers. Madurai needs to think like Hyderabad and clean up the city, only then will its entire heritage be seen in an impressive light.

There is an Indo-Saracenic architectural style to this palace and the massive white pillars are mammoths. The pillars measure twenty metres in height and have a circumference of four metres. It was King Thirumalai Nayak's grandson who demolished much of the fine structure and removed most of the jewels and woodcarvings in order to build his palace in Tiruchirapalli (Trichy); his dream never came true.

We returned for the sound and light show in English at 6.45 p.m; after which it is repeated in Tamil at 8.15 pm. This half-hour show at which one sits on chairs in the courtyard extols the virtues of King Thirumalai, particularly his passion for the arts, his victories in battle and his love for his subjects. It was well done, we had had to rush back to our hotel and have a quick shower to refresh ourselves and return in time. I very much hope the courtyard of the palace will be designed with care to give it a good ground cover – I think sandstone paving with large urns of green vegetation and perhaps a fountain would enhance it immeasurably. Sufficient room for seating for these shows would have to be planned and then in the future it could become a most elegant venue for public events or indeed private events, like weddings and celebrations. Presumably the Archaeological Survey of India is in charge of the renovations but whoever it is some of the work was being done, we thought, in a most amateur way; I just hope it is finished and not left in an incomplete fashion. Stucco art in India takes a battering from the elements but in this palace the beauty in the building is at eye level and above on its domes and arches.

The Gandhi Museum housed in the old Palace of Rani Mangammai depicts the highlights of the freedom struggle and contains a picture gallery of the Gandhian movement. This is worthwhile and one can also see the relics of the movement and khadi, the product of Gandhiji's spinning and weaving, and a village industries section along with a South Indian handicrafts section. I always find museums connected to Gandhiji immensely interesting and thought provoking. Nine kilometres south of Madurai there is a Meditation Centre dedicated to realising the ideal of Sri Aurobindo and Sri Annai or as she is known – The Mother; it is one of the oldest places of meditation in the region and can be visited between 4.30 pm and 8.30 pm daily.

On reflection the devotion and pilgrimage I witnessed at the Meenakshi Temple was similar to that we were to see in Rome around St Peter's Basilica when Pope John Paul II died ten days later.

We took our leave of Nandu, Aniva and the tourism officials once we returned to our hotel. As always when one has travelled with people there is an affectionate farewell; Graham and I made sure Nandu and the driver were suitably rewarded, upon which the tourism official started being obsequious in the hope of receiving some largesse. Nothing doing! He was merely doing his job for a short while. Nandu had accompanied us for days and though not the most brilliant intellectual and articulate of guides, nevertheless had always done his best for us. The following morning a jeep would collect us and drive us to Thekkady in Kerala. That night however we were then entitled to relax.

I am now going to include an account of my trip to Kanchipuram. It may seem rather odd to add it to this chapter, but in fact Kanchipuram is considered one of the sacred seven cities of the Hindus, and as it is situated quite close to Chennai, I visited it on my return once I was alone and Graham had returned to Britain. Anyone visiting Chennai and Tamil Nadu would be best to visit Kanchipuram from Chennai and on the following day depart from Chennai and visit Mamallapuram and then continue on the temple trail, as indeed we had done. Our visit has been mapped out by the Tourism Commissioner and for some reason he had not included Kanchipuram, but I knew it would not be right to talk about Tamil Nadu without a visit to this place.

The day of my visit dawned with heavy skies and by breakfast time the rain was falling in sheets; very soon Chennai's streets were almost knee deep in water and I wondered anxiously whether a car journey to Kanchipuram was a safe or good idea. It was neither, but I took a deep breath and went, accompanied by a female guide. She was friendly and helpful and very enthusiastic, but her English was halting and as I do not speak Tamil it was sometimes difficult to communicate – her friendliness made up for that loss. The car I very soon assessed was an old one with poor brakes and I swore under my breath at this stupidity; the driver employed a sort of peculiar jerking movement to stop or slow the car and I was not by any stretch of imagination a 'happy bunny'. The endless heavy rain moreover made the temperature plummet and the damp seemed to seep into my joints and I felt totally exhausted and cold by the time I returned to my hotel.

'Kanchi' is the shortened version of the name and most Indians would associate it with silk saris shrines and saints. From the 6th to 8th centuries it was the capital of the Pallavas who built numerous temples and founded universities. Subsequent dynasties also gave their royal patronage so the city continued to prosper right throughout the Chola, Pandya and Viyananagar reigns. Kanchipuram is sacred to both Shaivite and Vaishnavites and thus the town is divided into two distinct zones, with the Shaivite temples to the north and the Vaishnavite temples to the south east. There is also a goddess temple dedicated to Parvati, and this Kamakshi Temple was rebuilt in the 14th century during the Vijayanagar period. This is one of the three holiest shrines in India to *Shakti*, Shiva's cosmic energy depicted in female form, usually as his queen; and it is believed that Shiva and Kamakshi, the local form of the goddess Parvati were married in Kanchipuram. Kanchipuram's largest and most important Shiva shrine is the Ekambareshvara Temple which has a colossal white gopura which rises to almost sixty metres. It is said that the mango tree inside the temple is 2,500 years old and has four branches each yielding a different variety of mango!

The oldest structure in Kanchi is the Kailasanathar Temple built in the 8th century by Rajasimha and his son Mahendra. There are fifty-eight small shrines situated around the main shrine as a compound wall. I managed to go round this temple but in the pouring rain with the streets flooded which made walking difficult and dangerous, one didn't know what was under the water really and I felt that renovation work had been carelessly prepared and therefore builders' materials were making it even more difficult in the rain. On a good day it would have been enjoyable.

I have lost track of the temple in which it happened but I observed a little family that had come for a blessing for the children. They were friendly and shy and determined not to miss out on their objective, but truly it was a bad day to be abroad and I cannot even imagine walking around with a babe in arms and a toddler in floodwater that reached well above my ankles!

The Varadarajaperumal Temple is a Vaishnavite shrine which stands in a huge complex and is worth a visit though as a non Hindu one can only visit the outer courtyards and the wonderful 16th century pillared hall close to the western entrance gate.

I gave up pretty easily I am afraid as the lashing rain and cold made any photography quite impossible. I asked that we should visit a silk weaving factory. This proved quite amusing because the chosen workshop – factory is a rather grand word – was also difficult to reach but was quite obviously considered one of the smartest. When I finally reached the showroom after looking at the weaving shed I was proudly shown the photograph of HM The Queen who had visited this workshop – I think in 1997. HM looked a good deal happier than I felt and it had obviously been a dry sunny day. Kanchi silk is renowned and very beautiful and Indian ladies aspire to owning several Kanchipuram silk saris and outfits. I enjoyed talking to the proprietor and the girls and women serving. They were going to have a boring day with no customers and my guide obviously knew them well. I asked her if she would brave the elements and go back to the car and bring back my photograph album in a polythene bag. At a certain social level all Indians love looking at the background and family and

111

homeland of a visitor. They were delighted with the photographs of our grandchildren and of our younger son's wedding. I knew that both subjects would entrance them. Every detail had to be thoroughly dissected and discussed and some rather frank questions were asked but just to find out, not in any way to offend.

Being cold I asked if there was a cheap stole that I could buy; at home one has so many lovely pashminas and Indian woollen scarves that I did not want to spend a lot of money, but they good naturedly brought out a selection which was modestly priced and I immediately bought one and put it on; it is still very good and washes well. The proprietor asked for my advice as to how to make his stock more attractive to western visitors. I gave some advice on having a choice in more muted shades and drew some designs for him. I was trying to see something that I could buy and thus ensure honour was saved all round. I found a most charming soft paisley silk on a bolt. I said wistfully that had we the time this would look very nice made into palazzo pants. Time, he said excitedly, of course we had time; he would summon his tailor and the floaty trousers, which is the name he preferred, would be delivered to my hotel that evening. The little tailor arrived and took careful measurements of me and I paid for the garment. Sure enough that evening the reception clerk phoned me in my room and said a young man had arrived with a parcel from Kanchipuram. The reception clerk sent a bell boy up with the man who was thoroughly intimidated by the grandeur of Le Royal Meridien. I told them to wait outside whilst I tried on the pants, which were perfect and then I popped my head round the door and thanked the messenger and sent my best wishes. Easy as that!

Kanchipuram is worth visiting from Chennai and there are a number of hotels in which to have lunch. I do think however that a half day trip is all it merits unless a Hindu devotee; some would say that by this time I was probably 'all templed out' anyway coming to it at the end of my huge journey; and I would have to agree with that observation but I respect the fact that it is a religious centre for Tamil culture and learning and close by there is the University of Advanced Learning at Enathur; this too apparently has a very fine library.

Chapter Twelve

We Reach Kerala

Leaving Madurai was interesting as the festival of Holi and Good Friday in the Christian calendar had coincided. Holi is the big Spring festival in northern India and I last participated on a very happy occasion at the Regimental Headquarters of The Jat Regiment in March 1998. In the south however it is rather muted which was a bit disappointing for Graham who had not been present at the 'colour chucking' fun with Indian Army officers in Bareilly in 1998. Holi celebrates the end of winter, the destruction of the demon Holika and the veneration of Kama, god of love, and his wife Rati, goddess of passion. People mark the day by bombarding each other with coloured water, dye or, in poorer villages, watery clay and cattle dung and by drinking marijuana-based *bhang*. In Jaipur there is also a version called Elephant Holi, which must be rather special. In the south this festival has no real fervour, and we saw very few people covered in dye, whereas in North India people of all social classes 'play Holi' and have a fun time; sometimes it has to be said that festivities get out of hand and violence ensues at the village level where drinking and bhang play an enlarged role. As a child I had been prevented from participating in this festival as the parents, and indeed most Europeans denigrated the festival; those were the different days of the 1950s when life was, or so it seems upon reflection, all about status, deference and 'not being seen to let the side down...stiff upper lip and all that'. Hmm, well in these more enlightened relaxed times I can tell you it is an awful lot of fun when played in private surroundings like an officers' mess or someone's private garden or estate. I was absolutely covered in vivid yellows, reds and blues and there is a very memorable photograph of me used on the back of my first book India: The Peacock's Call. The dyes wash out with normal shampoos and detergents for one's clothes.

It was a great pleasure to be in a four by four vehicle with room to move and now only the two of us and a pleasant driver, who had been sent from Thekkady. Within minutes of leaving the outskirts of Madurai we realised just how beautiful the countryside was; gone was the arid dusty area on the eastern side of Madurai, now moving west it was green and prosperous with crop farming, flowering trees in their spring blossom, rice paddies and other cereals until we reached the first slopes of the Western Ghats; our destination at Thekkady was in the romantically named Cardamom Hills region of the Western Ghats.

We were not able to make the visit to Kodaikanal on this occasion but I know all who have been there really love this place. It is about 120 kilometres away from Madurai, and it is one of the few hill stations throughout India not to have been spoilt by reckless urbanisation. This rather charming summer getaway is set at an altitude of about 2,133 metres above sea level. The centre of Kodai is its sprawling lake spread over an area of twenty-four hectares, where you can fish and boat. There are wonderful long walks to be taken on special trails and trekking is a popular activity here. There are at least four separate waterfalls which make wonderful picnic destinations.

Ooty or Udagamandalam, or Ootacamound, to give the place its full name is a place that is synonymous with colonial life in India in times gone by. I know several lovely old people who still recall their early childhood which was partially spent in Ooty. It is a place created by the British as a hot weather retreat for Europeans for when the plains of Tamil Nadu or Madras State as it then was, became unbearable. Ooty is higher than Kodaikanal at 2,240 metres and can become quite chilly in the cool season. I have never been there and am mentioning it because readers who are familiar with the south of India would I think consider it sacrilege not to mention the place; it was quite beautiful and I am sure retains some of that old charm, though I suspect has been overbuilt. For most foreign travellers the spectacular train journey to the resort from Mettupalayam is the major highlight of the visit – it is referred to as The 'Toy' Train to Ooty. Seven vintage steam engines are maintained just for this journey and the line had been completed in 1887 and without it Ooty could never have developed, because in those days the only alternative to the train was ox cart. The journey from Mettupalayam to Ooty takes about four hours and thirty minutes, an hour less for the return. The little train stops along the way at stations with familiar names like Wellington and Runnymede and there are apparently no toilet facilities on the train itself. My family had no connections with Ooty and so I did not think it necessary for me to make a special visit.

The Periyar Wildlife Sanctuary on the borders of Tamil Nadu and Kerala was established in 1934 and was extended to its present area of 767 square kilometres in 1950. Its centrepiece is the man-made lake at a height of 615 metres, which covers 26 square kilometres; this was formed by the British who dammed the Periyar River in 1895. Water that had hitherto flowed south to the Indian Ocean was redirected eastward to flow, via a 1,850 metre long conduit, as the river Vaigai, supplying water to Madurai and irrigating much of south Tamil Nadu, before flowing into the Bay of Bengal. Now we understood why the land west of Madurai was so lush and green and the agricultural bowl of Tamil Nadu, in such sharp contrast to that on the eastern approaches to the city. Our drive, though quite long, was very enjoyable because of the comfort of the vehicle and the delightful scenery; we proceeded to climb quite quickly through a series of hairpin bends which then afforded us a very fine view of the Tamil Nadu plain. I have read somewhere that it was a Scots engineer who built the dam and that does not surprise me as the Scottish Diaspora was huge in India and the Scots have been famous for their engineering since the early industrial revolution; it is a good feeling to have two engineer sons, admittedly they actually do not work as engineers but they have the knowledge of mechanical engineering that made Scotland famous worldwide. I was very glad that we were approached Kerala by land on such a beautiful route; we had visited briefly before but on that occasion we had arrived by cruise ship at Cochin or Kochi as it is now called.

We arrived in Thekkady and drove up to Cardamom County in time for lunch. We received a warm welcome and were accommodated in a very comfortable cottage quite high up on the hill in this elegant complex. All around us were cardamom plants from which is harvested that wonderful spice of the same name. It is apparently quite a labour-intensive crop but I just love cardamom in curries and rice, and it is a very good addition to hollandaise sauce, or to flavour milk puddings and cardamom flavoured ice cream is sublime.

Cardamom County belongs to the Muthoot Group; Kripa Kurien's in-laws own this group of companies. They have a strong Christian ethic and the resort is without alcohol, which frankly I do not find a disadvantage, though quite a lot of people would. I approved of the fact that Muthoot Cardamom County promotes environmental awareness; a percentage of the room tariff goes towards the Thekkady Wildlife Conservation Fund.

Lunch seemed the most pressing thing on our minds and we were not disappointed in the resort dining room and with the cuisine. The dining room is named 'All Spice' which is apt for that part of the country. The chefs were friendly and the food was delightful. After lunch I had planned a laze by the pool and a swim and an Ayurvedic massage. It was a pleasant sunny afternoon and a very good opportunity to relax completely. I booked the Ayurvedic full body and head massage for late afternoon.

Graham and I were enjoying ourselves but the enjoyment was curtailed by the bad and loud behaviour of a party of Russian tour operators. They behaved quite disgracefully and were so rude and demanding of the waiters; Graham was so incensed that he went inside and told the management that he felt the waiters had coped in a very civil way with the aggression. I think Muthoot Cardamom County will have to be more discerning in the future as to whom they allow to stay at their very nice resort – in a complimentary fashion. The Front of House Manager was a particularly charming young woman called Devika Arvind; she was helpful without falling all over us and I liked her very much; her consternation at the Russians' behaviour was interesting. As she said they were on a tour to see and then promote Kerala in Russia but she devoutly hoped that other Russians would not behave in such a bellicose fashion.

I was happy to go away and enjoy some peace in the Ayurveda Centre called Ayura. This was an attractive building and the young doctor had a quick consultation with me and then led me through to the treatment rooms.

Ayurveda is a sacred vedic science of healing and rejuvenation. 'Ayur' means Life and 'Veda' means Knowledge. Its origins are 5,000 years old and can be considered as a natural herbal health care system which looks after both the body and the mind. I wanted to wait until undergoing Ayurvedic massage in Kerala to write about it specifically. Kerala it is believed provides the best ambience and natural surroundings to undergo ayurvedic therapies; more than 25 per cent of India's 15,000 plant species are found in Kerala and the year round abundant supply of herbs and medicinal plants together with the traditional healing techniques has made Kerala the heartland of Ayurveda. According to Ayurvedic philosophy your body is a combination of three *doshas* or bio-energies: Vata (air, the moving energy); Pitta (fire, the digestive energy);and Kapha (the energy that protects the sensitive tissues with mucus). Your personality is defined by the inherent qualities of these three energies. It differs in every individual and is as unique to you as your DNA or fingerprint. Ayurveda aims to retain the health of the well and to restore the health of the unwell; disease is believed to be indicative of imbalance and therefore equilibrium between the three energies is the natural state of health and wellbeing. All the physicians and masseurs at Ayura had been trained and received experience at a very reputable ayurvedic institute. I certainly enjoyed my full massage here, followed by a steam bath in a wooden cabinet and then a relaxing herbal gram shower to rinse off all the oils. The body feels wonderfully relaxed and the gram has this polishing effect which leaves the skin smooth and fresh. One leaves feeling very relaxed and serene. In everywhere that I experienced ayurvedic massage it was a soothing and comfortable experience; I wrote of it fleetingly when writing about Tamil Nadu but I do know how much it has helped friends who suffer from MS and all forms of arthritis. My only criticism is that if one tries to follow up through the website of the famous Coimbatore company and order more preparations there is no response. I really do not understand why they promote themselves as having a website if they do not employ people to monitor the enquiry and order-line.

The Chef was going to demonstrate some Keralan cooking that evening and this proved very interesting and enjoyable. I thought he did it so well and showed how easy it was that Cardamom County should produce a little cookbook of their Chef's own recipes that could have lovely colour photos of Keralan cooking and places visited; it would make an ideal gift for people to bring away with them instead of postcards.

After the cooking demonstration we had Kuchipudi Dancing demonstrated to us by a most talented young woman. Dance as a form of performing arts existed in India long long ago, and indeed sculptures at Amaravati dated to the second century, depict a number of dance poses. In the 14th century Siddhendra Yogi, of Kuchipudi village in the Krishna district of what is now Andhra Pradesh, developed this form of dance and taught Brahmin boys of the village. Teaching girls and young women was taboo as he had vowed to instruct only males; boys and young men used to wear female clothes and completely transform themselves. Now young girls and woman take their profession as dancers very seriously and it is the most fascinating form of movement. The subjects of the dance are invariably scenes from the great epics. Indian classical music and dance are celebrations of worship and life.

India has a number of different classical dance forms such as Kathak, a favourite dance at the royal courts of northern India; Odissi, developed in the temples of Orissia as an offering to the deities; Manipuri from the north east which enacts the legend of Radha and Krishna; Kathakali, which is Kerala's own special dance form featuring spectacular masks; Bharat Natyam which is from Tamil Nadu and has eloquent eye and hand movements, and of course Kuchipudi from Andhra Pradesh which we were to see on more than one occasion on this visit.

I love watching this form of art but about half an hour is probably the maximum time for enjoyment and the management had judged the attention span of their guests very accurately; we were able to go and have a delicious meal and relax for the rest of the evening.

The next morning we were up bright and early to go and spend time at the Periyar Tiger Reserve. It is just a short drive in a jeep to the edge of the Periyar Lake where we would embark on boats for a two-hour cruise on the lake wildlife watching. Sadly this proved to be very disappointing as we saw very little wildlife – just a couple of solitary elephants and a few birds. What was even more disappointing however was the way the boat trips were organised and the shambles that accompanied the whole endeavour. The lake after good rains can be twenty-six square kilometres or ten square miles of placid water but in March of 2005 it was very depleted through lack of good monsoon. I know many people who have thoroughly enjoyed their visit to Periyar and found it worthwhile but we were angry and disappointed as it was a poor contrast to the quality and efficiency of the wildlife parks in Madhya Pradesh and Corbett in Uttaranchal. I would say Ranthambhore is on a par with Periyar in terms of noise, pollution, and sheer foolish tourist behaviour; both Bandhavgarh and Khana in Madhya Pradesh and Corbett are professional about the park entry and behaviour of tourists. The litter at Periyar was irritating and the park authorities could very well have organised good litter disposal. The river launches are in poor condition and all the hoteliers agree, but when they have approached Kerala Tourism Authority the latter refuses to hand over administration and running of the boats to private enterprise; the general public has to contend with shabby outdated equipment. It is when I see that sort of negligence and complacency that I become very angry with Indian authorities who know that they are exploiting tourism instead of enriching the experience and maintaining good standards. I made my feelings known at the time and wrote it as well in the guest book for comments.

If one is hoping to actually see a tiger then I think the visitor will be disappointed; with that sort of shambolic noise and crowding no sensible tiger or leopard would allow itself to be visible, but there are normally plenty of other animals to see. The Malabar flying squirrel, gaur (the big horned bison), stripe-necked mongoose, sambar, wild pig, and Nilgiri wood pigeon, blue-winged parakeet, white-bellied tree pie, laughing thrushes and flycatchers are amongst the 260 species of birds present, and, most spectacular of all, herds of wild elephants. Usually from the lake one does see a small herd or two of elephants, maybe some wild boar and sambar deer; we were just a bit unlucky. Trekking through the reserve is also available for the resolute and elephant rides are also available, which is what I personally would recommend. There is no better way to see wildlife than from on the back of an elephant moving its stately way through the jungle, silent except for munching almost ceaselessly on its moving buffet of vegetation. One way of really enjoying Periyar is to stay at the Lake Palace, which is what the name suggests, the old hunting lodge of the Maharajah of Travancore. The ambience of a bygone era makes this a charming destination and one would be much more likely to see serious amounts of wildlife.

We returned for a very welcome breakfast but decided that the Russians were going to be an obnoxious addition to the day (some of them on our boat on the lake were beyond belief in apparel and behaviour). Fortunately we had received a very kind invitation from the management of CGH Earth Group to spend the day at their resort called Spice Village. It is just a few paces away from Cardamom County so that was really lovely. CGH Earth management have the right priorities with simplicity, elegance, comfort and conservation in their various properties. Both of us just loved it, probably because we both have a background of wildlife viewing and conservation going back to our childhoods. The Spice Village layout was spacious, green and eco-friendly with thatched roofed cottages and public areas, huge trees, spice bushes and creepers and fruit trees and winding paths taking you to your respective cottage set amongst six enclosed acres.

Spice Village exudes the spirit and ethos of wild India, tamed to enjoy but not exploited; here nature controlled the temperature and natural song was all one could hear – no piped music. The whole resort was modelled on a jungle village – the dwellings of the local tribal people. All the cottages are built with split bamboo and elephant grass. We were shown to the most sumptuous cottage imaginable, or so I thought! There was a veranda looking on to a private lawn, and inside a small hallway off which was a large simple but comfortable bedroom. In the middle of the cottage there was a luxurious bathroom, separate shower and loo. The other end of the small building has a very large lounge cum dining area and a simple galley kitchen. The soft furnishings are all very plain and unobtrusive and the flooring is tiled. Apparently one can have a private garden cottage or a spice garden cottage; there is badminton, tennis, yoga and meditation available plus ayurvedic treatments and a lovely ozone swimming pool. The resort shop is a good one and there is also an all day bar and café apart from the conventional open dining room. Alongside the dining room is a room called the Tiger Club, of which I heartily approved. There was a television set with DVD player and the room could take a reasonable number of people for talks or lectures on wildlife and the importance of conservation. The resident conservationist offered to give us a tour of the property and point out all the spices. This was immensely interesting and though we did not know all of the plants he showed us we were cognisant of quite a few. Pepper vines are the easiest to spot but the young man's extensive knowledge and passion about his subject made it a very pleasant hour. A great many of the old wives' remedies from my childhood were brought up and the most of them were based on good herbal knowledge. He then showed us the pepper drying area of the property where they process naturally their own pepper harvest. Wandering in a flock on the smooth green lawns were several guinea fowl; they were a lovely touch and apparently are extremely good watchdogs, as indeed are geese.

Lunch was excellent and that followed by a quiet swim in the slightly shaded large pool was a true delight. We then bumped into Jose Dominic, the managing director of CGH Earth and he introduced himself and was hospitable enough to ask us to dine with him. I would have loved another ayurvedic massage which was being urged upon me but I contented myself with just meeting the young physicians and looking at their herbal chest which is so fascinating. Spice Village also has Keralan cooking demonstrations which produced totally 'yummy' food and then the Kuchipudi dancer came and gave us a beautiful demonstration out on the lawn.

I think what I like about this sort of resort is that there is room, space, green lawns, small ponds of lotus or lilies, birdlife and tranquillity. Others would find it stultifying and dull and if you are fond of Ayah Nappa or the Spanish Costas then perhaps this is not the ideal destination for you! Sitting out under a thatched umbrella together with Jose and his charming wife, eating simply cooked seafood, looking up at the full moon was for us the best of travelling in India. I had asked the barman at the thatched roof café earlier in the afternoon for an iced tea; he seemed slightly thrown but then came up with the most wonderful delicately spiced iced tea, better than I have experienced anywhere else.

Our cottage had been the haven for a very well known celebrity couple quite recently; I could see why and because we visited three more properties in the group we saw their framed thank you letter of appreciation up on the wall wherever we went.

Jose Dominic explained to us how the group had come to change its name to CGH Earth and it is a story worth telling. Originally the Dominic brothers' late father had started a hotel in Cochin in the mid 1950s in partnership with a couple of friends. The Casino Hotel came into existence in 1957 and that generation of man thought 'Casino' was a good sophisticated name to choose. Funnily enough I can see why; it was about the time Grace Kelly married the late Prince Rainier and became that most beautiful of all princesses – Princess Grace of Monaco. Monaco was world famous for its Casino; it seemed to embody all that was sleek and sophisticated and possibly three or four men in distant Kerala thought this would be propitious for their new venture. As time went by the Dominics' father became very successful and the brothers' legacy has been extended and enlarged but: "Slowly the smile became a bit forced when people enquired, why was the group called Casino? We realized that all that we live for, the experiences that we offer, our values, our beliefs that are so precious to us are all radically opposed to the name that had been originally chosen – Casino. So why did they pick on the name Earth? Well it is a word that is simple, yet powerful. A word that captures the quintessence of the Kerala experience yet remains universal in content. The word earth, and for old times sake CGH Earth (Casino Group Hotels – Earth)."

I knew I was going to approve of this group's various properties. Sometimes when you meet an owner, a powerful man, you listen and talk and observe; sometimes one's perceptions have to remain confidential – some Indians talk a lot and make a great deal of noise enhancing their egos. Jose Dominic did not do that; I listened to his aspirations for the group and think they will do very well, and that Kerala is blessed to have them.

Graham and I returned to our beds because by now it was very late and we had an early start on Easter Sunday morning with a long way to go – by Kerala's standards – taking into account the state of the roads and the terrain which adds a lot of time to a car journey that in Europe would have been about three hours maximum plus a couple of short rest periods. Drivers boast about how short the journey will be with them driving; well we are very firm and want to arrive safely at our destination so insist that they drive in a moderate fashion and this adds a couple of hours to most journeys. It was to be a long day.

Chapter Thirteen

A Drive Across Kerala to the Sea

Driving away from Thekkady and Kumily, the latter being the actual small town in which most hotels are situated, the sun was shining and Kerala's hilly country looked beautiful and lush and covered in tea bushes along with pepper vines growing up tall trees in between the tea bushes. The whole affect is of green upon green and the hillsides look prosperous and well managed.

God's Own Country is the proud slogan of Kerala. 'Kera' in Sanskrit means coconut tree, and 'Alam' means land or location, hence Kerala is the land of coconut trees. We at this stage of the journey were still descending from the hill country where tea is the major produce. Interestingly there is an Indo-Swiss livestock project with a huge dairy farm at Mattupetty. On the roadside flowering bushes and creepers flourish and the whole drive is very colourful. There are many churches along the way but surprisingly I did not see any crowds, however it was still early and perhaps church going in Kerala is more popular in the afternoon or perhaps the cool of the evening. I suddenly saw what looked like a nursery garden with the most wonderful annual flowers so we asked our driver to stop and let us visit it. The house was a simple one but the people were friendly and their surname was also Kurien. I bought a few seed packets off them out of courtesy but sadly they did not germinate in our greenhouse last summer.

Kerala's economy can be best described as a socialistic welfare economy; I recall as a child reading that Kerala had become a communist governed state but it has evolved into a state with great emphasis on social welfare which has the spin off that economic progress has been rather slow. Sixty per cent of the GDP of the state is from the remittance of Keralans who work in the Middle East; we were constantly to meet men who had worked in the Middle East at all levels, either as young aspiring management trainees or as cooks and servants. Agriculture is the most important economic activity. Coconut, tea and coffee are grown extensively, along with rubber, cashew and spices. The spices cultivated include pepper, cardamom, vanilla, cinnamon and nutmeg, and much of Kerala's agriculture is in the form of 'home gardens', what we in Scotland would consider smallholdings or 'crofts' in the Scottish Highlands.

Livestock rearing is emerging as a very popular supplementary vocation in these small home farms or gardens; indeed it has always historically been part of the culture but now with modern veterinary science to assist. Rural women play a significant role in the development of the livestock aspect of the state's agriculture. It is thought that 3.2 million out of 5.5 million Keralan households rear livestock and because of the high level of literacy in Kerala, which has the highest levels of literacy in the whole of India, the females of the family are actively working in the livestock side of their home businesses and take the lead role in breeding, animal management and health care.

Kerala has a matrilineal family system which is called *marumakkathayam* whereby inheritance is determined through the female line. It is thought that this clever idea evolved from the 10th century when the area was going through a period of internecine war; men felt that by putting the inheritance through their women they could go to war knowing that their children's material well being was protected. Children thus bear their mother's family name and are identified as members of her family, with her brothers performing the role of father figure.

We had a charming personal experience of this custom; when we were dining in Cochin on our last night with Shilendran, the CGH Earth Group's manager, he was so excited and happy because his sister had that very day given birth to her first child, and he as the uncle was going to play a very significant role; indeed he left the dinner early to go to his sister's home to rejoice with them and the newborn. I do not know how much this custom is adhered to in modern times but apparently the Nairs were a warrior tribe who were known to favour this system and anthropologists think its origin is in the cult of the mother goddess widely prevalent in Kerala in past centuries.

On my last brief visit to Kerala we had remained at the coast so this drive across the state was enjoyable and interesting. We reached Kottayam.

This is a prosperous town and was the first to achieve 100 per cent literacy in India; it has become a centre for book publishing and is home to many of Kerala's Malayalam newspapers and magazines. Situated close to the foothills of the Southern Ghat mountains on which, as I have already mentioned, are grown tea and coffee and spices the main crop now becomes rubber and this product has brought this town its wealth. The name means 'inside the fort' and this is the centre of Kerala's Syrian Christians. I asked the driver to take us to the two most interesting churches, both dedicated to St Mary, that are really the tourist attraction of this place.

When I was writing about Chennai and Mylapore I spoke of St Thomas and the fact or legend that he had been martyred on St Thomas's Mount. I must say personally that I want to believe that one of Christ's apostles did reach the shores of India and was able to preach Christianity in this ancient country. That does not mean that it happened, but yet the evidence is very strong for believing it to be true. St Thomas is believed to have landed on the Malabar Coast in AD 52, and it is thought he founded seven churches. Muziris, his first chosen locality for preaching, is now known as Kodungallur, and there is a traditional account from Jews, who arrived there in AD 68 that they encountered a Christian community. Kodungallur is an important place though we did not visit there. This was the port known as Cranganore to Europeans and it was the historic capital of the Cheraman Perumals, monarchs of the Chera Empire. Situated at the mouth of the Periyar River this was the Malabar Coast's main port until a flood in 1341 silted up the harbour, after which Cochin or Kochi became the main port.

Kerala has a 21 per cent Christian population and people strongly insist that the religion arrived in the first century AD. When talking with Ranjit Jacob he just said with quiet authority, "No, Aline, we are St Thomas Christians... St Thomas came to what was one of the three Tamil kingdoms in those days – the Chera Kingdom; he came by way of Socotra."

The Island of Socotra was somewhere familiar to me through taking an interest in trees and their wonderful properties. Socotra is an island just off the Horn of Africa, about 150 miles (210 km) east of the north Somalian coast. The island is about 80 miles (130 km) from end to end which is in a west to east direction and at its widest is no more than 25 miles (40 km) across. Socotra has many strange tree species, two of which are the Sack-of-Potatoes Tree which is rather grotesque and human like with attractive pink flowers produced in winter, and the Cucumber Tree; it can shed all its leaves and withdraw into a white carapace-like trunk during periods of extreme drought. Socotra has been isolated from the African mainland and Arabia since Tertiary times (1.6 million years ago) and it has around 800 plant species over a third of which are endemic, including 25 trees. Pliny described this ancient mountainous island where dragons were thought to live. The myth was that Sinbad the Sailor was shipwrecked on this island where the monstrous bird called the Roc lived. Sinbad was a myth but Pliny most definitely was not and by the time St Francis Xavier landed at Socotra on his way to India in 1548 he heard from the natives of this special island that they "render special honours to the Apostle Thomas, claiming themselves to be the descendants of Christians begotten to Jesus Christ by that Apostle in these countries."

Now the population of Socotra which numbers about 50,000 is entirely Moslem of mixed African and Arabic descent. Arabic is spoken on the coast but inland the main language is Socotran which is a non-Arabic language and is related to the languages spoken in parts of Dhofar in Arabia. Up until the 17th century the island was Christian and archaeologists have uncovered the remains of at least one early church. The Portuguese occupied Socotra between 1507 and 1511, after which it was ruled by the Mahri Sultan from what is now the eastern part of southern Yemen. Since 1967 the island has become part of the independent state of South Yemen which united with North Yemen in 1991 to form the Republic of Yemen.

So, I am going to leave the controversy to wiser heads than me but if it is documented that St Francis Xavier went to Socotra in 1548 and found evidence of St Thomas having been there, then it is quite likely that he continued on his journey and reached the Malabar Coast of India in 52AD, as is claimed by devout Christians. There is also an unquestioned tradition in Malabar, which is corroborated by the customs of the place and by ethnological research, that the Apostle was very successful in the conversion of high caste Nambhudiri Brahmins. Four of the leading Brahmin families are believed to have been raised to the privilege of the priesthood.

These days the bewildering assortment of Christians in Kerala comprise: Nestorians, Roman Catholics, Syrian Orthodox Mar Thoma Syrians and the Anglican Church of South India. The liturgy of the early Christians was in the Syriac language (a dialect of Aramaic), but when the Catholic Portuguese arrived in a large community in 1498 a large community of Latin Christians developed, particularly on the coast, and came under the jurisdiction of the Pope. I thought from the evidence on Easter Sunday that perhaps Christmas is more important to the Christian community in Kerala, and indeed why not.

It was by now quite hot and midday; we went round the first church which is set on a hillock with good views over a cocoa plantation. Vailapally (the Big Church), which now is smaller than the Cheriapally (Small Church) is said to have been founded in the 9th century, but the present structure dates from 1550. It is very plain and I thought rather forlorn but we walked around and found a tombstone inscribed: "Rev. Fr. E C Lukose, Edavazhikal, Vicar of this Church 1088-1127, Born 1-12-1040, Ordained 4-2-1068, Died 11-5-1127 (reinterred 26.12.1951) R.I.P."

This tombstone or grave is extremely plain and unobtrusive and round the back of the main building; had one not persevered it would not have been noticed, yet here is evidence of a Christian priest born nearly a thousand years ago in the middle of Kerala. Twin altars in the chancel are brightly decorated, and a stone Persian cross has been inserted in the face of the north altar on the left. By tradition it was carved by St Thomas but scientists who recently examined the cross date it as 7th century work. The white inscription around it is in the Persian Pahlavi language. The visitors' book dates back to 1899 and has record of a visit from Emperor Haile Selassie of Ethiopia in 1956.

The Cheriapally – smaller church – is located about ninety metres away. Both churches were founded by Nestorian Syrians who, as refugees, colonized the area following their condemnation by the Council of Ephesus in 431. This church was built in 1579 but on the foundations of a 13th century church. It has a rather curious feature; an open covered passageway leads to the west door, from where the church is entered and where shoes must be removed, as is the custom in south Indian churches. The roof is typical Keralan style but there is an extravagant Baroque style façade. So much of religious worship goes on outdoors here in India and there was evidence of either a function the night before or preparations for one that night.

By this time we were both in need of some liquid refreshment – it had become steadily hotter and all I could think of was a nice chilled coke with lemon! We observed that the driver had become rather reckless whilst driving through the narrow lanes and roads around Kottayam and Graham thought he might be falling asleep. We told him to take us to a restaurant and then go and have a rest for one and half hours. His day had not been arduous at all but it just is not worth taking a risk and perhaps he had been celebrating in some form the night before. He found us a respectable air conditioned restaurant and we gave him money to feed himself and suggested a sleep in the jeep.

It was an odd sort of place because though it had everything one could want from a restaurant rather obviously the bar off the main hall was more popular and I was intrigued that by midday on Easter Sunday in Kerala that should be so. We were content with a light meal and watched other Indian families arrive in huge parties with three generations of family members. The sun was still high in the sky when we resumed our trip to Kovalam.

Very soon we were travelling on the main road down through the state towards Trivandrum and Kovalam. I have to say that I was very disappointed with the litter and general disorder the closer we drove to Trivandrum. The area between Trivandrum and Kovalam was really horrible and I now know why people are referring to it as the Costa del Kerala! Thirty years ago, indeed perhaps only twenty years ago, this must have all been very unspoilt and beautiful but now hotel groups have climbed on the bandwagon and more and more properties are being squeezed on to beach side land or not even that close to the beach. Trivandrum or Thiruvananthapuram's airport to give it the full name sees increasing numbers of international aircraft flying in as well as the daily domestic flights to the main southern cities and to Delhi and Mumbai. Unless the Kerala state government takes firm steps the piles of rubbish and general mayhem will very soon upset the discerning traveller who will go ever farther afield in search of clean pastures and beaches. I found it difficult to imagine how I would feel had I just arrived on a long flight from the West to see as my first impression the litter strewn main road taking me to my destination. These hotels are now quite expensive and promote themselves as the ultimate in relaxation and luxury. Indeed, they are very good, or at least some of them are, but at what price and people are increasingly conscious of their environment and how important conservation is to our survival.

We finally drew into the porch of The Travancore Heritage. Were we pleased to arrive, it had been a long day's driving and the last half of it had not proved attractive; indeed I would go as far as to say had that been my first impression of Kerala I would not want to return! I tried to convey this to the senior management of CGH Earth Group, because though they wisely do not have a property in this area they surely have huge influence in trying to pressure the state government to maintain clean and presentable roads around the capital city and approaches to the popular beaches.

The Travancore Heritage is an actual seaside resort in eight acres of lush green coconut grove and landscaped gardens at Chowara, south of Kovalam. The resort stands on a high cliff overlooking the Arabian Sea and a long, white, clean beach. It has been conceived as a heritage property to bring to life the age-old traditional architectural splendour of the region with its typical timber houses and 'Nalukettus' with tiled roofing. *Nalukettu* is the word for the traditional roofed open-sided communal living halls which usually are built round a courtyard. The main building is apparently a 120 years old palace. We liked it immensely and by the afternoon the sun's heat had diminished and it was such a pleasure to stroll around and then go down to the beach. There is a modern lift which takes one down to the beach and it was very empty and pleasant, with a church nestled into the cliffs at the base. The resort has cottages and semi-detached cottages which are all air conditioned with all modern amenities including open air bathrooms which I particularly like. There are two luxury pool mansions with private pools set in the courtyard of each villa. We however had been accommodated in a small semi-detached villa which we found both small and dark. I think it had originally been designed for single occupancy and greedy management had put in two large single beds, with the result that we kept knocking our shins on the bed post which led to some choice language from both of us. The bathroom appeared bigger than the bedroom and I hate anything that is dark. I am sure there were nicer villas and I liked the general atmosphere, but the management were a little laid back and inefficient which was a disappointment. The hotel was full of British couples and families and it is a popular resort with both a lovely pool with jacuzzi and the sea to choose from; however, I think the sea would have its challenges and might not be all that safe, other than for walking through the spent waves and sunbathing on the beach. The gardens were probably the highlight for us and we enjoyed lying back in a hammock and looking at all the papayas and orchids and other blooms. I really liked getting up early, making a cup of tea and sitting out on the wooden porch and watching the place come to life. The food was quite good and I am sure with careful imaginative management it could become a very good resort but as it stood I found it a little disappointing despite its very charming architecture and position. Like any country India does take its hospitality and tourism seriously but there is no doubt that a hotel group with a good ethos will inspire its staff, and the management of this resort were nowhere in evidence on a most busy day; that is not commendable and leads to all the 'little mice' just playing or talking to each other instead of getting on with the business of ensuring good hospitality to their paying guests.

Kovalam has all the natural attributes for a perfect beach holiday but I think now one has to be quite discerning. Kovalam consists of four successive arc shaped beaches. There is Kovalam Lighthouse beach where most people spend their time; there is Eve's Beach in the middle, and Ashok Beach and Samudra Beach to the north. There is something to meet everyone's budget but we as a couple have very clear tastes and criteria for a beach holiday, namely that the grounds of the hotel must be spacious and therefore one never feels overcrowded, and the beach must be easily accessible on foot and be clean and relatively safe from hawkers and general public harassing one. I know a great many people just like to 'chill out' by the pool and have a lazy dip and drink cool drinks and sleep and read; that is absolutely fine and wonderful for those people, but we like to be able to walk and move around and not feel as if we are in a tight little enclave.

Kovalam's tourist development actually preceded that of Goa but because it was only a few hippies and did not attract vast numbers the area retained its charm. Having the natural coves greatly enhances the area and the picturesque headlands give a sense of drama whereas long flat beaches can begin to seem boring. Kovalam the village is unremarkable and does not really feature, but each curve of beach has its own community. Four steep roads descend to the beaches from the main Trivandrum highway, but, apart from these roads there are only linked footpaths, which mean that much of Kovalam's accommodation cannot be reached directly by motor vehicle. Apparently the real name for Eve's Beach was Hawah Beach but *hawah* means Eve in Malayalam and this was a reference to the young European females who came and bathed topless and sometimes totally nude. The locals were horrified but I supposed intrigued; however it is not a good idea to bathe topless in India – except in one's own private pool in luxury accommodation!

Kerala's capital Thiruvananthapuram or Trivandrum which is infinitely easier to say and indeed write was named after the Serpent God, Anantha, on whom Lord Vishnu reclines. There is a statue of Vishnu at the 2,000 years old Padmanabhaswamy Temple in the heart of the city. This temple is located within the walls, or fort that encircles the town, and is the only temple in the state with a huge *gopura* which was so much part of the temple architecture in Tamil Nadu. This is an interesting temple but quite muted by Tamil Nadu standards and I think the six metre long reclining figure of Vishnu is probably the most striking aspect. King Marthanda Varma, founder of Travancore, made Trivandrum his capital and even after his rule ended the city continued to be the capital of the state of Travancore. When Kerala was formed as a state in 1956 the city was unanimously chosen to continue as the capital continuing two centuries of tradition. There is a lot to see in Trivandrum and it is a small city by comparison to the other state capitals and thus retains its charm.

The Government Arts and Crafts Museum which was formerly the Napier Museum named after a former governor of Madras, John Napier, is in a red and black brick Indo-Saracenic architecture designed by Robert Fellows Chisholm in the 19th century. The exhibits including bronzes, stone sculptures, exquisite gold ornaments and a temple chariot were all from the locality when part of the ancient kingdom of Travancore. This and the Shri Chitra Art Gallery, which is a beautiful building, are very worthwhile visiting and at the Natural History Museum there is a fine replica of a typical Kerala Nair wooden house – the *nalukettu* – as we had experienced in The Travancore Heritage resort.

Mahatma Gandhi road is the city's main road and runs from the Victoria Jubilee Town Hall to the Anantha Padmanabhaswamy Temple; this road has many impressive buildings including the Secretariat, which is the headquarters of the state government, the

University College and the Public Library. The latter would probably be a bit boring to the average tourist but it houses 250,000 books and documents in Malayalam, Hindi, Tamil and Sanskrit. Trivandrum is a short distance from Kovalam and the obvious place for shopping as well as sight seeing; it is certainly worth a visit, but to see the really beautiful Padmanabhapuram Palace, the seat of the Travancore rulers, one has to travel south of Trivandrum and ironically it now is part of the state of Tamil Nadu, though the Kerala government maintains it beautifully!

This palace is one of the finest examples of traditional Kerala architecture and is well preserved. In the 14th century Trippapur Moopan, the head of Trippapur Swaroopam fiefdom built a palace and a mud fort and named it Darpakulangara. The palace had undergone a massive renovation during the 18th century and the mud fort was replaced with a four kilometre long granite wall. The then ruler of Travancore, Anizham Thurunal Marthanda Varma renamed the entire premise as Padmanabhapuram, honouring Lord Padmanabha (Lord Vishnu) the patron deity of the royal family of Travancore. This place and this building remained the royal seat until the capital was moved to Trivandrum in 1780. In fact this is a huge complex of fourteen palaces and is spread over six and a half acres. This is a well preserved set of buildings and worthy of a morning's visit.

We were on our way to something that I had long wanted to do. I had a fascination with the tip of India since I was a child; in 2003 on New Year's Eve we had sailed round the tip of India, which is called Kanniyakumari on our way to Sri Lanka. Now I was determined to go and visit it. Kannyakumari is actually in Tamil Nadu, as is the palace of which I have just written. When the Indian states were variously reconfigured these odd things happened. It is much easier to reach Kanniyakumari from Kerala than from Tamil Nadu. The very tip of India, the great sub-continent, is considered one of the nine holy rivers of India. Along with the Ganges, the Yamuna, the Saraswati, the Sarayn, the Godavri, the Cauvery and the Payokshini, Kannyakumari is sacred as it is the confluence of three seas – the Arabian Sea, the Indian Ocean and the Bay of Bengal.

Kanniyakumari was also battered by the tsunami waves and we were able to see the damage for ourselves. It is a great pilgrimage destination but was thankfully not crowded on this particular day. It is said that in April on Chaitra Purnima one can see the full moon and the sun at the same time and this is truly special but I think it is probably special at every sunset; sadly however we were there in the middle of the day and it was very hot. This place is believed to be the abode of Kumari, the Virgin Goddess, who is supposed to have done

The tip of India at Kannyakumari

penance here so that she could marry Shiva. The marriage however did not take place and she was doomed to remain a virgin here to save the world. Her temple Kumari Amman Temple is a very popular pilgrim destination, which was built by the Pandya kings in the 8th century and was extensively renovated by the Chola, Vijayanagar and Nayaka rulers.

The Gandhi Memorial is what drew our interest. This shrine is where Mahatma Gandhi's ashes were kept before immersion in the ninth sacred river of India i.e. the confluence of the oceans. The building is designed so that every year on Gandhiji's birthday – 2nd October – at midday, the rays of the sun fall on the exact spot where his ashes had rested. This shrine was hit by the waves and the workmen were rebuilding on the sea side of the building. The custodian greeted us and I explained what I was doing and he very kindly allowed me to photograph inside. It has rather strange architecture which I think was meant to look like a modern temple, but it is clean and fresh and spacious inside.

As always with Gandhiji I was moved by all that he achieved and all that he stood for. There was no-one else there so Graham and I enjoyed ourselves in silence looking at everything; there is an inscription on the

Gandhiji's memorial at Kannyakumari, the very tip of India

bronze depiction of him writing which says:

"I am writing this at the cape, in front of the sea, where three waters meet and furnish a sight unequalled in the world. For this is no port of call for vessels, like the Goddess, the waters around are virgin." Dated 15-1-1937

That wonderful little man to whom India owes so much; I know these days it appears unfashionable to venerate him, but why I ask? Nelson Mandela is the current icon of the masses, but his time will also pass and will he be dismissed as well? Gandhiji was a good man; I am not saying that he was an easy man with whom to live or to have as an ideal, but he was a good man and helped to steer India through tumultuous times in her history. When a country has matured and is thriving it is easy to 'forget' the struggle and the challenges and the dark days, but India experienced those in her freedom struggle and Gandhi was the true guiding light – the others were all merely politicians.

On the way in a man stopped me and asked me to buy his offerings. I was about to politely decline but I saw that he had some really nice shells on which he carved. So I asked him to carve the names of our grandsons, one on each shell and paid him. When I came out he had done a lovely job and we have those for Piers and William for when they are grown up. Who knows, they too might wish to visit the very tip of India?

Just off the coast on a rocky island is the Vivekananda Memorial which marks the spot where Swami Vivekananda meditated before attending the World Religious Conference in Chicago in 1893. It was visible from the ship when we were sailing past the point; I believe that people were marooned on the rock by the tsunami and had to be rescued by helicopter. Nearby is the memorial to Tiruvalluvar, the forty metre high statue of the 1st century BC Tamil poet. He wrote an epic poem in Tamil called Tirukural which is considered one of the great classics of Tamil literature.

This place has such huge appeal for Indians and I do not suppose the authorities consider they have to do anything to improve its appearance, but actually were it to be slightly redesigned I think western visitors would find it a worthwhile destination. I am constantly pleasantly surprised in Scotland when some European funding is used to enhance a tourist area and with imagination, and modern building materials plus the addition of trees or shrubs, a quite ordinary perhaps dull place is transformed. What we did not know at this point was that later in the day there was going to be another full scale alert for a second tsunami.

We returned to Kovalam for a much needed rest and lunch, which was quite late in the day! I asked the driver to take us to the very new Taj Green Cove Resort, which had only opened in December 2004. It is an interesting and very luxurious resort set in ten acres; the architects decided on a Balinese architecture and landscape with lots of stone used in the construction. The building belongs to the Muthoot Group of companies, the conglomerate that belongs to Kripa Kurien's in-laws. It is very beautiful and the welcome was warm and the food was delicious. This was a very luxurious place and the management kindly took me round. Instead of Ayurveda they offer a Jiva Spa with Indian aromatherapy treatments. It all looked very inviting as did the infinity pool and the outdoor hot and cold Jacuzzi; my criticism however is that the architects have tried to put too much on a small area of land and therefore it is all a bit suffocating with lots of hot stonework which positively gives off the heat of the afternoon sun; I want a sense of space and freedom when I have travelled thousands of miles – nor is it all that appealing to bump into half of Sloane Square.

Very reluctantly we climbed back into the jeep and headed north. Our destination was Marari Beach and there was quite a long way to go. One lovely experience on that tiring drive was that as evening fell I suddenly saw on the side of the road a bunch of caparisoned elephants. We had missed the annual big festivals and I had not been optimistic about seeing elephants decked out in all their finery, but here it was right in front of me – a little prayer answered. I asked the driver to find a safe spot to stop so that we might walk back and photograph the elephants and see what was happening. It was rush hour and difficult, but he managed to pull up safely and Graham and I really enjoyed ourselves and the photographs have been successful. There were about six elephants, all beautifully adorned with their keepers; I don't think in this instance the word 'mahout', which is the correct word for the elephant keeper, really is appropriate because we were in Kerala and that is a Hindi word.

I had so hoped to see a wild herd of elephants at Periyar but had been unlucky; at least here I could photograph the ceremonial beasts and maybe we will be lucky when we go to Karnataka and visit Bandipur and Nagarahole and see them at close quarters in the wild!

Chapter Fourteen

Beautiful Memorable Kerala

We were driving through the afternoon sun and then quite suddenly it was dusk and quite stressful as the equivalent of 'rush hour' took place all along the main road driving north. Because of the sheer multitude of people and cars and huge lorries, let alone livestock and ceremonial elephants Graham and I try to keep vigilant in the back seat. Some drivers have that sense of spatial awareness and good judgement that means one does not have to worry at all; unhappily on this occasion the young man was inclined to take risks and we had to be firm and tell him not to endanger our lives. We have been driven literally hundreds of miles, indeed over the years that I have been travelling to India it must now be thousands of miles, but I can still recall quite clearly all the very good drivers and the excellent relationship we established with each one. This young man was likeable but I think had not yet accepted that driving is what he does for a living and to become a trusted experienced driver one has to reduce one's impatience and quickly establish confidence in one's passengers! Let us just say he failed.

It was dark by the time we arrived at the Marari Beach Resort owned by CGH Earth. I was tired and grumpy from some of the danger on the road. The welcome was warm and friendly, and in no time we both realised we had arrived in Keralan heaven. Had someone asked me prior to my arrival at Marari Beach what are my criteria for a good luxurious beach holiday I might have listed a few obvious requirements, but even in the dark I could see that Marari Beach was enchanting and I began to feel relaxed. The management guided us to our villa through the grounds on well lit paths which went over little bridges and I could see pools of lotus; the configuration of the individual villas looked interesting and there was this great feeling of space.

They had been kind enough to provide us with a deluxe pool villa of which they have about three, and then they also have pool villas and ordinary garden villas, something to suit everyone's budget. This villa

Fishermen at Marari Beach, Kerala

was spacious and elegant and simple; yet again the management had used simplicity with lots of white and very pale soft furnishing to give a tranquil air. The front door on the veranda led into a hallway that became a sitting room with a small dining table; sliding doors opened on to a secluded walled garden with a lovely pool with underwater lighting. There was a conventional bathroom and then a huge bedroom with its own sitting area and dressing alcove which had a door into the outside bathroom. I love these outside bathrooms with a gravel garden enclosed by a brick wall; a young banana tree was growing out of the bathroom's gravel garden. Through the wall was a little wooden door so one could enter the garden and pool from the bathroom. We were totally enchanted and promptly divested ourselves of hot sticky clothes and went for a nude swim.

One of the most memorably happy times in this huge trip was that evening swimming nude under the moon and the stars, totally relaxed with my fatigue being washed away; one end of the pool acted as a jacuzzi. Looking up, floating on my back the silhouettes of palm trees and fruit trees could be seen but nothing else and no noise whatsoever – total bliss. Reluctantly we went and showered and dressed to go and explore and have some supper. The Grill and Seafood restaurant was under a thatched roof not too far away from the sea and the atmosphere was very relaxed and simple. We feasted on the most amazing large grilled garlic prawns followed by a mango ice cream. Four of these prawns left one totally sated, and we just relaxed and enjoyed the candle-lit atmosphere of soft breeze, gentle sound from the ocean and a delicious meal.

Our beds were calling but I just slipped into the pool again and relaxed and enjoyed a memorable day reflecting on all that I had seen and experienced. Little did I know that the management would be up all night with the threat of a full scale tsunami alert; we did not want the news or television to intrude so remained in blissful ignorance of this worry.

Marari Beach at sunrise was quiet and misty; I made us some tea and then went on a walk through the grounds down to the beach. Thirty-five acres of grounds gives the feeling of space and tranquillity with waving palms and fruit trees, large pools of pink lotus through which kingfishers darted, provide focal points for villas; a heron gazing down intently looking for fish and the raucous birdlife synonymous with an Indian garden were the only signs of life as the sun came up. The beach is a nice one with clean sand and a beach guard's high chair to help him monitor bathers. Very soon the yoga and meditation area filled up with people intent on achieving relaxed serenity; this was quite close to the beach and perfectly situated. I was alone and loved the feeling of solitude yet I knew I was in a safe eco-friendly environment; furthermore no-one would come and hassle me or try to sell me trinkets or beg. During my early years in India as a child when we went as a family to the beach at Puri in Orissa this same feeling was present, but that was nearly fifty years ago, so today if one is able to recapture that sense then you know you have come to a special place.

Graham strolled down to the beach and then spied the fisherman on their own stretch of sand to the left of the hotel's beach; we wandered over to watch them launching boats or bringing in the catch. I realised that I had a dilemma when having arrived amongst the fishermen it soon became clear that these folk were busily engaged on their morning 'toilet'. I was embarrassed as this had never happened to me before in Orissa or Andhra Pradesh or Tamil Nadu. It soon became clear that the actual sand was studied with 'dumps' and the individuals were busy in the shallows washing their respective posteriors! I said to Graham that this was no place for me and being the robust veterinary surgeon that he is he just grunted and said something like, "A man has got to do what a man has got to do..." and carried on looking at the construction of the fishing boats. The fishermen appeared not to mind my presence but I did not wish to intrude so hurried away with great care as to where I placed my feet. Obviously, when the tide came in it would wash the shore line clean; however I had never seen quite this degree of unsophisticated behaviour before. Their village was situated literally yards away, and indeed had there been a tsunami wave would have suffered accordingly.

I decided that I would have another private swim and wait for Graham to return. Breakfast was in the large open sided dining room which looked onto the main hotel pool. As ever it was a magnificent spread and that was when we heard about the tsunami threat from the manager Erine.

Graham and I know that we could spend a whole week, or indeed two at Marari, doing nothing on the beach, exploring village life, cycling, learning to cook the Keralan way. There is tennis available as well as the yoga and meditation class, plus one's own pool if the budget allows, and of course the large swimming pool when one wishes to be sociable with other guests. The Ayurveda centre looked very inviting and I think I would have a daily massage to top up the luxury! Alleppey is just round the corner to have a walk round or visits to places of interest can be arranged; if I had arrived by air at Cochin then a couple of days spent in Cochin sightseeing would be ideally followed by a week at Marari Beach.

The management took the trouble to show us around the whole complex and now in daylight I could see the attractive circular drive and reception centre. Each of these resorts has a very good shop with a discerning buyer and the clothes, book and art work are worth purchasing and naturally they also stock items such as toothpaste, or films and suntan lotion. I always go round hotel shops because in India they are usually well sourced and this group has obviously maintained a high standard of gifts and clothing. In places like Mexico the hotel shop very often is ridiculously priced but here the prices were affordable; I saw so many lovely books but those are the one thing really one cannot load up with when flying.

The hotel management arranged to have us driven to the place from which we would embark on our Spice Boat Cruise. It was a very short pleasant drive and the *kettuvallam* was ready and waiting for us. The embarkation area is attractive and we came across an old man weaving coir rope from coconut fibres. People who have arrived from the airport are driven to this point to embark on the spice boat or to take the rather elegant launch that ferries guests to Coconut Lagoon, to which we too would be going after time spent on the Spice Boat.

Kettuvallams are the huge famous boats synonymous with Kerala; they are giant country craft measuring up to twenty-seven metres long (80 feet). They are built by joining huge planks of jackfruit tree wood together, without the use of a single nail. *Kettu* means a bundle, while *vallam* means big boat. Each jackwood plank is sewn to the next plank with coir rope and then the completed craft is coated with a tar-like substance that has been extracted from boiled cashew nut kernels. (You may recall I mentioned this when we came upon the folk on the side of the road in Tamil Nadu processing freshly harvested cashew nuts). I can quite see that with careful maintenance the boat would last for generations.

We embarked on the CGH Earth Spice Boat and were introduced to the crew of three. Joseph was the cook and he was also the 'purser', as his name implies he is Christian; Gopalakrishna was the 'captain' and Kunjumon was the 'engineer'. We waved to John the Manager and the boat slid away. I was enchanted. The accommodation comprised an entrance passage with led round to one double bedroom and its en-suite shower, loo and basin. Towards the prow was a sitting area and at the prow was a large reclining area on top of which the captain sat on a wooden stool when he was required to navigate something special. Most of the time one had the living quarters entirely to oneself. The second bedroom and its ensuite were towards the rear and then there was the galley kitchen and a WC for the crew. From what I could see kettuvallams are constantly being reconfigured to provide more and more luxurious accommodation, some indeed seemed to be partially double storey. We however were delighted with the comfort and simplicity of ours.

Kuttanad: that is the actual name of the backwaters of Kerala and the next twenty-four hours were to provide a most memorable experience that anyone can also choose to do – it can be expensive but it need not be and though I would recommend a night on board,

Our spice boat in Kerala

Flocks of ducks on the backwaters in Kerala

if the budget does not allow just spend a whole day lazily traversing the Kuttanad. There are 44 rivers, 41 of which flow west and 3 flow to the east in Kerala, and the Backwaters are the large inland water bodies consisting of an entire network of lakes, canals and estuaries which measure nearly 1,900 kilometres. The Backwaters provide water for drinking along with irrigating the lush paddy fields; a Spartan yet thriving economy exists on the borders of these water expanses. The waterways connect isolated villages to the urban settings and one sees the huge craft transporting men and materials, let alone the agricultural produce and sometimes livestock. Over 900 kilometres of this labyrinthine water world is navigable and the largest backwater expanse is Lake Vembanad, which flows through three districts and eventually opens out into the sea at Kochi. The second largest lake is Ashtamudi Lake (which means having eight arms) which is further south and considered a gateway to the backwaters.

Graham and I sat back in comfortable chairs and just watched. Joseph came along and suggested a cool drink which was expertly poured – a clever combination of mango juice and lemonade and the 'captain' took his seat and navigated the start of our tranquil journey. This boat has also been used by the same very famous couple who had stayed at Spice Village and Marari Beach; they had signed a letter of appreciation that was framed as a picture on the coconut matting wall. People come on honeymoon but I would suggest that one night would suffice, if one is on honeymoon! You see though the boat is spacious and comfortable I suspect any advanced 'intimacy' would not be ideal in rooms made of coconut matting...but each to their own and we recalled that our own Hamish and Vicky had spent one night of their very happy Kerala honeymoon on a spice boat. I was in seventh heaven with so much to watch and photograph and just quietly comment upon to Graham and write up my notes. I would not want to be reading a really good book as inevitably one would miss interesting bits of Keralan life on the banks.

It is reckoned that there might be 400 kettuvallams in existence and some of the waterways are as wide as a motorway and others are very narrow canals, and then one will empty out into a lake or lagoon. There are rules of the road or waterway and hooters are sounded. Most of the time the canals are above the level of the adjoining fields and the water is contained by stone dykes which also form the pathways between the canals. I loved the lushness of coconut trees, some at strange angles, and vegetation dipping into the water; it was spring time so laburnum trees, hibiscus and other flowering shrubs and plants were in full blossom. Overhead there were fish eagles and cormorants and on the water literally hundred of huge flocks of floating ducks. They floated in vast circles and all stayed together.

Water hyacinth is also present and is a cause of serious ecological problem since untamed growth has clogged the waterways; I recall as a child that water hyacinth was an increasing scourge of inland waterways and indeed in Central Africa it is having a hugely detrimental effect on the big lakes.

According to legend Parasurama, the sixth incarnation of Vishnu, created Kerala by throwing his battle axe into the sea. We both found it totally enchanting and more enjoyable than the Mekong Delta in Viet Nam, which was also a wonderful experience. Children playing, or returning from school, then bathing or just having fun in the water; old men reading their newspapers, women preparing the family meal, dogs barking, ducks waddling, mothers doing the family washing, indeed all of rural Keralan life going on like an ever changing lush tapestry in front of your eyes. The ferries reminded us of the Vaporetti in Venice with people patiently standing whilst being transported to their destination, and there were boatmen with large tanks of fresh water on their craft distributing them between the various villages.

Joseph's lunch was a total delight and was preceded by a chilled beer or fresh lime. This is excellent Boat Peoples' cuisine and very tasty too. Toddy tappers scale up the coconut trees and tap the sap which is fermented and made into 'Toddy', an alcoholic drink. I am told the first 'brew' is delicious but it becomes ever more potent with subsequent fermentation, we did not wish to try it! Joseph told us what he planned to cook for our supper that night and then asked what we would care to eat for breakfast. We mentioned our great favourite papaya and his face fell; no matter, he said we would go shopping for some fruit and other groceries.

Homes, farms, churches, mosques and temples could be glimpsed amongst the trees as we sailed by; with a keen eye we spotted kingfishers and the odd green parakeet. The cormorants would stand on a log and open up their wings to dry them in the sun and the fish eagles continued to wheel and turn and sometimes dive for a fish or a frog. By this time the sun was low in the sky and one could observe that life was winding down from the day's work or routine. The sun cast a rich glow on the vegetation and little houses and I drank a welcome cup of tea and waved and responded to calls from the bank.

As well as the famous kettuvallams the Kerala *chundanvallam* or Snake Boat is quite magnificent. A master craftsman assisted by a team which is traditionally drawn from different religions builds the boat. No nails or metal pieces are used; only wooden pegs and joints hold the parts together in this craft. Snake Boats were thought to have carried warriors originally but now they only participate in ceremonials and the famous Snake Boat Race. The prow of the boat is normally manned by four boatmen. Then there are oarsmen, singers and men holding the ceremonial umbrellas. The *Amaram*, the stern, is decorated with brass studs and inlay work. Boatbuilding is an ancient craft in Kerala and a boat is usually started on an auspicious day in the Malayalam calendar, and is marked by a special invocation to the gods. The most famous Snake Boat Race is for the Nehru Trophy Race which was introduced way back in 1952.

Snakes play a big part in the religious life of the state. Malayali folklore speaks of a wooded rural land inhabited by Nagas (snakes) who are considered the Lords of the Underworld. Indeed even I clearly recall in the rest of India that if there was a snake hole in a village clearing people would lay milk and fresh flowers to appease the deity. Vishnu's sixth incarnation, Parasurama, declared the snakes be given divine status after he vanquished them with the help of Brahmin settlers. Most temples would have a niche for a snake god and groves of trees often provide a shrine for the snake deity.

Joseph asked the captain to put into port and this was interesting as we nosed our way into the jetty and moored. Graham and I sat and watched all that was happening on the shore. We reclined on the prow cushions and kept the mosquitoes at bay. Joseph invited us to go with him but it was frankly more fun just sitting there watching all

Luxury Villa with pool at Coconut Lagoon

that went on around one. He was not that successful with his shopping and felt the mangoes were better than the papayas, we told him not to worry. A man was putting up posters advertising something; we don't know what as the script was Malayalam. Then there was a huge cloth banner advertising a bio enzyme toilet for households, which seemed altogether a good thing!

Eventually we set off again and the captain took us out into Lake Vembanad. As the light failed and the moon and stars came out it was lovely to be in the middle of this huge lake with total peace. We looked for a shooting star but did not see one, though other passengers writing in the visitors' book obviously had been fortunate. Joseph suggested some chilled white wine and then presented a beautiful meal. After eating, yet again, without any exercise we felt totally satisfied and just lay on the white mattress on the prow and fell asleep to the sound of fish jumping and nothing! Joseph had made us some coffee and it was welcome because the temperature cooled but we suddenly realised that we were asleep out on the prow. I somehow suspected that Joseph normally slept up there having moved the mattress and bolsters away. So we sleepily moved into our bedroom. Sure enough, Joseph very quietly moved up to the prow and settled himself. What happened next was quite funny. I was lying on our bed and almost asleep and

Clam fisherman on Kerala's Lake Vembanad

then I heard the loudest snores and 'trumpets'. I could blearily see Graham was still washing his teeth so I said in alarm, "Graham there is a man under my bed." He laughed and didn't take me seriously but as it went on I became more alarmed and rather short with Graham. Indeed as he approached the head of my bed he too heard its volume. Then we heard Joseph moving about behind our curtained windows and he obviously went up to the captain or the engineer and told them to move. The snoring man was right on the other side of my head with just a coconut matting wall dividing us! Joseph, we got the feeling, shook him awake and he was told to move off and resume his noisy sleep elsewhere. We fell asleep with the fans going at full tilt.

In the early hours as dawn approached we heard the muezzin calling and before sunrise we rose and sat on the prow which Joseph had remade with the cushions and bolsters. The great lake was silver-grey with just the odd kettuvallam moored far way; this is a good idea because it prevents any intrusion or robbery if the craft is moored out in the middle of the lake away from prying eyes and light fingers. The early morning bird chorus and the sun rising through the mist along with a cup of tea made it all so special; moreover this was Graham's birthday and therefore a special day.

We went and had showers and prepared for breakfast but were fascinated by the clam fishermen who were working nearby. Joseph asked them to come alongside us and explained that the fisherman dredges manually with a long pole with rake and a scoop net. They extract the clams and eat the flesh and shells accumulate, as has been found in ancient civilisations worldwide. When the shells have grown into a big enough pile they are sold to cement factories to make into lime.

Joseph had quite a conversation with us at breakfast after delivering beautifully segmented and sliced fresh fruit and fruit juice followed by a tomato omelette and tea. He is a Latin Catholic, and considers he is a follower of St Peter. To help the family income he had gone and worked in Bahrain some years previous. It had been an awful experience because though he is obviously a very good cook the wife of the man for whom he worked was jealous of his culinary prowess and treated him badly and the family did not pay him, and like all migrant workers he was prevented from moving about freely and was virtually a prisoner in his leisure time. He had resolved to come home but was still without his pay; fortunately the son of the house agreed to pay him his outstanding salary and he was able to return to Kerala. Here was another tale of exploitation by some of the cynical greedy and lazy people in the Middle East which by now did not surprise us.

All too soon our Spice Boat cruise was at an end and we gently glided into shore and alighted at Coconut Lagoon. We thanked the three men and gave a good tip between them and I have a lovely photograph of the trio and such happy memories.

Coconut Lagoon is another CGH Earth resort which is loved by all who have been guests there. Indeed I was told by one email correspondent whom I have never yet met that I could not go to Kerala without staying at Coconut Lagoon. It can only be reached by boat and is set on an island at Kumarakom. Here amongst the backwaters and the lake's edge sits a tile and timber mansion and all the cottages are similar. The mansion is called a 'tharavad' which has been painstakingly transplanted and restored. Many of the villas have also been transported and rebuilt here and are so interesting architecturally. We were both enchanted with the system of little canals with small craft gliding under bridges and green lawns and mango trees and exotic blooms. Everything is immaculately maintained and intriguing. The management uses Vechoor cows, which are an endangered species to 'mow' the lawns, thereby helping to preserve the breed. They are feisty little beasts because when Graham wanted to go up close to inspect one he was given short shrift!

The resort has a Butterfly Garden and access to the local bird sanctuary. Vembanad Lake is the largest backwater in Kerala. The lake along with the adjacent wetlands over the eastern and southern sides forms the largest wetland of Kerala; five rivers drain in to the lake and a good portion of this wetland has been converted in to cultivable paddy fields, which remain water logged for half of the year, this is the area to which I referred earlier as the Kuttanad.

Again friendly efficient management took us to a lakeside villa which also had a private but smaller pool. This villa was equally well equipped and the pool looked very inviting. I asked them if they could possibly do a quick wash of some of our clothes and they were marvellous and returned them at our departure. I would have liked nothing better than to have stayed at Coconut Lagoon for a week. What could be more beautiful than swinging in a hammock, looking out onto the lake and from time to time going into the courtyard and having a skinny dip in the private pool? The main pool was very lovely and all the amenities provided were excellent. I liked the musician who was seated near the reception area playing an instrument and inviting people to have a try and he would teach them.

The Ayurvedic Centre was unusual because it looked on to paddy fields and countryside. The perfect holiday for me would be a week at Coconut Lagoon followed by a week at Marari Beach, and, if I had not already experienced it, a night between the two spent on the Spice Boat.

Lunch was a splendid affair because the management wanted us to eat special prawns and whatever we wished and then the staff brought out a birthday cake made by chef for Graham and sang Happy Birthday to him which was such a thoughtful gesture. We were able to talk to the resident naturalist who was a keen young man who certainly knew his subject and became very excited when I told him of whom I had written in my second book when talking about conservation and tigers. I noticed that quite a lot of guests were for lunch only and then departed by launch; presumably they were staying at other properties but knew that Coconut Lagoon was worth a visit. There are other very good resorts in the area but again I stress the elegant simplicity and attention to detail; in rural surroundings one does not want any sort of 'bling' or ostentation.

I still remember it clearly on this cold February day in Scotland as I sit writing in my study with a drizzle falling and no sunshine: I was sitting in a deckchair facing out to the lake with no sound, just watching a heron and a cormorant and hearing the odd splash of a fish, a kingfisher was sitting perched on a branch close to me; we were enjoying a cool drink and knowing that yet another delicious meal awaited us after a dip in a private pool – truly this was our kind of holiday heaven.

Chapter Fifteen

Cochin and the Malabar Coast

We stood on the Mizzen Deck and watched as the captain slowly and carefully steered the ship into Kochi, or Cochin as we are used to calling the hub of Kerala. It was another glorious sunny morning just after Christmas 2003 and we were arriving at a place that had long held a fascination for me. Coming in by ship into the huge harbour and lagoons of Cochin is the best way to arrive. If one is fanciful then the imagination can roam over its history and fame through centuries past. On this second occasion in 2005 we approached by road fresh from our blissful time spent relaxing on the beach, the spice boat and at Kumarakom, and indeed we departed on this occasion by air from the new international airport. Definitely sailing in by ship is the most attractive way to arrive, and we considered ourselves very blessed to have had that wonderful opportunity to cruise down the west coast of India and round to Sri Lanka.

To understand Cochin we need to turn our minds back to the legend of St Thomas's arrival and the trade that was conducted between this coast and the Mediterranean. Then in 712 AD the Arabs conquered Sind, the area of India around the Indus River, much of which is now in Pakistan. For four centuries thereafter Sind remained under Arab rule, thus permanently moulding the Muslim character of the population. Arabs once again somewhat later began as traders and sailors to settle amongst the people of the Malabar Coast, much further south than Sind and those descendants of the original Muslims are called "Moplahs". India's first practical contact with a western European power however came when Vasco da Gama landed at Calicut in 1498.

Trade and the ability of a country to trade extensively and boast of its trading routes was what the 14th and 15th centuries were all about. Modern terminology has coined the phrase 'Mercantile Imperialism', circa 1500-1780 which is considered the Pre-Industrial Age. This really began with Portugal and Spain staking out colonies in the New World and trading with India, China and the East Indies. Their motive was mainly the desire for gold, silver and trade – and they did not scruple to plunder or exploit native peoples. The Dutch, French and British later supplanted them, acquiring colonies that helped in trading operations and sending emigrants to settle them. By 1780 Britain had outrivaled France and Holland and held by the far the largest empire.

To digress a little it is worth mentioning that when studying 'imperialism' there has been outward migration from Europe for a very very long time; indeed Greece probably was the first country to embark on it and there is evidence to suggest that Greeks sailed round the British Isles in 600 BC. The Greek city states were enormously wealthy and they continued to flourish for a long time after the 'glories of Greece' were past. The rise of the Roman Empire led to the decline of the Greek City States and the Romans established colonies in North Africa and Britain, but failed to subdue Galicia in Spain. The Romans as we have seen in Tamil Nadu and Andhra Pradesh had established trading with southern India. There have been recent discoveries of a Roman ship north of Rio de Janeiro – the relics prove that the ship had actually sailed from Italy. However, Roman ships were not actually able to tack into the wind; the ship had probably been driven far out of its intended course to the coast of South America as a result of navigational error probably due to storms. Gradually the Roman Empire declined and by 312 AD the Huns defeated Rome and the northern races like the Vandals, the Goths and the Visigoths became powerful. By 330 AD or thereabouts Roman troops were withdrawn from the British Isles and the geographical knowledge and experience disappeared and the early Middle Ages saw a reversion to thinking the earth was flat with the rise of Christianity and the power of the medieval church throughout Europe, which lasted for centuries.

In the 11th, 12th and 13th centuries an enormously profitable trade flourished between the west coast of India and the great merchant cities of Italy. Arab ships carried that trade because the Arabs had achieved undisputed power and therefore passage over the direct sea-route. All of those waters were bordered by Islamic power. Portugal, whose maritime prowess was developed over a century before that of Spain, England and France was determined to try and seize some of that wealth but His Catholic Majesty disguised his desire for wealth through trade with India and the East with an urgent desire to 'save the Hindu soul'. Accordingly, Vasco da Gama was sent to the Malabar Coast, but out of sight from inquisitive eyes, he set sail round the coast of Africa and approached rather stealthily. His ships were tiny caravels, smaller than the famous Mayflower, and in the summer of 1498 Vasco da Gama reached the port of Calicut, the richest port on the Malabar Coast.

The famous old sailor worked his way down the west coast of Africa, then up to Dar as Salaam, where he probably picked up an Arab pilot and then sailed across to Calicut. That part of Kerala as we now know it was under the rule of Zamorin of Calicut; he received da Gama with courtesy, and probably not grasping the significance of a little marble pillar typifying Portuguese conquest and claim of possession that the visitor quietly set up on the shore – his shore. The Portuguese probably behaved themselves on that occasion and when he sailed away back to Portugal da Gama had in his possession a letter from the Zamorin to King Manoel written on a palm leaf that read:

"Vasco da Gama, a nobleman of your household, has visited my kingdom and has given me much pleasure. In my kingdom there is abundance of cinnamon, cloves, ginger, pepper, and precious stones. What I seek from thy country is gold, silver, coral and scarlet."

When da Gama returned to Calicut, again at the command of his king, the time of courtesies has passed. He bombarded the Zamorin's palace. Contemporaneous Portuguese chronicles tell the story; I just have to reproduce the extract word for word because only then will you appreciate just how appallingly the Europeans behaved. Incidentally, the word *Zamorin* is a Portuguese corruption of the title *Samoothiri*.

Brunton Boatyard Hotel's pool looking out onto Cochin's harbour

"It befell one day, that a boat from Calicut came alongside da Gama's ship, carrying under a white flag, a letter from the Zamorin. Da Gama allowed its bearer, a Brahmin, to come aboard, promising him safe-conduct back to shore. Meantime, the letter being interpreted, da Gama conceived a suspicion that it did not cover the Zamorin's whole intent. Therefore, he put the Brahmin to torture, to discover the truth. Under torture the Brahmin finally admitted that his orders were to observe whatever he could, on board the ship that might be of interest to his master. He then begged to be killed at once, since otherwise he must kill himself for shame of having betrayed his master's confidence.

The situation left no two ways open. That heathen dog, the Zamorin, if ever he was to learn the fear of God, must first learn fear of His Majesty of Portugal. Da Gama, seeing the picture clearly enough, hastened to project it. First he cut off the ears of his ship's dog, then those of the Brahmin; after which he caused the dog's ears to be sewed 'with many stitches' to the Brahmin's head. Then he cut off the Brahmin's upper and lower lips, so that the teeth showed as in a canine snarl. Which completed, with some further details that must here be spared, the messenger was shipped back to his master as Portugal's complete answer to heathen insolence. Yet, for good measure, bombardment of the town followed."...

"Against such visitations the Indians, both then and always, were powerless, having no sea strength able to cope with that of the foreigner. It also chanced that da Gama lay before Calicut when a fleet of twenty-four little native sailing craft, bearing rice from farther down the coast, swung into the harbour. Escape from the Portuguese caravelles being impossible da Gama easily robbed the fleet of all its cargoes. Then he ordered his own people to cut off the hands, ears and noses of every man in the native crews, and to tie each man's two feet together. After that, lest they untie with their teeth the lashings that bound their ankles, he had their teeth knocked down their throats. This duly done, he ordered some of his victims to be hung by their heels to their own mastheads; after which the rest, roughly numbering eight hundred, were flung into their boats in heaps and the heaps covered over with mats and dried leaves. Finally, all sails being set for shore, the inflammable stuff was fired and the little craft sped forward, blazing. As they sped, under the eyes of great crowds of horror struck natives gathered on the beach, the Portuguese cross-bowmen, from da Gama's decks shot arrows into his still living victims as they swung head downward from the masts into the blaze."...

"While this was in progress, several other small vessels, unwarned and unsuspecting, swept into the harbour, to be likewise seized. But from aboard these later comers certain natives called out to their captors,

begging 'for the sake of Thomas' to be made Christians. Now the Apostle Thomas the Doubter is believed to have spent the last years of his life on the eastern coast of India, where, before his martyrdom, he made converts. The cry of the helpless raised in St. Thomas's name from pity was repeated to the Captain-Major (da Gama), who ordered them to be told that even though they became Christians, still he would kill them. They answered that they did not beg for life, but only to be made Christians. Then, by order of the Captain-Major, a priest gave them holy baptism. There were three who entreated the priest, saying that they wished for once to say our prayer, and the priest said the Pater Noster and Ave Maria, which they also repeated. When this was finished, then they hung them up strangled, that they might not feel the arrows."

The full descriptions of these awful barbaric acts carried out in the name of His Catholic Majesty the King of Portugal are to be found in the *Lendas da India* by Gaspar Correa, chronicler of the voyages of the famous Portuguese navigator and in other old Portuguese records.

I have the details of all this in a priceless book that we own and I showed it to my history tutor Dr R Simmons when I was learning about the History of Imperialism. Ray Simmons fell upon the book with awe, because he had been a lecturer in history at the University of Coimbra in Portugal; Coimbra, which I too have visited in 2001, is the equivalent to Portugal of Oxford or Cambridge to the United Kingdom. When he had been teaching there he had had free access to the archives of the university and much of the work from which he taught was not published in English but in medieval Portuguese. Even in the 1960s much of the work was largely unclassified, but of its day the University of Coimbra was one of the largest universities in Europe. Ray Simmons was appalled at what he learned from my book; he explained that modern Portuguese historians like to draw a veil over the exact atrocities that were committed in the name of their monarch and indeed Christianity. Indeed, perhaps another crime for which a modern pontiff might consider apologising?

The ancient theory was that around 300 BC the Chinese philosopher Mencius attributed imperialism to man's greed, especially to the power lust of princes, advised by ambitious ministers. Something like this view has been expressed again and again down to modern times when similar motives have been attributed to rulers of national states.

Mussolini expressed his views as 'a theory of a struggle for survival'. "The tendency to empire is a manifestation of vitality; its contrary, or the stay-at-home mentality, is a sign of decadence". J A Hobson, the English economist advanced the theory in his book Imperialism in 1902, "...that the industrial nations of Europe *grabbed* for colonies after 1870 because their economies were in difficulties: capital was accumulating faster than it could profitably be invested, and the easiest, quickest solution was to invest it in the colonies where the rate of interest was high than at home..." he probably had a point; in 1854 total British investment overseas was £300 million; in 1860 £650 million; in 1875 £1,300 million; in 1914 £4,000 million.

I doubt much thought was given to the long term in the Middle Ages, and Christianity was obviously used as an expedient excuse by which to aggrandize a nation's wealth and excuse barbaric behaviour to non believers, i.e. the heathen – never mind the fact that they were devotees of a far older religious faith. Interestingly, in our current age modern powers can lose sight of their consciences and occasionally behave or allow their soldiers to behave in a reprehensible manner until the world's press exposes the facts; though it has to be said that currently western military personnel must be experiencing the most challenging of soldiering i.e. trying to help restore order in an ancient land that is wracked with ingratitude and vulnerable to its own insurgents.

By 1540 the City of Lisbon had become the most important financial centre in the whole of Europe with sixty-two commodity markets and a money market. The other interesting point to note was that in those days the Muslim universities and seats of learning were far in advance of the European universities which were constrained by religious Christian thinking; the ancient universities of India were responsible for mathematics, early engineering, hydraulics and medicine. The Bodleian Library in Oxford has a most wonderful collection of early Muslim books such as The Book of Curiosities of the Sciences and Marvels for the Eyes, composed probably before AD1050 and copied in 1200. There are ninety-six pages of maps of the heavens and the world's rivers, cities and oceans, the book is an unparalleled insight into the learning of the time: a guide to stars used in navigation and weather prediction, a discourse on comets, a circular map of the world, the Mediterranean trade routes, plans of the cities of Tinnis in the Nile Delta and al-Mahdiyah in Tunisia, diagrammatic maps of Sicily and Cyprus and the anchorages of Byzantium. The book maps five river systems: the Nile, Oxus, Euphrates, Tigris and Indus. Some are mixed up, with the Indus shown as part of the same system as the Ganges and Brahmaputra; this suggests however that the Muslim traders of the 11th century knew the overland route between India and China. It even refers to a small island in the West labelled in Arabic *Inghiltirah* – believed to be the first map showing Britain with that name. Written in the Golden Age of Islam when Baghdad was the seat of the Caliphate one thinks of it now when sadly Baghdad is once again a focus for world attention. Now however seven centuries later we have fanatical Muslim believers

Customary tranquil bowl of flowers to welcome guests

The five monolithic stone temples at Mamallapuram

Temple offerings in Tamil Nadu

Dilli Haat – wonderful craft market in Delhi

Wild dogs

Happy young Muslim boys

Elephants

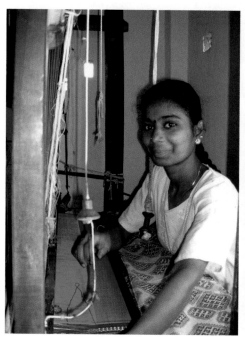

Young woman weaving beautiful silk

Thanjavur's colourful Royal Palace pillars

Ghandiji memorial at Pondicherry

Interior of a spice boat

India: The Elephant's Blessing

Gangaikondacholapuram Temple in
Tamil Nadu

The peacock in his glory

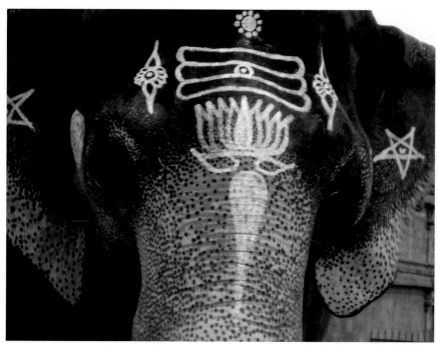

Typical temple elephant

The tigress resting

Elephant greeting at Thanjavur Temple

Cobras

Author eating The Bangla's delectable lunch
on a banana leaf

Part of the great temple at Madurai

who are attempting to try and dominate the world with their theocratic principals through terror and suppression. No doubt were their busy zealots not flying about the world hell bent on creating carnage and mayhem their 'wise men' might even be tempted to declare that the world is flat!

Happily Vasco da Gama did not succeed in seizing Calicut (the modern Kozhikode) and turned his attention to Cochin, which became the site of the first Portuguese fort in India in 1503. Cochin's strategic position enabled them to break the Arab monopoly of trade with western India. Unlike previous traders they introduced new agricultural products such as cashew and tobacco and they were the first people to recognise the importance of the coconut and its by-products of coir rope and matting. Calico, white, unbleached cotton, was a product introduced to the world from Calicut, and is still produced to this day.

Kochi was known curiously as the 'Queen of Arabia' and because of all the traders and invaders has a fusion of folklore and customs that stem from as far as China, Africa, Holland, Portugal and Britain. Probably its most famous icon is that of the Chinese fishing nets. The harbour is one of the finest in that part of the world and the topography is unique in that it is built on numerous islands and peninsulas. It can be bifurcated into the modern city of Ernakulam in the east while the old districts of Mattancherry and Fort Kochi are on a promontory to the west. People travel between the two on a complex system of ferries.

The Chinese fishing nets are a legacy of the early Chinese visitors to the Malabar Coast who came from the court of Kublai Khan. The nets are believed to have been erected between 1350 and 1450 and they are a set on huge teak wood and bamboo poles. Vasco da Gama Square is the ideal place from which to view the nets being lowered into the sea and the catch being recovered. Vasco da Gama Square is not what the name suggests but a narrow walkway facing the beach and along much of the sea front, the square is lined with small stalls selling fresh seafood, prepared in front of you and served piping hot. There are some old colonial mansions on two sides of the square and they represent a good blend of Portuguese, Dutch and Kerala influences. The house in which Vasco da Gama lived is one of the earliest mansions in Fort Kochi. Another place that we visited and found really interesting was Bishop's House. This property was originally built in 1506 as the residence of the Portuguese Governor. Its large gothic arches and circular driveway with flowers and spices is attractive and that is where I first saw a pepper vine. The building was acquired many years later for the use of Don Jose Gomes Ferreira, the powerful 27th Bishop of the Diocese of Cochin, whose authority then extended throughout India,

Chinese Fishing Nets – iconic to Cochin

Burma, Malaya and Ceylon.

We had a rather amusing experience when visiting Bishop's House. This was organised by the cruise line and they had ordered masses of three wheeler vehicles to come and meet the ferry and transport us to the various historic sites. Graham and I loved it as we often use these in Delhi if we want to nip somewhere and have not ordered a car and driver for that day. However, there were passengers on that particular cruise who were so in love with themselves that they felt it was a great inferiority to be seen trundling around in such a quaint vehicle; whereas most passengers thoroughly enjoyed themselves there were those who were so 'camp' that they spent most of the time whining about the indignity of the transport! Having said that there was a German couple of great material wealth who never once boasted or complained but enjoyed themselves enormously, and so did the friends whom we made on that trip and with whom I am glad to say we are still in contact.

After Bishop's House we visited St Francis's Church, which is arguably India's oldest place of European worship; it was built by the Portuguese Franciscan Friars in 1503. The church was rebuilt in 1779 because originally it had been built in wood. It became an Anglican church in 1795, but Vasco da Gama's mortal remains were buried in this church in 1524 and exhumed and taken to his homeland and re-buried there fifteen years later, but the tombstone remains to this day.

Kochi has one of the oldest Jewish settlements in the world. The Jews are estimated to have moved down to Kochi about 1,000 years ago. The first families are thought to have landed at Cranganore (as I mentioned with regard to St Thomas) and started businesses and flourished. Now there are perhaps a dozen families remaining from about 2,500 Jews who, mostly post World War II, emigrated to the new state of Israel. India's oldest synagogue is tucked into a cul-de-sac at the end of a narrow lane in the heart of Jew Town. Originally their settlement was called Shingly but persecution from the Portuguese forced them to migrate to Cochin, where they settled on land donated by the local raja, and they built a synagogue in 1568. However, in the wall of the current synagogue I found a stone tablet inscribed with the date of the earlier one going back to the 14th century. The Cochin Jews were divided into two distinct groups: the Black or Malabari Jews who claimed to be descendants of the original settlers, and the White or Paradesim Jews who came here from the Middle East, and after whom the synagogue is named. A third, smaller group was the Brown or Meshuhurarum Jews, descended from converted slaves, many of whom were in the spice trade. The present synagogue was rebuilt in 1664 with Dutch help after the Portuguese destroyed it in 1662. The treasures

The Pardesi Jewish Synagogue in Cochin

within include beautiful silver and gold Torah scrolls, a multitude of hanging oil lamps and crystal chandeliers and a very fine brass pulpit. The floor is covered in lovely blue and white tiles which were brought from Canton in the mid-18th century by a powerful merchant called Ezekiel Rahabi.

Coming out of the synagogue and moving slowly down the narrow street we came across a very good book shop and found it really fascinating. Our German friend bought a number of books but we were mindful of our air journey home. However nearly next door I espied a narrow simple shop which called itself a Wives of Fishermen Co-operative. In there we found the most beautiful embroidery and promptly bought all our family lovely table napkins in sets of eight. One can never have too many table napkins and they always add elegance to even the simplest of meals. I like buying something which I know will directly benefit the people who have worked hard and who are very disadvantaged. Fishermen live a hard enough life, but their wives have to work just as hard maintaining their families and the incomes are far from guaranteed.

It was quite interesting because when we were returning on the ferry to the ship one of the most wealthy passengers starting ridiculing some of the shops she had seen that afternoon and was dismissive of the quality of the goods on display; I have heard of cruise passengers who dismiss all that they see and experience instead of enjoying it for what one learns and experiences – they really should not leave their 'comfort zones'. Yet she had spent a lot of time ostentatiously showing all and sundry what wonderful jewellery she had bought in Goa; apparently the necklace she liked had not been designed with sufficient gems in it originally and she instructed the jeweller to add a whole lot more. That arrangement was agreed on Christmas Day and accomplished twenty-four hours later; truly the jeweller must have thought all his Christmases had rolled into one! It was a great source of amusement to the rest of us.

The Mattancherry Palace built by the Portuguese in the mid 1550s was given to the ruler or Raja of Cochin as a token of goodwill in exchange for trading rights. It is an odd sort of building and in no way matches the magnificence, exuberance or charm of other palaces, but then of course it was built for the wrong reasons really. Today it houses a rare collection of murals and royal artefacts and is worth visiting but we had the misfortune to go on a very hot afternoon and with so many visitors the place was stifling and one of our Indian female guides had the voice of a peacock, all of which led one to rush through the experience and exit as quickly as possible.

The Kochi International Pepper Exchange is however a unique

establishment; the cacophony of sound of a morning is truly something with all the traders shouting their prices – truly this is a sight worth seeing. The Pepper Exchange is closed in the afternoons.

Kathakali is Kerala's classical dance-drama. The word literally means 'story play' and is a highly evolved classical form of dance, drama and music which is both vocal and instrumental. Male actor-dancers in voluminous colourful skirts and elaborate headdresses and jewellery and ferocious face make-up enact stories from the Puranas (old books) and epics, mainly the *Mahabharata*. The make-up takes four hours to perfect and helps to identify characters and define their roles. There is no speech and meaning is conveyed by *mudras* (symbolic hand gestures) and facial expressions with great eloquence. I enjoy watching a little of this but am not a great fan of hours of classical dancing because very probably all the subtlety is completely lost upon me!

On our second visit in 2005 we had the great good fortune to stay in a most palatial suite in The Brunton Boatyard in Fort Cochin, situated right on the water's edge. It is a perfect position from which to watch all the maritime traffic and the people and the business of a great port. The building was indeed a boatyard and the owners CGH Earth have managed a most sympathetic conversion to boutique hotel. There is a shaded courtyard through which one enters and all the best rooms look out to the harbour. Harbour side there is an excellent swimming pool right on the edge of the property which lends enchantment. The restaurants are also very good and the general décor is one of using colonialism's relics and furniture which makes it totally different from a normal modern hotel. Ayurveda is also offered though I did not have the time on this occasion to enjoy it. The group's first ever hotel is the Casino hotel situated on Willingdon Island and it is renowned for its seafood restaurant. Happily we were able to have a most delicious dinner there and enjoy the most wonderful halibut, simply grilled and sauced.

The Lakshadweep Islands archipelago is off the Malabar Coast and truly the most wonderful of natural treasures. They are the smallest Union Territory of India. They comprise twelve coral atolls, three coral reefs, and five banks of coral. The total land area is thirty-two square kilometres. and they are located between 200 and 300 kilometres off the coast of Kerala. Ten of the islands are inhabited, seventeen are not, and there are numerous islets which are not included in these numbers. The inhabited islands are: Agatti, Amini, Andrott, Bangaram, Bitra, Chetlat, Kadmat, Kalpeni, Kavaratti and Minicoy. The main island is Kavaratti with a capital city also called Kavarratti. Agatti has a small airport which takes planes from Kochi and the name Lakshadweep means literally a hundred thousand islands (laksha= one hundred thousand, dweep = island). If you have ever been to The Maldives then just try and imagine something even more beautiful because the islands are so carefully monitored. Flying in a small aircraft and seeing the azure blue sea with these lovely atolls dotted amongst it is so beautiful. The people of the islands speak a dialect of Malayalam and almost all of them are Muslim (as indeed is the case in The Maldives). It is a folk belief that they are descendants of traders who were shipwrecked on the islands during a heavy storm. Bangaram Island has the only hotel open to non-Indians and it is run by CGH Earth, who tendered for the opportunity long ago and were rewarded because their approach was to create a resort with a minimalist approach but building on nature's treasures. The accommodation is in standard or deluxe huts, there is no television or 'luxury' of that sort. The cuisine is of the Lakshadweeps and coastal India with lots of beach barbecues. Scuba diving, snorkelling, deep sea fishing, boating/kayaking and island excursions are the activities along with Ayurveda, yoga and meditation. Our idea of pure heaven: we adored The Maldives and were on the southern most atoll on that occasion; the Lakshadweeps are even more special because the authorities have been very careful with what they allow and there is only this one hotel for non-Indians with absolutely no ostentation.

Typically, the first westerner to visit the islands was Vasco da Gama, but the English were the first to explore the islands and it is also mentioned in great detail in the stories of the Arab traveller, Ibn Batuta. The Portuguese established a fort in 1498 but the inhabitants rose up and chased them out of the archipelago, which subsequently became a suzerainty of the Ali Raja of Cannanore in Kerala.

All too soon our visit to Kochi was over and we flew out of the international airport on a very comfortable Jet Airways flight to continue our epic journey of southern India.

Chapter Sixteen

Memories of Mysore

We flew into Bangalore and spent some time first at The Windsor Sheraton and Towers, another great ITC Welcomgroup hotel. Bangalore had been our home as a family in 1952 but none of us had happy associations with the place because of a serious accident I suffered as a small child. I fell down the outside of some terrazzo stairs on to the terrazzo floor about fifteen feet beneath and fractured my skull from ear to ear. It must have been an intensely worrying time for my parents and I recall the feeling of worry surrounding me for a few days. However a solution was found to the problem of how to keep me from jumping around and generally behaving as any normal healthy five-year old would. The parents employed an elderly European nurse to be my daytime companion and somehow this worked terribly well! Mrs Hogg was a poppet and a grandmother herself so she became the nearest thing to a 'granny' for me for a short time. This proved providential in as much as she knew she had to keep me occupied and still and so set about teaching me all manner of things like sewing, embroidery and gardening. I have her to thank for my interest in these occupations which serve me to this day, she was a very fine old lady. Thankfully after six months my skull knit again and I was pronounced fit and with no after effects and my sedate ordeal was at an end!

Bangalore in the 1950s was a truly garden city with plenty of parks and palatial hotels and wide avenues; now it is probably India's fastest growing city, or was and maybe now is being overtaken by Hyderabad. The Windsor Manor is a charming hotel in that the swimming pool area is gracious and the hotel itself has wonderful internal architecture and gives a great feeling of space and light. Moreover, the hotel has a 'ladies only' floor which is nice for female executives. We had lunch with Thomas who is manager for Trails of India group of hotels and both Graham and I could see why he is so good at his job – he has that enthusiasm that marks him out from others who merely go through the motions.

I had no wish to linger in Bangalore but do still clearly recall those days; in particular I recall the day that King George VI had died in February 1952. My late father came into my bedroom where I was being dressed and told mother, "B...the King is dead..." and she burst into tears. My mother's brother-in-law had been the anaesthetist at the King's last operation in the autumn of 1951 and my parents knew some of the things that had been kept secret about his health, so it was not a surprise that he had died, but nevertheless very sad in one still young.

People consider that Bangalore offers a wonderful architectural snapshot of the British in India. Cubbon Park, comprising 300 acres, was laid out in true Victorian fashion in 1864, and close by is St Mark's Cathedral, and the cricket ground. Bangalore Palace was built in 1880 and was modelled on Windsor Castle complete with fortified towers and turreted parapets; it fell into disrepair when under dispute over its ownership, but now thankfully it is fully restored and returned to the Wodeyars (the Mysore hereditary rulers), who rent it out for weddings, film shoots and concerts. In my thinking Bangalore is a place for business but not for leisure, I found the whole pace frenetic and a bit materialistic.

There is however a new building that is worthy of interest; the Vidhana Soudha which is the Secretariat and Legislature of Karnataka State. It was built in 1956 and is India's largest new legislative building built out of granite and porphyry. Apparently at that time when India was so influenced by the Russians it had been said that India's buildings were too 'European' and thus to rebut this criticism this modern building was designed to incorporate architectural styles from all over India. It is not open to the public but on Sunday evenings is floodlit – perhaps it is Bangalore's way of competing with Mysore which has a stunning palace that has been floodlit through the decades.

I think because my parents knew they would not be in the south of India long and also as a way of doing something interesting with me Father arranged a couple of visits, which today would be considered 'tourism'. We went to Mysore and the surrounding area and as I still recall those adventures I was determined to repeat them just over fifty years afterwards!

The road to Mysore is one of these days going to be really good as a huge amount of work is being done; but like quite a few projects in India unfortunately the work is allowed to drag on and in the meantime what should be a lovely dual carriage way is anything but and makes the journey tiring and vexing. The Bangalore-Mysore Infrastructure Corridor Project or BMICP once completed will reduce a four-hour journey into one and a half hours but it has run into political problems as well; there are accusations of the company violating environmental regulations and amassing land beyond its requirement. The Bangalore-Mysore Expressway was conceived to fight congestion in India's IT capital by providing entrepreneurs with an opportunity to move capital and investments to cities outside Bangalore and to townships along that road. With a population of over nine million and burgeoning vehicular traffic the civic infrastructure of Bangalore is deteriorating and narrow roads and water shortages are compounding the difficulties. The road was destined for completion in 2007 but will not meet that target and it is a great shame if the whole project falls completely into disrepute. This was the largest BOOT (build-own-operate-transfer) project and the expressway should include a peripheral road that will connect the expressway to the NH4 which is the Bangalore-Pune road. What is worth mentioning is that the BMICP paved the way for other BOOT projects in India by amending eighteen pieces of legislation. If the developers are to be believed they plan to restore 251 lakes and ponds and replant trees. Moreover this project has evolved over a decade and has seen at least four chief ministers and five Public Works Department ministers take office in the state government. I mention all this because those of us who live in the UK know that it too is a crowded, but little place with constant controversy regarding maintenance of our motorways and development of even more roads. Governments of different persuasions promise us they will address 'the traffic problem' but then discover what a thorny issue it is and how many votes can be lost, and our own 'Green Lobby' tries very hard to preserve the countryside. In India road building is of vital importance and in this last decade of travelling all over the country, mostly by road, I have seen the huge differences it has made. Without an adequate new road network India will not be able to sustain her achievable ambitions as a twenty-first century economic super power.

The rural roads programme launched by the previous national government in 2000 has become a popular and successful project which has already shown huge benefits in the rural economy nationwide. The present national government would have been very foolish to overturn the earlier decisions and have actually enlarged the project because it makes such good sense. Instead of providing just 'the last mile' close to a village or enclave the entire road network will be upgraded to build farm to market connectivity. This in combination with e-choupal of which I wrote in my earlier chapters will make a huge exponential difference to the rural economy. Eighty per cent of the rural roads funds will go to ten states with poor internal road networks. Already it has proved successful in Madhya Pradesh and Rajasthan where farmers have taken to livestock farming and keeping dairy herds as they are now able to send their produce to urban markets and processing plants. The knock-on effect has been in social services like education and healthcare which have improved because of the connectivity. My heart sings when I hear of all this because the great rural masses are the ones who so seldom receive a 'trickle down ' benefit, but at last it would seem things are changing for the better in India's rural heartland.

We finally arrived at Mysore feeling hot and tired and a bit grumpy! Because of changing my plans due to sheer fatigue I instructed the driver to take us to the Lalitha Mahal Palace Hotel. This pretty building was commissioned in 1921 by Krishnaraja Wodeyar IV and completed in 1930 for the Maharajah's most important guests; the Maharajah was a devout Hindu and remained a non-drinker and vegetarian all his life, but he was determined that his important guests should stay in complete comfort. As a small child we had stayed there in 1951 when it still operated as a Maharajah's Guest House. People had told us recently that it was a bit of a relic and not to expect too much and voiced a number of negative comments. We arrived and I told the driver not to take the luggage out but just to park the car. We went in and asked if we might have some tea. The management were immediately courteous and helpful and asked if instead of tea we might prefer lunch. It was late by the usual lunch times but yes, of course we would love lunch as we had been travelling since about 06.30 hours with just an airline breakfast. I replied of course lunch would be most welcome but surely the kitchen would be closed by 2.40 pm. No, we were taken into a

Lalitha Mahal Palace - one time maharajah's guesthouse

huge colonnaded dining room and assured of our welcome. Lunch came and was very good; it was not sitting in a lukewarm buffet but quickly made for us and all the more welcome for that. Graham and I walked about and went upstairs and looked at the view. It is a truly splendid building built in a grand style with lots of marble and wide staircases and columns and domes – just what one would expect for a Maharajah's Guest House! Apparently the architect E. W. Fritchley was inspired by the dome of Wren's St Paul's Cathedral; as well as the Banqueting Hall, which is now the dining room, there is a ballroom that is used for conferences.

I again approached the management and gave them my name and they immediately recognised that in fact we should have arrived the next day. We were given a very pleasant suite with a huge bedroom, slightly overdone with a sort of doily décor (perhaps the designer had a doily/lacework factory), a dressing room and a huge bathroom which had been modernised. The only relic was the bath with a wonderful old shower that obviously had been built in the 1930s. I recognised the design from some old houses in Edinburgh. Today we have the modern equivalent of these sorts of showers that spray one from all sides but they cost a huge amount of money. We had a wide communal balcony outside our suite with a good view; there was a swimming pool and spacious gardens; with a little thought that whole garden area with a new swimming pool would make it so gracious and charming. Graham and I were so tired that we decided to stay for three nights and just take it easy. This hotel could, with careful improvements and some money lavished upon it, rival the Rambagh Palace at Jaipur, but then the tariff would rise accordingly. Ashok Hotels, which belongs to the Indian Government owns it or leases it from the descendants of the last maharajah. As it was we were very comfortable and I did not think it at all expensive. Yet, in the evening tourists would arrive, have a drink and walk around and depart to their hotels. The barman explained that it was thought too expensive. Again, I detest that idea of thinking that everything in India should be accomplished on a shoestring. I found the staff helpful and friendly; perhaps they too would benefit from a little more training but considering that they worked for a government-owned organisation I found them very pleasant. The washing and ironing was beautifully done for us.

There were about three shops within the Lalitha Mahal Palace and I had no real wish to shop, but out of courtesy I went into one when diffidently approached by a young man. Once in I knew I must buy something and he had some charming items. We talked and it became clear that he had very few customers – I could see why because so few people actually stay in the place. I bought some gifts and mentioned in the passing that we needed to send some things home by parcel through the post office and what a bore it would be to organise this. He immediately offered to do the packaging for us. I know what this involves; usually one takes the items to a man near the post office who will wrap it all up and sew it into a parcel for posting. This young man promised he would return the following night and sew up our parcel, which he did, with a bit of help from Graham. I am ever so glad because having been given a lot of wonderful books by the various state tourism departments I did not want to have to jettison them at the end. At first he said he would take nothing, it was just enough that I had bought from his shop, but we said very firmly that he had helped us greatly and we were not going to see him go unrewarded so he shyly accepted the money. We then urged the hotel to have a porter take it to the post office and send it and bring back a receipt for us on which we would reimburse them; they rather grudgingly agreed to do this and in due course within a month of being home the parcel arrived at our home in good condition. Had we messed around trying to do it ourselves the costs would have risen because of the simple fact that we are European and it would have taken a lot of our precious time.

On our first evening I enquired about the Brindavan Gardens and if the light show was still being performed. The answer was yes, so we asked the driver to take us and I indulged in memory lane. The gardens had been laid out beneath the great wall of the Krishnarajasagar Dam which had been built by Krishnaraja Wodeyar, Maharajah of Mysore. As a child I had been enchanted by the floodlit fountains and coloured lights once the sun had set. That evening we experienced a most spectacular sunset. Now they still have this performance thrice weekly. In terms of sophisticated entertainment it is very tame, but I had not thought so as a child of five and now I watched other little ones in their family parties. We in Britain have the various functions and entertainments that we consider family events at which to relax and enjoy ourselves; I like to participate in similar Indian pastimes because it is a way of interacting with Indians and inevitably people shyly come up to us and ask why we are there or something to start a conversation. Then when I explain my past they are delighted and listen and all the children talk to one very shyly or just stare, depending on their age. I had to pinch myself that here I was fifty-two years later in the same place but now the population was prosperous, with lots of cars and other signs of India's general wellbeing. In big cities Graham and I always try to participate in something that is the local custom; in Paris it is enjoyable on a Sunday afternoon to just go and 'hang out' on the lawns near the Eiffel Tower, or in front of Les Invalides. French families congregate and talk and play ball, walk little dogs and generally relax. In Spain or Italy one can see this to some degree in their public parks but more especially in the 'pasagiata' that takes place most evenings. In Mediterranean countries it is all too easy, in ours one has to wait for some good warm weather and then yes, Londoners and the good citizens of Edinburgh and Glasgow come out and sit with their faces pointed at the sun, inevitably wearing too few clothes and becoming redder by the minute! At least in Edinburgh we have the wonderful fireworks display at the end of August which usually falls on a fine late summer evening and then about a quarter of a million people take to the streets and parks to view the fireworks. We once queued for tickets for Princes Street Gardens (which are not at all expensive) and took about ten people as our guests to supper and then the Fireworks Concert; it was sheer heaven lying back on the grass on a warm summer evening looking up at the might and majesty of Edinburgh Castle lit by the most humungous fireworks to the accompaniment of popular classical music. There is also the Christmas and New Year Festival of Edinburgh which has a fabulous New Year's Eve firework display at midnight, but though I loved it initially now it has become too big and anyway it can be truly freezing!

We drove back the sixteen kilometres to the hotel and had a leisurely supper in the great balconied dining room, which I itched to redecorate by reducing its frills and furbelows! We sat on the impressive colonnaded veranda upstairs and thought of princes and potentates, viceroys and governors who would have all at some time pre World War II have graced these halls.

Mysore was a beautiful small garden city and one can still see so much of that charming past today; I just wish the local authority would follow Hyderabad's lead and have a good private contractor really maintain cleanliness and tidiness. The roads are wide and one can still see all the old colonial houses, some of which appear to be so neglected, which seems odd in a country where people are forever looking for housing. The city has a race course and is well laid out with the most beautiful buildings, all in the neo-classical style of our hotel with domes and towers and colonnaded balconies. It is a relaxing town famed for its sandalwood, incense and silks. Graham and I love incense and frequently buy the wonderful fragrances of sandalwood and patchouli and jasmine from one of our favourite local shops in Biggar which is a cornucopia of jewellery, toys, puzzles and items that other folk collect. It is funny to think that most of the incense we buy in Biggar was probably made in Mysore. Incense making is a good cottage industry.

The neo-classical Manasa Gangotri building is the campus of Mysore

University, which is the largest university in Karnataka and the Oriental Research Institute houses a collection of Sanskrit manuscripts; driving by one of the new glass and steel buildings we were so amused to see a great eagle looking at his own reflection and tapping the glass, and it cheered us that a bird of that size did not feel too threatened by this urban environment. Chamundi Hill which is close to the Lalitha Mahal has a great monolith of Nandi the Bull dating from 1659; carved out of a single boulder it is 7.5 metres long and 5 metres high. The Chamundeshvari Temple at the summit of the hill was built in the 17th century by the Wodeyars. It houses a beautifully decorated idol of Chamundeshvari the family deity of the Wodeyar royal family.

The Devaraja market is a most colourful place and as with most large Indian markets just a pleasure to wander through. Dazzling stalls are stacked with pyramids of fruit and piles of powdered spices, and the air hangs with the scent of fresh flowers displayed in baskets for people to purchase to adorn their chosen deities. I love the jasmine, but also am fond of marigolds because I know how much they represent India in their gold and orange hues. We use marigolds in our vegetable garden to ward off pests such as carrot fly.

The Railway Museum is another good place to visit though one has to be aware of the opening times. Sometimes in India one feels that the museum or building is open at times that are more convenient to the custodian than to the viewing public!

The great focal point of Mysore is its very grand Amba Vilas Palace in the heart of the city. Mysore was the capital of the Wodeyar rulers, who had been vassals of the Vijayanagar kings from further north on the Deccan plateau. From 1399 until Independence in 1947 the Wodeyars had ruled almost uninterrupted except for the 38-year old interregnum of Haider Ali and his son Tipu Sultan in the 18th century. I will tell you more about them in due course. At the time of his reign in 1793 Tipu Sultan raised the old city and built the city as we see it today with obvious additions through the colonial era. Mysore has in fact seen twenty-four rulers since 1399 but until Raja Wodeyar in 1578 it was a small vassal kingdom, but the Vijayanagar rule came to an end in 1565 and that is when Mysore came into its own. According to the Mysore royal family archives there are records to show that since the 14th century Mysore has had a palace but not necessarily a truly grand abode. The wooden palace that burnt down in 1897 seemed to have been a rather odd and not very prepossessing building, and as was the way in those days the palace had a jumble of ordinary buildings very close to it. The rajas of those days certainly did not seem to have enjoyed any space or privacy. In order to establish grandeur at Mysore the Maharani Vanivilasa Sannihdhana, who was a

The Maharajah's Palace at Mysore

regent for her son, decided to build a new palace on the foundations of the old palace. Henry Irwin, architect of the Viceregal Lodge at Simla and consulting architect with the Government of Madras State (where he was responsible for some very fine buildings) approved the construction of the building which the Maharani inaugurated. The building was completed in 1912 and there were two outstanding features: namely that as far as possible local materials were utilized and fireproof methods of construction were to be an essential feature of this grand Indo-Saracenic building.

The palace is very visible in the centre of Mysore and has huge ornamental gateways; the area in front behind the boundary is huge, rather like parade grounds but all that contributes to a feeling of exotic grandeur. It is well maintained but I felt that they should have a modern tourist's shop at which to buy good postcards and books; as it is there is nothing really and one is not allowed to photograph inside the building. We employed a guide who was very good in his own way. There are at least five temples in the palace grounds that all predate the palace; the Lakshmiramana Temple was built in the 15th century. The Varahaswami Temple, built by Krishnaraja Wodeyar III is immediately to the right of the south gate through which tourists enter. It was built reusing material from an ancient Hoysala temple, and the gopuram of this temple inspired the design of the gopuram for the temple on Chamundi Hill.

The palace can be divided into two parts, one of ceremonial and the other residential. Sri Srikanta Datta Narasimharaja Wodeyar, the descendant of the royal family of Mysore lives in the private quarters. As with all of India the locals continue to think of the various incumbents in royal palaces as royal and accord them respect and loyalty. India is a hierarchical society and people need to have someone at the top of the 'pecking order' and, as in other countries where wealth is equated with power and appears to have superseded royalty and nobility, inevitably these folk too are found to have their own frailties and feet of clay.

As a child I saw the palace lit up at night with thousands of light bulbs. This tradition continues but only on a Sunday night and high days and holidays – it seemed like fairy land to a small child. In the front is a Seating Gallery that was designed so that people along with the Maharajah could watch the annual Mysore Dasara procession. The highlights of the tour are the very richly decorated Public Durbar Hall or Divan-e-Am which is decorated in gold and turquoise – truly it is the opulent India of which we have all heard. It is over forty-seven metres long by about thirteen metres wide. On its rear wall there are a series of charming paintings by Raja Ravi Varma who was noted for depicting royal family groups as well as other subjects. The Ambavilasa Hall, known as the Private Durbar Hall or Diwan-e-Khas, is smaller than the Public Hall, but as sumptuous and perhaps more intricate and delicate; the marriage pavilion or Kalyana Mantappa is on the ground floor and is roofed with stained glass imported from Glasgow. The central part of the ceiling is supported by cast-iron columns and arches. Walter Macfarlane Saracen Foundry of Glasgow manufactured the pillars and the stained glass which had been designed and decorated by local Mysore artists. The dome is supported by clusters of triple cast-iron pillars at intervals. The main theme of the stained glass decoration as well as that of the mosaic floor is the peacock, hence this hall is also called the Peacock Pavilion. Sadly the foundry went out of business in 1965 and all the records were destroyed in a huge fire. Apart from the stained glass decoration, which is the central attraction, the walls of this pavilion are covered with murals depicting the famous Mysore Dasara. When I am fortunate enough to see this standard of Indian architecture and art and be informed by someone knowledgeable about all the intricacies I realise sadly how so many of our colonial forefathers missed out on these pleasures because of their rather supercilious attitude – it has taken so long for the majority of people in the West to realise, appreciate and truly respect the beautiful man-made features of this ancient country.

The Dasara Festival or the Festival of Ten Nights was first celebrated on a grand scale by the rulers of Vijayanagar at Hampi. Graphic accounts of these festivities can be found in the accounts of the then contemporary foreign travellers such as the Portuguese Domingo Paes and the Persian Ambassador Abdur Razaak. After the disintegration of Vijayanagar rule the tradition passed to others like the Wodeyars of Mysore; the piece de resistance in the Mysore palace is the Golden Throne or Royal Elephant Throne, but this is only taken out and placed in the rear octagonal part of the Ambavilasa (small Durbar Hall) during the nine or ten days of Dasara every year – sadly otherwise the public do not have the opportunity to see it and I have not seen it. I tried to explain Dasara or Dussehra as it is spelt in the north of India in my second book India: The Tiger's Roar. Briefly I will explain that it annually celebrates the goddess Durga's slaying of the demon buffalo Mahishhasura. On the tenth and last day of the festival a truly magnificent procession of mounted guardsmen on horseback and caparisoned elephants, one of which will carry the family deity of Chamundeshwari on a gold howdah, marches the five kilometres from the palace to Banni Mantap. There is also a floating festival in the temple tank at the foot of Chamundi Hill; a torch-lit parade at night takes place followed by a firework display and scenes of great rejoicing.

The paintings depicting the Dasara procession of 1930 I found very attractive and interesting because they are fresh and full of detail and really show the panoply and magnificence of the time of the Indian Maharajahs and the colonial era. I am sure tourists would buy a set or series of attached postcards reproducing these glorious scenes.

Gateway to Tipi Sultan's summer palace at Seringapatam

One of the most impressive things I saw on that early trip in 1952 and that I still recall is Srirangapattana or as we knew it Seringapatam. This island fortress in the Kaveri River was very important to Tipu Sultan known as the 'Tiger of Mysore'. We went and spent an afternoon at Seringapatam and learned all about him. He was nicknamed the Tiger of Mysore for his resistance to the British though ultimately he was defeated by them and died at the last battle in 1799. The island fortress had however been the capital of the Mysore Wodeyar rajas.

Tipu Sultan was the son of Haider Ali a general in the Mysore ruler's army who deposed the Wodeyar rajas in 1761. Father and son were responsible for transforming this area into a major Muslim power. Born in 1750 of a Hindu mother Tipu Sultan inherited his father's military skills but unlike his illiterate father he went on to become an educated cultured man who introduced major agricultural reforms. He hated the British and wanted to rid India of their rule and so he flirted with the French. He had sought an alliance with the Marathas and the Mughals without success and his dalliance with the French came to nothing as well. France had suffered losses in the Seven Years' War and just at the time when he was hoping for success through alliance with France the country was overtaken by the French Revolution. He invaded the state of Travancore in what is now Kerala, and of which I have written earlier, but this sparked a third Mysore War, which resulted in a resounding defeat for him. Napoleon's landing in Egypt in 1798 was intended to threaten India, and Mysore was a key to that next step. The British took the threat very seriously and Lord Arthur Wellesley – later to become the Duke of Wellington – marched into Mysore in 1799 and besieged the capital Seringapatam. On May 4th the British forces broke through the defending walls and Tipu Sultan died of gunshot wounds near the gates of his fortress. This victory was the turning point in Arthur Wellesley's career, and the rest, as is said, is history!

Richard Holmes' book *Sahib – The British Soldier in India 1750-1914* is one of his most recent books and he covers this whole story in such an interesting way; he further deals with the Indian Mutiny or First Indian Revolt in 1857 very well.

The Daria Daulat Bagh or former summer palace which is a kilometre from the fort was used to entertain Tipu's guests. This I recalled from 1952 and there it is today; at first sight one might feel unimpressed but it is a very worthwhile building. I feel the Archaeological Survey of India could do a great deal more to preserve it and enhance its environs but nevertheless it is interesting. The low wooden colonnaded building seems unremarkable, but one should consider its age and the interior with its ornamental arches, tiger-striped columns and decoration on every inch of teak walls which is unique. There is a mural depicting the victory by Haider Ali over the British at Pollilore in 1780 and upstairs there is a small collection of Tipu memorabilia. It infuriated me that the counter selling pamphlets and other items was unmanned and by and large there was no sense of marketing the place as being so special. One officious little chap kept telling us all that we must not photograph anything, which is perfectly understandable, but surely the Indian authorities could work out that people would like postcards reproducing the murals and buildings. I only have photographs of the exterior. We then visited the Gumbaz mausoleum built by Tipu Sultan in 1784 to commemorate his father and later also it served as his own resting place. Much of the interior of the mausoleum has been untouched or renovated and therefore the décor with the tiger stripes is the original. In the Victoria and Albert Museum in London there is a model of a tiger killing a British soldier which is entitled Tipu's Tiger which was made for him out of wood and metal in 1795. The Nehru Gallery at the V and A is full of wonderful Indian pieces and indeed it is the largest collection of Indian art outside of India. There is also a painting of the death of Tipu Sultan that is owned by, or lent to, the National Gallery of Scotland which is a most impressive art gallery at the foot of The Mound in Edinburgh. Graham then visited the notorious dungeons within the fort itself, but it was very hot in the afternoon sun and I just looked out at the river and thought of over two centuries ago when a desperate battle took place where I was standing.

Tipu Sultan in many ways stands head and shoulders above other Indian rulers who were his contemporaries. He was a man before his time with aspirations for India that did him credit; he was a shrewd diplomat and a scholar and poet as well as a soldier and administrator. In Bangalore there is all that survives of Tipu's Summer Palace, which he had built in 1789; it is rather similar to the one at Seringapatam. I recall a picnic there in the grounds of Haider Ali's fort that took place in 1951. The monkeys were very bold and came and looted the picnic basket; this is still quite a clear memory but wrestles with the only other one of being shown huge iron hooks let into the fort's great walls and being told that apparently his prisoners would be thrown off the ramparts to land on the hooks and die a slow agonizing death – so, he was not any sort of saint!

On all my travels in India there is usually one special moment that I recall – usually something to do with children. On this occasion when we parked and were preparing to visit the mausoleum I stopped to look at the horses standing close by. They were in very good condition and I thought it rather odd that someone should offer riding to locals and overseas tourists, who most probably would not be dressed appropriately – it just cheered me up that the animals looked in such good condition. Then a young boy approached hopefully and diffidently offering me a set of postcards. He behaved so politely and without being pushy that I bought them, for the asking price. Well, it was worth it just to see the sheer delight in his face and eyes and he kept saying thank you. Then a bunch of youngsters approached and surrounded me and begged me to buy from them in the usual raucous manner, but he did not crow or boast of his success, he just looked at me across their heads with twinkling eyes as if to say, "We share a big secret". I never did say anything to the others as they would have probably put pressure on him to share his money. When we departed I just waved – again we just grinned, sharing our secret.

Chapter Seventeen

Bandipur, Kabini and Elephants!

I am sitting writing in my study on a sunny spring morning, hardly able to believe that exactly three weeks ago today we had flown out to India and embarked on another huge journey by air and road. Now I am once again back in Tweeddale and Raju is sitting beside me as close as he can be because when I return from these trips he does not like to let me out of his sight for more than a few minutes. The spring garden is just waiting to burst into bloom with hundreds of daffodils and crocus and frittilaria, plus the hellebores. It has been another very cold night with just a touch of late snow and the birds demanded my attention, with hen pheasants walking up and down the mown paths between the daffodils and the little birds desperate for some breadcrumbs and seed on their tables.

Dear old India, it was good to return there and equally good to come back to our beloved home in Scotland. The purpose of this trip was to go and experience the many attractions of Karnataka and write about them in this book, and in the doing thereof have a really wonderful holiday!

Two weeks ago we flew to Bangalore from Delhi and then travelled by air conditioned four by four to Bandipur, which is eighty kilometres south of Mysore. It was a long drive not made any easier by the fact that I had obviously contracted some awful 'Delhi Belly' the night before and thus the air journey followed by the road journey was, to say the least, a challenge. These are the hazards one encounters and I almost immediately took the antibiotic prescribed by our doctors to expedite my recovery; we always travel with a full course bought in Scotland. Our favoured antibiotic is Ciproflaxin and it is available in Indian pharmacies but having heard of the horrible 'scam' that is perpetrated on innocent Indian victims, who sometimes buy in good faith and do not know that the pills they are taking are under strength and therefore unlikely to cure the affliction, we try to ensure our safety by buying medicines before travelling. This notorious trade is something that the Indian Government will have to eradicate with stringent protection laws.

We finally arrived at the Bandipur Resort run by Jungles Lodges & Resorts, a Karnataka state-owned enterprise. The sun was setting and the almost full moon was already high in the sky. We sat and had a welcome cup of tea followed by a coke to help rehydrate me. The bedroom and bathroom were comfortable if a bit sparse but modern and clean. The location of this accommodation is not ideal because it is built on the main Mysore to Ooty road with the ceaseless noise of traffic. I was a little surprised by it all and disappointed.

My memory of Bandipur Park goes back to 1952 when as a child of five I visited it with my parents and stayed as a guest of the Maharajah of Mysore. On that occasion we stayed in his lodge in the actual park and that was wonderful. It was in fact my first ever visit to a wildlife sanctuary and made a powerful impression on me. I can still recall the night and looking out in the dark and seeing a thousand eyes looking at me reflecting the light in the bedroom; chital, the spotted deer came right up to the building and were quietly grazing right under our windows. The other things I remember are the Maharajah's bedroom with an enormous old fashioned bed with a purple bedspread, and in the garage a huge wonderful purple Rolls Royce! Purple was undoubtedly a favourite colour!

Looking round this small resort which had been renovated in 2004 and reopened with a marble slab marking the occasion I reflected that Karnataka State Tourism is really in a bad way. I have seen and enjoyed so many of the beautifully published brochures and pamphlets but the reality on offer is second rate and inexcusable really. Perhaps the various governments of the state have been complacent because of the burgeoning city of Bangalore and the revenues it undoubtedly brings in to the state's coffers. As a photographer I know only too well how one can romanticize a subject in photography and this is indeed what the tourism department has done; moreover they do not respond to communications and I would not even have been there but for the dogged determination of Thomas Cherian who is the Marketing Manager of Trails India and the group that owns the beautiful Orange County Resort in Coorg. It was Thomas who pestered the Commissioner for Tourism's office to arrange our visit. Sadly that is India; there are so many people who have a jobsworth attitude in state government and rest largely on the laurels achieved by other states who really try hard to entice foreigners to India. Now I come to think of it, there is a similarity between them and the Visit Scotland department in the Scottish Borders; all our local entrepreneurs cannot find a good word to say about them, and indeed I too have found they spend more time informing one how busy they are, whereas actions always speak louder than words. We in this lovely little corner of Scotland which is so under populated badly need to publicize our attractions to a wider world.

The next morning was our reward for coming all this way. I firmly told the naturalist that I wanted to be in the jeep by 06.20 hours and we achieved this. The sun was coming up and the air was cool enough for me to wear a cashmere sweater. Driving along in the jeep we had a feeling of anticipation which was fulfilled.

Bandipur National Park is 865 square kilometres and is part of the larger Nilgiri Biosphere which encompasses Bandipur and Nagarahole in Karnataka state, Mudumalai in Tamil Nadu and Wynaad in Kerala. There are a few roads through some of the forest because it is a huge area overall and home to the Indian Elephant as well as all the other denizens of the Indian Jungle. The core area of Bandipur however is very well maintained and a joy to experience. It was one of the fifteen parks selected across the whole of India to be part of Project Tiger, the scheme launched in 1973 to try and save the tiger and its habitat.

The naturalist explained that the area had experienced some really good heavy rain within the last two weeks and the evidence was there in good clean fresh spring growth which made it all look beautiful. Within minutes we saw herds of chital and groups of wild boar in the Forest Department area. They are so tame they just graze around the various buildings. Setting off down the rough tracks almost immediately we saw several more herds of chital, then sambar, the big red deer of India, wild pig, monkeys, mongooses and a barking deer. Quite suddenly with the sun shining on the grass verge and track we came face to face with a huge pack of Dhole, the wild dog of India. This was truly amazing. Dhole are largely secretive creatures and very rarely seen, let alone as a pack; here we were with the jeep silenced sitting and watching and they literally came and played around the jeep. There were about fifteen or sixteen of them with about five pups. The latter were hesitant but they soon joined their parents and it was difficult to imagine how ferocious and feared these animals are when sitting calmly and quietly they sat or played within six feet of us. Graham and I were able to take all the photographs we wanted which have come out very well and acted as proof to others we subsequently met at Kabini and Dandeli to substantiate our claim. It was such a rare sighting. It is recognised that even tiger and leopard will leave a kill on which they are feasting if Dhole appear in a pack and make it clear they wish to feed. I have seen wonderful wildlife films showing a pack working a pincer movement to hunt down their prey.

The Indian wild dog is a predator; mostly diurnal it hunts in packs and feeds on chital or sambar, but it has also been known to attack gaur, the Indian wild buffalo. People thought of them as vermin in times past but they are now recognised to have highly efficient hunting techniques and a complex social structure; large family groups stay together and help to look after succeeding generations of young. We felt so 'chuffed' with this sighting and reluctantly drove on slowly and left the pack to their early morning frolic in the sunshine. How my late father would have enjoyed that sighting. He in fact wrote an article on Dhole for The Field magazine published in London way back in 1954 and tried his best to educate people about this creature and eradicate the idea of them as vermin.

The peacocks were in full feather and looking absolutely gorgeous sitting in the trees or displaying their wonderful tail feathers and Graham and I now think that March is the best time to visit wildlife parks and see the chital with their fawns, the dogs with cubs and birds in 'full fig' ready for mating.

The blue sky, sunshine and bird calls were so entrancing here in the peace and quiet of the core area of the forest; the Indian Roller or Blue Jay was flying about, there were Hoopoes, woodpeckers and langur monkeys and the peacocks calling. The velvet on the antlers of the chital stags was something we had not seen previously and all the animals looked in such fine fettle. Sometimes in India one receives special gifts; an indifferent resort, a long journey and a fragile stomach all disappeared with this enjoyable morning in Bandipur. The park

Kabini River Lodge, Karnataka

itself is in very good condition and its proximity to Mysore should make it a strong attraction.

My recommendation however is that Jungle Lodges & Resorts work a little harder on their hotel; it could become charming with a properly planted and maintained garden area and lotus pond that would attract birdlife; a hedge of banana trees and other vegetation would drown out the noise of the road. The indolent manager should be replaced and the staff trained and hey presto! A new invigorated destination would attract visitors from within India and foreigners as it is only eighty kilometres from Mysore and therefore a feasible place in which to stay for one night and allow at least one if not two wildlife drives through the park and forest. The road from Mysore moreover is an attractive one showing rural India at its best.

After a rather indifferent breakfast we took our leave and proceeded on our journey to Kabini River Lodge. Our driver Pratap was a nice friendly man who was gaining confidence with us and as he spoke Hindi it made things easier and more relaxed between us. The journey over Karnataka's poor roads was slow; at last the infrastructure is being developed and renovated which is essential if this state is to flourish.

Two and a half hours later we arrived at Kabini. It is a lovely place and well run. Rated among the top five wildlife resorts in the world by Tatler, the British magazine, Kabini River Lodge offers a lush slice of wildlife paradise. The greatest attraction here is the convergence of spectacular wildlife and birdlife to the banks of the Kabini River in spring and summer. The Kabini is a tributary of the River Cauvery (one of the great sacred rivers of India) and it surrounds the River Lodge. It is located at Kharapur near the Nagarahole Wildlife National Park which is formally known as the Rajiv Gandhi National Park, but nobody ever refers to it as such, and the Lodge itself has grounds of fifty-five acres that are well maintained and very attractive.

The man who inspired and worked so hard along with one other to establish Kabini is Colonel John Wakefield. Graham and I had the great pleasure of meeting and socialising with him on this visit and we have a huge respect and affection for him. John Wakefield or 'Papa' as he is known affectionately around Kabini is now exactly ninety years old. Like my own family his had a history of working and living in India throughout the colonial era. He was born in Gaya, the birthplace of the Lord Buddha; his father was in the employ of the Maharaja of Tikari. His great grandfather had gone to India in 1826 to join the Bengal Army. John loved the Indian countryside and indeed grew up treating the Maharajah's private forest and hunting ground as his own. He shot his first tiger at the age of nine and his first leopard at the age of ten. These in this modern responsible world sound shocking achievements, but that was the way of life amongst colonials in another age; fortunately John Wakefield was converted to the whole idea of conservation and helping to preserve India's wonderful wildlife, not least of course the big cats.

The story goes that as a child of seven John went on a hunt with Sir Maurice Hallett (later to be Governor of Uttar Pradesh); when a tiger roared and charged down a hill slope, John tapped him on the back and whispered, "Don't be afraid Mr Hallett, I am here." Sir Maurice recalled the story many years later. Coincidentally Sir Maurice Hallett was the chairman of the board of governors at my public school Saint Swithun's, Winchester, in the 1950s. John Wakefield converted to conservation after a career in the Indian Army which he only left in 1954. His son-in-law is the distinguished photographer Toby Sinclair who has photographed so much of India's wildlife for the various BBC programmes such as Land of the Tiger. Sadly, as is the case so frequently in India, though a chief minister of Karnataka suggested that he help to establish a wildlife lodge in Karnataka such as the famous Tiger Tops in Nepal, others in the bureaucracy were jealous and suspicious of his aims. However, thankfully he and a man called Ramesh Mehra succeeded and they found this ideal location for a wildlife lodge, on the premises of the Maharajah of Mysore's hunting grounds. The Maharajah had built two hunting lodges in 1929 especially for the viceroy's visit. Lord Irwin and his entourage travelled to Kharapur by Rolls Royce and Bentley to witness the annual khedah, in which a herd of wild elephants was captured – from what I have read it was a rather brutal and vicious business. The various well known maharajahs like Jodhpur, Benares and the famous Maharani of Cooch Behar and the Prince of Persia were also present on this occasion. The old buildings have been carefully renovated and preserved and new chalets and tented accommodation built. Whereas we had been the only occupants of the Bandipur resort Kabini is thriving and full of foreign groups as well as Indians enjoying their own country; in fact one has to book weeks if not months in advance.

Kabini is sandwiched between Nagarahole and Bandipur and is one of the strongholds for the Asian elephant and home to the largest single population of elephants throughout Asia. Elephants congregate in large numbers during the dry season of February to April on the banks of the Kabini River. Nagarahole is also home to tiger and leopard, dhole, sloth bear, langur and even crocodiles, plus gaur, chital and sambar. There are over 300 species of birds present in the park.

Our chalet down by the river bank was excellent and well furnished and we went to lunch in the 'gol ghar', which means round house, which has just a roof and is open all round. There are hides built into the tall trees and areas from which to sit and watch birds and animals. The food was good – these jungle camps do not pretend to be providing five star cuisine; it was however good and wholesome. We went on the afternoon wildlife safari accompanied by another couple and an Indian family with a tiny girl. I wondered how things would work out with a fractious toddler but she was very sweet and good.

Almost immediately we had the great good fortune to see a big tusker elephant right on the side of the track. This was amazing for us as he was so close. Graham took a lot of photographs of him and the naturalist, who was a very keen young man, explained that the animal had obviously just knocked down the tree sapling and was intent on eating the bark. He stopped and looked at us, but decided that we meant him no harm and calmly continued his late lunch. I was enchanted as were all the others. We have seen plenty of African elephants in years gone by but had not seen Indian elephant in the wild close up.

I first experienced elephants in India at the age of six weeks when my parents took me into the jungle for a shooting weekend. Naturally I do not remember that event but I certainly do recall my encounters with elephants since the age of three. I was taught to be respectful of them and their huge size and weight, but as a small child I was encouraged to climb bare footed up the trunk of an elephant and sit just behind the head – this I have to say was a prickly experience as elephant hair is about two inches long and quite spikey!

Indian myth and legend and history have featured elephants and indeed the favourite deity Lord Ganesha is Lord Shiva's eldest son and resembles an elephant and is enormously benevolent and therefore loved. I made sure I bought Ganesh statues for our close relatives as gifts. I have two very favourite statues in our home; one carved minutely in soapstone and the other in brass.

Elephas maximus is the Asian elephant – the majestic creature that appears in art form and sculpture from around 2000 BC and is still deeply revered in Indian religion and culture. However, poaching for ivory and sheer population pressure are the two major threats to this wonderful animal. Conservationists and like-minded individuals are working intensively to try and preserve its endangered habitat as India's population continues to expand and farmers and tea and coffee planters behave aggressively towards wild elephants when they feel their livelihoods threatened by marauding wild herds. Uneducated and even educated but greedy people do not care about the consequences for us all if the elephant is driven to extinction in the wilds of India, even though this is a land in which the animal is revered as a god. Elephants arriving on the banks of the Kabini frequently carry the scars

Wild tusker at Kabini near Nagarahole in Karnataka

of shotgun pellets, fired at them by the irate owners of coffee plantations whose land the animals have trampled through – they do not feed on the coffee bushes. Many are blinded by the pellets or maimed by crude electric fences connected to high-tension cables.

India is emerging as a great economic superpower but its governments and peoples must never forget that they are custodians of their land and its animals; Indian politicians are for a large part a duplicitous bunch who say one thing to appear responsible but then allow a blind eye to ignore flagrant poaching or persecution of wild animals provided their own 'vote banks' are rich.

In a country with a population exceeding a billion people, there is scant place for animals as large as an elephant to survive in the wild in great numbers. From a distribution which spanned most of the Indian sub-continent, elephant habitats have shrunk to a few scattered forests in northern, eastern and southern India. The healthiest population by far exists in these diverse forests of South India. Ranging from dry teak to tropical evergreen, these habitats are home to about 15 per cent of the world's wild Asiatic Elephant population.

Elephant society is typically headed by the eldest and most experienced female in a herd, known as the matriarch. The matriarchs know, through experience, which areas will have a certain variety of food in a certain season, the location of water in the dry season and areas where they will be safe. Over the centuries, herds have followed rigid migration routes that take them through areas of optimum food and water during the course of the year. These routes are ingrained in the matriarch's memories. However, in modern times, these routes are being fragmented by man-made obstructions such as coffee plantations, farms and human settlements. As a result, elephants are increasingly coming into direct conflict with man. The fallout is human casualties injured by elephants desperate for food and water and elephant deaths due to poisoning and electrocution. In a land dominated by a large and hungry human population elephants are seen as pests by some and have little local support.

Despite a bleak prospect, there is hope for these gentle giants. In South India, the elephant still has a fighting chance at survival. That chance lies in the Nagarahole National Park where we were visiting, which as I have indicated is part of the larger Nilgiri Biosphere Reserve. Elephants are able to migrate between Nagarahole and Bandipur in Karnataka and Mudumalai Sanctuary in Tamil Nadu and the Wynaad Sanctuary in Kerala, along with several smaller sanctuaries and protected forests.

For the Nagarahole elephants, the migration routes go through either Kerala in the south or through the Brahmagiri Hills in the west and north. These migration corridors which are still reasonably intact, allow the elephants a relatively safe passage between the lush monsoon forests in the hills and the grassy banks and abundant water of the Kabini Reservoir in the summer. This reservoir which forms the southern boundary of the Park provides sustenance to a whole host of animals, elephants included, during the hot dry summer months.

Every year, around November, the waters of the Kabini Reservoir are gradually drained to provide irrigation to the farmers in the catchment areas around the city of Mysore. The resultant mudflats are rich in silt washed down from the Western Ghats and, by the time the forest dries up in April, there is an abundance of fresh grass to sustain the elephants. It is perhaps a unique phenomenon, where a reservoir which has drowned some twenty-five thousand square kilometres of forest, has actually benefited the ecology of that forest. Indeed the seasonal movements of the Nagarahole herds are intrinsically dependent on the annual drainage cycle of the reservoir.

By the beginning of March, the now lush banks of the reservoir start to fill up with elephants. As summer advances, more and more herds descend from the hills to partake of this annual feast of grass. This is also a social aggregation for the elephants as matriarchs meet each other and the meadows echo with the rumblings, squeals and trumpets of elephant vocalisations. Calves that were born the previous year are now old enough to eat the soft nutritious grass and they too get a rare chance to play, tugging at each other's trunks and tails and butting each other. Younger calves stick close to their mothers or gambol playfully with their elder siblings. Adult elephants are remarkably tolerant of their young. The big bull elephants that are normally solitary mingle with the herds, getting a chance to mate and pass on their genes. Conflicts occasionally occur as is wont to happen in any society, but these are soon resolved by the matriarchs and peace returns to the vast sea of grazing elephants.

Towards the end of May, the grass has worn away, leaving behind short, dry stubs. These too are kicked up by the elephants, leaving bare dusty patches of soil. Soon the rains will come and the reservoir will once again fill up and it will be time for the matriarchs to lead their herds back up into the cool green heights of the Brahmagiri hills. The lone bulls remain behind, feeding on the bamboo and fresh leaves of the teak forest.

Elephas Maximus by Stephen Alter is a portrait of the Indian Elephant, a book that was published in 2005 in India by Penguin and I can truly recommend it. I salute Stephen Alter for his fine work and find it very readable. "*He charts the elephant in art, religion, folklore and the everyday world of India, bringing to life the complex past and troubled present of this majestic creature while offering hope for its future.*" This is a quotation from the cover of his book which encapsulated his achievement.

Reluctantly we drove on and left the tusker busy with his bark stripping; now I could recognise where an elephant had brought down a young tree and one saw evidence of this several times throughout the afternoon. We then came across a gaur and her calf; the Indian form of wild buffalo is a fine beast that I have seen before but they too are quite shy and on this occasion we soon came upon a magnificent bull gaur. Then we saw more and more elephants and some chital and sambar. The next big excitement was a beautiful Malabar giant squirrel high in a tree overhead. We had never seen these before and found them so handsome and big. There were wild pig, mongooses, hoopoes, kingfishers and blue jays to delight us.

Suddenly the naturalist thought he had come upon a tiger resting up in a particular bit of the forest. He was confident from the various alarm calls that he was right, but sadly though we sat and tried to be very silent the tiger wisely kept his cover and we moved on...only to be rewarded by the sighting of a leopard as the light was fading. That was exciting because leopards are secretive lonely creatures who do not usually allow one to see them.

The full moon had risen and the light was fading. This was the full moon of Holi, which I have already mentioned in the book; it was so beautiful that I asked the driver to stop the jeep so that I might have an opportunity to photograph it, which I did but then we heard a crashing sound and sure enough there was another lone elephant having a quiet feed quite close to us.

Driving back in the twilight with the moon ahead was lovely with everyone feeling very satisfied with the afternoon safari. The early morning drive the next day was not that successful for us but we felt grateful for all that we had seen. I would seriously recommend a visit to Kabini River Lodge. In the morning there was the opportunity to go in the motor launch on the lake and we came close to a lone tusker in the morning sunlight having a peaceful drink on the far shore; the birdlife comes into its own as seen by motor launch and some people tried out a coracle ride. This park is open throughout the year so would be a good destination in the monsoon months when the wildlife parks in central and northern India are closed to visitors.

For those who have not ridden on an elephant before there is also an opportunity to experience this briefly, though disappointingly there is no opportunity to actually experience wildlife viewing on elephant back as happens at Corbett National Park in Uttarranchal. I love wildlife viewing from an elephant because it is all so silent and the animals allow one to approach really close. Three hours on elephant back can be very comfortable and enormously rewarding. Do not however drink very much before you set out as obviously though the elephant will kneel down and allow you to 'disembark' it is not so easy to return to the howdah without a mounting stepladder!

Graham and I left with reluctance and wished John Wakefield happy birthday for his forthcoming 90th. There are pictures taken of him in the company of celebrities and others and the old gentlemen has much of which to be proud; he cares passionately about India and its conservation development as indeed do I; the fact that so many of the young men refer to him as 'Papa' in their conversation with me gave me a good feeling. One said in Hindi to me that all he had been taught had come from Papa, even little things about strangler vines and the way they grow. The young do not always want to admit that they learnt anything from their elders so he surely got it right at Kabini!

Chapter Eighteen

Orange County in Coorg and Hoysala Temples

We had travelled by car to Orange County Resort in Coorg in early April 2005; on that occasion it had been from Mysore, rather on a whim to have lunch, a look around and get a very superficial feel of the place. The management had been very welcoming and urged us to return on another visit and experience all their hospitality; thus we were driving to Orange County which is situated near Siddapur in the region of Kodagu, which was formerly known as Coorg and was a unique little state which has been absorbed into Karnataka.

This drive took us about three hours because of the poor roads; it was nevertheless interesting to see the huge development going on. The countryside is prosperous with a lot of house building in an around the villages. These new homes are double storey brick houses, tiny by European standards but I am sure just what the occupants have been dreaming about. The predominant colour that is used it seems in the whole of rural Karnataka is a very pleasant bright turquoise and certainly freshly painted and adorned, some of the villages looked very attractive. They are by no means all attractive but what does one expect? I can think of a lot of boring little British villages which really are quite depressing, and in the central belt of Scotland that seems to have been the aspiration of the local planners – grey and grey and unremitting grey, made altogether worse by our rather harsh weather!

The lush countryside with tanks of water (artificial small lakes), palms, coconut groves, rice fields and well worked fields with brassica crops looked very pretty. The fields had plenty of red tractors working away and yet the old form of transport was also evident – the bullock cart with two patient beasts going about their work and toil. The schools were freshly painted and have murals that are intended to teach the pupils the fundamentals about India and its patriots I think. Occasionally there was the rather lurid mural suggesting the use of some basic form of hygienic practice – Graham and I would chuckle

Luxury pool villa at Orange County, Coorg

about these, I just refuse to go into details, but if they achieve their aim then everyone will be a lot healthier!

As it is springtime we had the added attraction of beautiful blossom on the jacarandas, acacias, tulip trees and flame of the forest, along with laburnum. The bougainvilleas were in brilliant display and the ponds had masses of pink lotus in bloom.

Once we drove into Coorg the coffee plantations are the major crop with tall silver oaks covered in pepper vines climbing up the trees amongst the bushes to give them shade; it is a very clever use of land, two different crops in one area, with perhaps the added value of timber in due course. The coffee bushes were resplendent in white blossom; truly it looked amazing as if there had been a fall of snow and the snow had lingered on thousands of coffee bushes. Last year it had not been like this and clearly the signs for a bumper crop of coffee beans were evident. Coffee bushes require water to achieve pollination and because ten days previously there had been very good rainfall the flower was in full force. Usually artificial watering is necessary throughout the plantations and this year the natural rain was so welcome and would have saved a huge amount of money that is normally spent on pumping the water continuously for about ten days.

The coffee story it is thought dates back to the period of early Christianity. By the end of the 3rd century allegedly Christian monks fleeing from persecution in Rome travelled to Ethiopia to escape torture and death. It is commonly believed that coffee plants were first discovered in the Ethiopian province of Kaffa. Legend has it that a young shepherd named Kaldi noticed that the sheep he was tending on the hillside became hyperactive after eating red berries from a plant native to the area. Kaldi decided to try the berries to see what effect they would have on him and he also became hyperactive. Apparently the monks noticed this and became the first coffee enthusiasts because the stimulant allowed them to stay awake for long periods of time to pray and meditate and fulfil their duties. The name of the province influenced the name and Kaffa became coffee. Ethiopia continues to grow coffee to this day. The Galla tribe from Ethiopia had used the berries but not as a drink. They would wrap the beans (berries) in animal fat as their only source of nutrition while on raiding parties. The Turks were the first country to adopt it as a drink, often adding spices such as clove, cinnamon, cardamom and anise to the brew. In about 1000 AD coffee was transported from Ethiopia to Arabia where it began to be cultivated in plantations in the Yemen. Hence the name: 'coffee arabica'. It became a very popular drink but up to the 17th century coffee was a treat that could only be found in Arabia, and it was prohibited for coffee plants to be transported outside of any Muslim nation. Many feel that the popularity of coffee in these early centuries was fuelled by the Islamic prohibition against alcoholic drink. By the 17th century coffee plants began to appear in India and legend has it that a revered Muslim holy man from India named Baba Budan smuggled several coffee beans wrapped around his stomach out of Mocha after discovering the drink during a pilgrimage to Mecca. He returned to India and planted them in the rolling hills of Chikmagalur in Karnataka. The hills to this day bear his name 'Baba Budan Hills' or 'Baba Budan Giri'. Coffee Robusta evolved from the favourable climatic conditions and cross pollination.

The British became very interested and they started large coffee plantations in Coorg (Kodagu) – 'coffee arabica' in North Coorg and 'coffee robusta' in the South. India only contributes 3 per cent of the world's coffee crop, but Coorg and Chikmagalur in Karnataka are the largest producers of commercial coffee in India.

Kodagu, the new name for Coorg, which I find I return to as does everyone else, is set amid the forested hills of the Western Ghats. It was independent until subsumed into the new state of Karnataka in 1956; as it is only a little over 60 miles or 100 kilometres from Mysore it is a must when visiting Karnataka. Madikeri is the capital town situated at 1,500 metres (4,921 ft) and the whole atmosphere is different. Coffee plantations with the pepper vines, cardamom and orange plantations are the major crops and everywhere you look it is lush and green and shady. The Kodavas are the people of Kodagu and they are a distinct ethnic group and have their own language, Coorgi. Curiously they were historically quite a martial race and to this day the Indian Army has many distinguished soldiers and famous generals from Coorg. I can think of two who particularly stand out in my time – General Thimmaya and General Kariappa. Both I can recall became commander-in-chief of Indian Forces. I knew General Thimmaya, who was a friend of my late father's. He distinguished himself as a United Nations commander in Cyprus in the early 1960s.

The Ramapuram family started Orange County Resort, and they originated from a small town called Pala in the district of Kottayam in Kerala. Emmanuel Ramapuram was born in 1892. He struggled through the difficult years of the early 20th century and was appointed as a ranger in charge of South Kanara and Coorg districts, then under the Madras Presidency of British India. While working as a ranger he fell in love with the landscape and culture of Coorg. Later Emmanuel suffered a severe bout of malaria but he survived and had to return home to Kerala. In 1926 at the age of thirty-four he returned to Coorg and was able to purchase Chikkanahally estate in Siddapur and Kaimakumbatta Estate in Pollibetta from a Mr Percy Glover Tipping. Mr Tipping was the managing director of Consolidated Coffee Estates, a company incorporated in Great Britain, with its registered office at 71 George Street, Edinburgh. Orange County today is part of that Chikkanahally Estate; here again is a Scottish connection.

In addition to being one of the oldest coffee plantations, Chikkanahally Estate was also the first trial plantation of rubber by the British in India. There is a great deal that a guest can do at Orange County Resort. The sightseeing options include the Raja's Seat, the lovely Abbey Water Falls, the Omkarashwar Temple, and Talacauvery – the birthplace of the River Cauvery, which is one of India's sacred rivers.

At Kushalnaga there is also a huge Tibetan settlement. At Valnoor Fishing Camp the opportunity to fish for the world famous Mahseer fish is very attractive. We however decided that we would just relax at Orange County and only visited the Dubare Elephant Camp, which was a totally delightful experience.

We received a wonderfully warm welcome from the management of Orange County, some of whom we had met briefly previously. They gave us one of the new villas that had not been ready a year ago – this has its own small pool and jaccuzzi. The planning and décor of these villas is delightful, elegant and simple but with everything one could wish for and very spacious. The architecture is based on the traditional Coorg form of house with wooden features. I have a passion for outdoor bathrooms and this one was cleverly designed with French doors to a small courtyard but one could have the doors closed yet receive the impression of the outdoors, which is probably a very good thing in the cool season up in the hills. There were all sorts of thoughtful touches. Last year we had experienced The Camp, which meant we had been given a luxury tent with every comfort which had its own en-suite luxury shower room and was air conditioned. The original cottages are in a Tudor style which I think was the result of the British link, though in Scotland, as it was originally owned by a Scottish company, we do not have black and white timber houses except now in an ersatz form from modern builders. Still, the thatched, black and white cottages look very attractive and truly there is accommodation to suit everyone's budget. The views from the recent additions of luxury tents and pool villas are lovely facing the serene lake which is in the midst of 300 acres of coffee and touching on the 50,000 acre Dubare Reserve Forest.

The main dining room is about to be renovated to incorporate more dining area and it has a lovely conference facility and fitness studio beneath. The original pool is very nice and The Camp has its own beautiful infinity pool right on the edge of the lake which is stunning. We however luxuriated in the privacy of our own pool with flowering coffee bushes forming a boundary beyond the fence. I imagined I heard a wild elephant at one stage!

The Ayurveda Village at Orange County is housed in a traditional ancestral Kodava house, complete with a central courtyard and exquisite woodwork, and indeed it has three villas which guests can choose to stay in with their own private pools; I had seen these last year. If one comes for some serious ayurvedic treatments, perhaps as a sufferer from some serious chronic disease such as multiple sclerosis, or Parkinson's disease or suffers from arthritis or injuries I could see living close by in a luxury villa and just having to walk a few paces to the treatments would prove very helpful. I was only too keen to experience yet again a full head and body massage done by two girls simultaneously from each side. It was excellent and I particularly love the herbal gram mixture with which one scrubs down afterwards which leaves the whole skin feeling smooth and polished – it rather resembles a gritty spinach puree!

One of the funny things about writing is that from time to time characters met in one's travels sort of jump out of the memory. For my first book there was a soldier in the Indian Army called Gurung, a Nepalese man, who is still in his regiment – the Jat Regiment stationed at Bareilly, my birthplace and the headquarters of my late father's regiment. Gurung, whom I have met on numerous occasions, is just a special man and is generally liked. In my second book there was a naturalist at Ranthambhore working for Tiger Moon called Rakesh who had the same qualities for me and helped me to see my first tigers in the wild as a mature adult. Here in this book there is a young man called Ganesh whom I had met on our first trip to Orange County; he had impressed us both with his natural enthusiasm and friendliness. His job is to interpret all the natural encounters that guests may experience and educate them gently. He bounced up to greet us on our arrival and we too were delighted to see him. His English has actually been learnt from listening and talking to the children who visit Orange County and it is pretty good; I think the management should help him and send him on various courses because his eagerness and loyalty is what every management team would like to encounter in their staff, and yet he does not push himself forward – naturally I have told them so. I am making this point because it is so easy for sophisticated knowledgeable professional people to swan around the world perhaps slightly patronisingly, but here were three good men, all experts in their particular field, a lance corporal in charge of serving officers in an elite officers' mess of the Indian Army, a naturalist who within twenty paces could tell you what fauna was around you and almost invisible to the eye, and young Ganesh who speaks with pride and knowledge about the fauna and flora of Orange County and elephants and is ever eager to learn. It is unlikely that any of these three men will actually have the pleasure of travelling internationally themselves yet they bring a certain sweetness to their encounters with others that make them each memorable in their own special ways.

Another two new additions are the Reading Room and the Vegetarian Restaurant. The latter is very well placed with a beautiful view of the lake and serves table d'hote vegetarian food on a thali; we enjoyed it immensely at lunchtime. The Reading Room has been built on stilts and looks out on the boggy ground and little lotus pool and receives the last rays of the setting sun. I think it is a lovely idea to go and sit and look out; no loud noise or music is allowed. There are some wonderful books in which to delve and at the same time have a delicious coffee from berries grown on the estate that is made on the spot in a special new cappuccino machine. Along with all these attractions there is a hen, duck, turkey and goose house which would have an obvious attraction for small children and the resort also grows thousands of anthuriums for use themselves and for export to the rest of India. When I am on holiday in India I tend to be rather languid because naturally the heat becomes a little challenging, but for Indians or young people there is the opportunity to power walk, jog, bicycle, play golf or swim for exercise – and then collapse gently in a hammock on the lake's edge.

The Dubare Elephant Camp was a twenty minute drive away set in beautiful surroundings on the banks of the River Cauvery. In fact one has to cross the river by little launch to reach it. This is a charming spot and I am sure that Jungle Lodges will develop it well. If one has not had any other experience with elephants this can be the most joyful first encounter or enrich one however many times elephants have crossed one's path. These are trained elephants which are no longer used for logging duties, but they do a useful job helping to keep wild elephants away from the coffee plantations. The naturalist in charge gives a small talk on elephants and encourages people to take an interest in them and explains all the challenges facing the elephant population of India. We watched a special food supplement being prepared in a huge pot boiling away. This gram mixture is then, after hours of cooking, formed into huge balls the size of an old fashioned cannon ball. The elephants love being fed by hand and people like us love the experience too. In fact whilst we were inspecting the boiling mixture one old elephant was sidling up to us to become first in the queue, except it is a little disconcerting to turn round and find a huge pachyderm breathing down one's neck, rather like a child trying to steal cookies from the kitchen. The keepers and mahouts just shouted at him to keep back, but each time their back was turned he would creep, if you can imagine an elephant creep, forward. We had gone to visit the elephants with Ganesh, who is so aptly named and he just loved the encounters as

Three wise beasts waiting to be fed at Dubare Elephant Camp

much as we did. Then the mahouts would lead them down, or tell them to go down to the water's edge to have a daily bath. I was urged to go down into the water and help scrub them. This I have done with Tara the famous elephant at Kipling Camp at Kanha and I have the most marvellous memories of the whole afternoon, which I explained in my second book India: The Tiger's Roar; however, on this occasion I was a little hesitant and I thought I would just stand and photograph the whole ritual. I am glad I did because with such a lot of elephants they tend to behave like a herd, and guess what, the first elephant lifted her tail and deposited a huge dump just in the water and then hey presto, just like a herd of cows (I am a vet's wife) the others did too. Somehow the idea of wading around in elephant 'poo' did not have an immediate appeal. Tara was slightly more refined and never did anything so unladylike within our view on that happy occasion in 2002. So, I was happy to snap away with the camera and have some wonderful photographs as a result.

Watching, learning and participating in various activities involving elephants is such a good thing for young Indians and their children; I had done this from a small child myself, though in truth had never washed an elephant and entered the river myself when small, but if these wonderful animals, the world's largest terrestrial mammals, are going to be given a realistic space in which to flourish then India's young thrusting population must be educated as to their needs and intrinsic beauty, not just as an occasional exotic living ornament for a festival or marriage day. It is interesting to find in research that in centuries past men who came to conquer India were all amazed and delighted when they discovered the Indian Elephant, and those rulers of India who rose through the various Indian dynasties were men who valued the elephant for itself, not just as an early fighting machine or ceremonial animal to enhance their stature amongst their subjects. The current rulers of India should consider their proud history and remember their own role as custodians of their country's magnificent animals and birds – denizens of the great Indian jungles; otherwise they will find that future generations of humans will suffocate in their own man-made concrete jungles.

At the risk of repeating myself I will quote Gandhiji:

"All creatures have an equal right to live on this earth."

With great reluctance we took our leave of all at Orange County who had made our stay so happy; we continued to Hassan and just past Hassan we arrived at The Hoysala Village hotel. This is a strange hotel that belongs to Trails of India, one of the Ramapuram enterprises. We received a warm welcome and were comfortable for one night. I can only think the owners bought this rather strange conglomeration of rooms set in a pleasant garden with swimming pool from someone else. The food was actually quite good and the place was overrun with French people. The French, and I have a quarter French blood in me through my grandmother Aline, have a capacity for bowling round India, talking loudly, never smiling, taking over all the chairs, commandeering the majority of whatever facility is on offer and caring not a jot for other guests – moreover they almost shout in French to bemused young Indians who are just supposed to know what they want; I had thought it was only the British who ran around the world imperiously shouting demands on the basis that if one shouts doubtless the other race will understand better! As for learning a few gracious words, goodness me no, even President Chirac walked out of a press conference because a junior colleague dared to respond in English, so young men who speak Kannada, and then some English, perhaps Hindi too, if they do not understand French are not worthy of consideration – a rather sad reflection really on a proud country.

We had come to this area to visit the famous Hoysala temples of Halebidu and Belur. There is a third equally wonderful temple at Somnathpur built in 1268, which was the last of this great architecture; Somnathpur is quite close to Mysore and thus very accessible for anyone who spends a few days in Mysore.

Hoysala architecture is characterised by its star-shaped plan and rich surface decoration. Hoysala kings during the 12th and 13th centuries were responsible for this particular architectural flowering. They embody a fusion of the curving towers (*shikharas*) of North India and the columned *mandapas* of the south. Hoysala mandapa interiors have massive highly polished lathe-turned columns and sharp ridges, quite unlike other temple column architecture. Every surface of the exterior is richly carved and sculpted with religious and mythological scenes and bracket figures. Halebidu is a small town beside a tank (lake) called Dorasamudra, which apparently was also the town's original name. Certainly it is a perfect location and I think one of the hotel owning groups should try and secure some land and build a beautiful small hotel on the banks of the water. The Halebidu temple of Hoysaleshvara was begun in 1121 by King Vishnuvardhana, but never finished. This structure consists of a pair of identical temples, each with its own east-facing linga sanctuary opening on to a hall and a screened porch. Each temple is also preceded by a pavilion with a huge statue of Nandi, the bull on which Shiva rides. The sheer beauty and intricacy of the carvings is breathtaking. I enjoyed my visit but was put off by a very grumpy custodian who was rude. This is a sin that besets so many in

Hoysala temple at Halebidu

officialdom in India, and is unforgivable on what are essentially tourist
sites. However, unless someone in authority makes routine checks
and disciplines individuals it will continue. The site was pleasant
and we arrived early in the afternoon so the sun was at its zenith
and I had forgotten to bring any socks; being a religious building
we were required to take off our shoes to walk around. In the end
I did not, it was roasting to the feet and I remained on the ground
at this particular temple. I was also disgusted to see that locals who
had used the offices of a local caterer then just discarded their paper
plates and detritus in the temple grounds; I glared at the supervisor
of the caterer, who promptly officiously ordered the female to pick up
the litter but naturally did nothing himself. Funnily enough the whole
incident soured my impression; what is the point of coming all this
way to look at wonderful ancient beauty when modern India behaves
in a disgraceful manner; this is a conundrum for Indians themselves to
solve. We were the only foreign visitors to this and the second living
temple at Belur.

The Belur temple called Chennakeshava was built in 1117 by
Vishnuvardhana to commemorate the Hoysala triumph over the Cholas.
The entrance to the temple is marked by a huge gopura erected by the
kings of Vijayanagar in the 16th century. Inside is a spacious paved
courtyard surrounded by subsidiary shrines and colonnades, much
like the great temple complexes we had experienced in Tamil Nadu.
It was all very beautiful and well maintained. I did take my shoes off
but my goodness though they had rather coarse red mats on which to

walk it was still like walking on hot coals because the mats did not stretch everywhere and sometimes one just had to bound to a place in the shade just to cool off. Again, that sort of thing should be properly thought out because it is not only unpleasant but actually puts tourists off who will tell others not to bother to put themselves through pain and discomfort. Coconut matting is just the cheapest thing in India and the authorities could buy a whole new comprehensive set at the start of every season or perhaps replenish it every two months.

This is a wonderful piece of intricate architecture. In the centre is the main temple with a single star-shaped sanctuary opening onto a columned hall fronted by a screened porch. The entire exterior surface is again intricately carved. I was inclined to photograph all the friezes involving elephants. We employed a guide on this occasion and he was good; when returning to collect our shoes I bought a few postcards and came across a man selling small brass statues of deities. I try always to buy something from these folk because this is their livelihood, so I asked him for diminutive Vishnu and Lakshmi figures; he had them and now I have put them on my mantel shelf. The Belur temple is a temple dedicated to Vishnu, which pleased me.

Khajuraho would be the place most similar to these in the intricate exterior sculpting and carving of every available space. It is apparent that the arts, music, dancing and sexuality were all seen as interrelated in worship and pleasure. The arts were used to display religious fervour, the joy of a victory in battle, or simply to give domestic pleasure and it is also evident that women played an important part in all sides of life with prominent female participation in public affairs. Curiously we in Europe went through a sort of Victorian prudery, and currently in India all forms of sexual contact like kissing and hugging in public is severely frowned upon but in Europe there is a return through film and television of flagrant sexuality. It seems that humanity goes through expressive and repressive cultures be they in the east or the west.

There is one more wonderful ancient place I must record. Sranvanabelagola is one of the most ancient and important Jain pilgrimage centres in India. The huge naked statue of Bahubali (Gomateshvara) is said to be the world's tallest monolithic statue. It overlooks the town of Sravanabelagola; the name means the Monk of the White Pond. The simplicity of this statue is in complete contrast to the intricacy of the two temple complexes. It is thought that Chandragupta Maurya came here with is guru, Bhagwan Bhadrabahu Swami, after renouncing his kingdom in the 3rd century BC. Bhadrabahu's disciples spread his teaching all over the region, and thus was Jainism established in the south. The Gangas who ruled this part of India became powerful patrons and Jainism reached the zenith of its influence in the period between the 4th and 10th centuries.

Every twelve years the Gomateshvara statue is the subject of a spectacular ceremony. During this extraordinary event this small town becomes the centre for pilgrimage and for tourists from all over the world who worship in the Jain faith. The statue's head is anointed with thousands of pots of coconut milk, yoghurt, ghee, bananas, almonds, poppy seeds, milk, saffron and sandalwood – and gold coins. Devotees reach the head from the top from scaffolding that is especially erected for the purpose. The clean up procedure afterwards must be a huge operation; the last such ritual took place in 2005! Again, I should warn that this statue is only reached by climbing 614 rock cut steps which can become scalding hot.

I was glad that we had decided to visit these historic sights, but our main interest was to the north and we knew we had a long hard road ahead of us to reach Hampi, and indeed we were right – it took over six hours with just a short stop at Chitradurga. Chitradurga has a wonderful old fort, but is otherwise a truly ugly industrial town, a sort of crossroads in Karnataka with developing highways crossing at this point. We had been advised to stop and stay at a particular hotel but when we arrived it was so truly awful that I considered the advisor either does not have a clue, or was playing a joke; I was just thankful that we were only stopping for lunch. As it was, the place was so dreadful that we just had a coke out of a bottle with a straw and used

Temple carvings in Karnataka

the facilities! Curiously we met some American non-resident Indians who were touring with the help of a map of India; I mean a map of the whole of India so they had no idea of how huge the distances are and thus had grand expectations that would never be met! Quite extraordinary really we thought to be so ill-prepared.

Chapter Nineteen

Hampi or Vijayanagar – the City of Victory

At the very end of the 19th century Robert Sewell a British civil servant discovered the ruins of Vijayanagar; he quoted a 16th century traveller in his book A Forgotten Empire, "Never perhaps in the history of the world has such havoc been wrought, and wrought suddenly, on so splendid a city teeming with a wealthy and industrious population in the full plenitude of prosperity one day, and on the next seized, pillaged, and reduced to ruins, amid scenes of savage massacre and horrors beggaring description".

Sadly, Robert Sewell was speaking before the various atrocities witnessed in the 20th century where speed, stealth and total devastation have become synonymous with savage acts of war, when inevitably and most cruelly the weak, vulnerable and innocent become the tragic victims as well as the defeated armies of an enemy.

In 1565 Vijayanagar suffered just such a disastrous onslaught from the combined armies of Bijapur, Golconda and Ahmednagar and the empire went into terminal decline and this most beautiful of cities was left to rot and disintegrate after systematic pillaging and vengeful destruction. I have long wanted to visit Hampi – as it is now known but it is quite difficult to reach and requires time and patience to absorb. Unless one is a backpacker or serial traveller ordinary life sometimes does not allow for these journeys. Now we would be reaching our destination soon and I was so pleased at the prospect.

However, continuing our drive from Chitradurga was quite interesting in its own way. Essentially one is travelling by this time on one of India's national highways, NH 13, which would take you up to the north, and the road is very busy with huge lorries. The early part of the journey until Chitradurga had been very challenging from Hassan. Pratap was excellent but we had to drive across country sometimes on the top of dam walls to reach a really decent road. I knew that Karnataka's infrastructure was poor but for the ordinary western traveller this was a case of returning to the India of my childhood and sometimes quite worrying; had we reached some sort of immovable obstacle despite being in a 4 x 4 vehicle it would have been a long way to retrace our tracks. I think the majority of tourists come up by night train from Bangalore, and indeed that is a sensible way to travel, particularly in first class and our first thought, but as Thomas pointed out there really was no guarantee that we would find a reputable driver and roadworthy vehicle to then take us all the way west and out to Goa. So we had abandoned the train travel idea, but I noticed that a party of French came by train as did another pair of westerners. These package tourists come up by train, spend two nights perhaps, usually only one, and return to Bangalore; that is not what I recommend because there is so much to see in this area of Karnataka and realistically it can only be achieved by road. I am hoping that in a couple of years the roads will have improved enormously judging by the road works, which though rather 'cottage industry' by western standards are achieving improvements generally, though painfully slowly.

The countryside had changed dramatically and was now quite arid but with the addition of sunflowers as a crop along with cotton; the rocky landscape is quite spectacular. Goats in large herds were to be seen everywhere, usually with a young goatherd lazily making sure the kids were safe and not straying into the path of the traffic. There were huge wind turbines all along the ridge of hills in the distance. They seemed to be the spikes on the spine of peninsular India. I hope they will prove useful in adding to the nation's energy solutions, but I do know that here in Scotland where they seem to be proliferating people actually have a very negative view of them and the forecast for their value as energy providers seems quite muted.

At long last we reached the outskirts of Hospet where we would be staying. It is a busy but totally underwhelming town full of institutions belonging to the region or indeed the whole country, and were it to be seriously cleaned up it could have some attraction; as it is for most travellers it is the railhead and jumping off point to visit Hampi which is about twelve kilometres away.

We asked for directions and finally found the Malligi Hotel. It is the only 'game in town' and I have to say quite awful. Sometimes when I write I find a euphemistic way to describe something which I found ugly, dirty or unappealing. Well this time I am going to say that this is the most awful hotel I have experienced in recent years; it is dirty decaying and totally repelling. There are two parts to this hotel. One that had been built in the 1950s I think which resembles a gaol. Sadly we had been consigned a room with bathroom in this old decrepit wing. It was so dreadful that for a few minutes Graham and

I just looked at each other before we could find some reaction. From time to time in dire movies one finds a character living in a sleazy hotel in whatever country – well this place should audition for location shooting. Moreover there are all sorts of minions who just hang about doing nothing. The hotel was full because it is the only place in town and recommended by Karnataka State Tourism. I cannot think what French, Germans and others find to say when they arrive after a long tedious journey. We decided to go and look around and I looked at the grounds where preparations were being made for some evening entertainment to do with a convention. The swimming pool nearby asked people not to 'allow urine in the pool' and the idea of entering it was totally repellent! I decided to voice my extreme dissatisfaction – now that is a euphemism; the management took in what I said and called a Front of House manager who apologised and said they were totally full but he would see if he could move us the next day. Eventually the General Manager came and introduced himself and waffled on. We decided to be firm but as polite as we could. The only thing to do was to get out of there and into the fresh air of Hampi in the setting sun. We asked for Pratap who also signified that he thought the place a total dump. I was determined that this very bad experience

Iconic stone chariot at Hampi – Vijaynagar

would not overshadow this visit to see Hampi which was really the focus of this huge trip.

Driving to Hampi is pleasurable through villages and pleasant countryside with all the relics of a past empire around one. The area is covered in rocky outcrops but has lush groves of bananas and coconut in between which gives a wonderful contrast to the beiges and pinks of the rocks. We arrived and just started walking about and almost immediately the magic of the place took over and we forgot the vexed hotel. The sun was low in the sky and all the ruined buildings and walls and statues and rocky hillsides were being bathed in a rosy glow that always enhances. Our photography has worked really well and it was so peaceful with very few people around. Pratap then drove us to the parking area near to the actual Hampi Bazaar and then we walked through the street, the actual medieval street that is now thronged with modern day India. We did not stop to look at the various shops but just walked up the steps to find a perfect vantage point from which to look over the whole vista and landscape and watch the sun set. There was an eclectic mix of people doing the same thing but in no way was it crowded that evening. The pie dogs played around and frightened a young Japanese man and then they lay down almost as a dance routine and lapped up the warmth of the rock; monkeys frolicked about and people murmured and enjoyed the experience.

The buildings and relics of Hampi or Vijayanagar's imperial city are spread over twenty-six square kilometres and include a citadel area, a temple area, bazaars, fortifications, river landings and gateways. This place is not the size of Fatehpur Sikri, or Orchha or Mandu, it is so much bigger; and indeed the famous quotation from the Portuguese traveller Fernao Nuniz who wrote, "What I saw...seemed as large as Rome and very beautiful to the sight..." is apt. At its zenith this place had the same population of renaissance Rome, half a million people, and to India it had immense importance as the nucleus of a large proud empire that ruled the whole of peninsular India very successfully – it was in fact the last great Hindu empire.

Merchants and ambassadors from foreign lands used to travel to Vijayanagar to do business and conduct diplomacy and each and every one of them wrote in their journals about the beauty and prosperity of the place and its peoples. Sitting on the warmed stone I looked around and realised how the magnificent granite boulders acted as a natural fortress for Hampi. Some of them are believed to be at least a thousand million years old. It is quite easy to see why wonderful monoliths were carved from the big ones. The Tungabhadra River itself is very beautiful and is considered sacred and a pilgrimage site.

The original capital of this area was at Anegondi which lies on the opposite bank of the Tungabhadra River. There is a bridge under construction but because Hampi is a UNESCO World Heritage Site there was understandable controversy about whether the increased traffic that a new bridge would encourage would destabilise the monuments and ancient buildings. Apparently this has been resolved and the bridge building will continue but in the meantime one has to cross the river by coracle. There is apparently quite a good place to stay on the other side but that would have meant ferrying everything across in a coracle and leaving Pratap on this side with the car. We preferred to stay in our awful lodgings but in close contact with Pratap. Hampi is a mecca for young travellers who stay in the simple lodgings in Hampi Bazaar; they usually arrive by bus and some stay for days if not weeks just walking around soaking up the atmosphere. There is a peace about the whole place that if one is not restricted by time would make staying on attractive and people can hire bicycles or small motor bikes and move around freely. However, this is not a developed attraction and indeed Karnataka State Tourism should manage it more seriously and productively along with The Archaeological Survey of India. Fortunately I know that Orange County and maybe even CGH Earth are planning resorts somewhere close which will help to make it the new Khajuraho for foreign tourists and maybe an Indian honeymoon destination. Certainly if the airport that exists somewhere near, which I never found, could be developed this would become a wonderful tourist destination. I read that 'millions' of people visit Hampi in boastful literature published by Karnataka State Tourism; the overall figure for tourist numbers is about four million visitors to India in total annually so I do not see how these claims are justified.

As luck would have it just as I changed my film, having snapped one lovely photograph of the sun setting, my camera jammed with a sort of gritty sound. We have a digital camera that Graham was operating and my trusty 35 mm camera; the latter ground to a halt and I think sadly is not worth repairing. The air was tinged with blue not pink around me at this point, but thankfully that last shot of the sun on the old film is very good. I found a disposable camera in the hotel's shop which I used the next day with amazingly good results and have had it developed together with a disk.

In the early 14th century when large parts of northern India were under Muslim rule this area in peninsular India was part of the Hindu kingdom of Kampili. Mohammed bin Tughlaq, the ruler of Delhi defeated and killed the king of Kampili in 1326. Two brothers, Harihara and Bukka, were among the thousands taken prisoners and they were forced to convert to Islam. Some years later the Sultan sent the two brothers back to the area as governors of the province. In 1336 they strengthened their position, and laid the foundation of an independent kingdom, reverted to Hinduism and renounced allegiance to the Tughlaqs. That was the inception of the Sangama dynasty with its citadel in Vijayanagar. It is thought that the original name was probably Vidyanagar after the great Hindu wise man Vidyaranya.

The zenith of this empire was in the reign of Krishnadeva Raya who ruled from 1509 to 1529; he was the greatest of all the monarchs and travellers from Arabia and Italy came to his court as did the Portuguese from Goa, but it was the secular and tolerant attitude of all the Vijayanagar kings that made it such a special place with the coexistence of different forms of worship, Jainism, Vaishnavism, Shaivism, Naga (snake) and Tree worship, all coexisted with the Advaita school of thought and also Islam. The various saint composers and the minstrels and religious poets who spread devotional messages to the population were also revered, with many shrines built to commemorate them. The architecture that evolved over three centuries was fashioned in the later Chalukyan and Jaina styles.

Portuguese engineers were reputed to have created the ingenious irrigation system of stone aqueducts and gravity led water channels which allowed this barren land to flower into a lush place of orchards and rose gardens. Graham and I saw one of these ancient aqueducts

Looking out over the ruined city of Hampi-Vijaynagar

still working very well amongst some of the roadside fields and banana groves.

The Persian Abdur Razak has written in the 14th century, "The City of Bijanagar (Vijayanagara) is such that the eye has not seen nor ear heard of any place resembling it upon the whole earth. It is so built that it has seven fortified walls, one within the other…the fortress is in the form of a circle, situated on the summit of a hill…from the third to the seventh fortress, shops and bazaars are closely crowded together…there are four bazaars, situated opposite to one other…" Looking at its ruins over 400 hundred years later I can understand what he meant. Just to give you an idea of the size, we had to drive about eight kilometres to reach the Vitthala Temple from the Royal Enclosure. There is a shorter way along the river bank but that does not allow for a vehicle.

After the fall of Hampi in 1565, seven more rulers, powerless and struggling, presided over a reduced and tattered empire till its end in 1646. The Mysore Wodeyars and the Keladi Nayaks grew in influence. The rest of the south of India was fragmented and ruled by local chieftains and the Bijapur Sultanate. Eventually the Mughal Sultanate of Delhi under Aurangzeb, and the Marathas under the great patriot Shivaji gained control of the entire Deccan.

It should be remembered that at its zenith with around 300 large and small ports *Vijayanagara* had a flourishing overseas trade; cloth, rice, precious stones, iron ore, timber and spices were exported to Portugal, Southern Africa, Abyssinia, Persia and Arabia in the west, and to Burma, Malaya and China in the east.

Art and culture and architecture had flourished with the Hampi temples; those at Sringeri, Lepakshi and Vellore are also amongst the best examples. Vijayanagara kings gave generously to embellish and add to the famous temples about which I have already written at Chidambaram, Madurai and Kanchipuram in Tamil Nadu. The music which I described earlier, Carnatak classical music, evolved its form in this age and some of the greatest Kannada and Telegu works of literature were written in this period of domination.

The Vijayanagara navy defeated the Sinhala ruler in northern Sri Lanka between 1424 and 1446. An Italian traveller Philippo Sasseti wrote in 1585 after the sack of Hampi that, "Vijayanagara had such great traffic going through the streets that it was beyond imagination, and that there dwelt in it very rich people not (merely) as rich as the people of our country but as Cresus (sic) and other rich in days gone by…"

After the sun had set we strolled through the Hampi Bazaar, but we were tired and decided that we wanted to return to our dreadful room and shower and have something to eat. Pratap had driven for so long that it was inconsiderate to keep him vigilant when he too just wanted to relax. Driving back in the twilight is a time I like watching village life winding down for the day and seeing all the beasts – buffaloes, cows and goats – going home virtually by themselves.

We went to discover the restaurant, which was very busy with locals eating out as well as travellers and the noise of the rowdy convention alongside. On close inspection the hotel restaurant was pretty awful too, shabby and falling apart, but the waiters were helpful and friendly and the food turned out to be quite good and multi-cuisine. That first night in the gaol-like room was passable, but the air conditioner stopped functioning though fortunately the fan worked once the electricity came into force again; there were wrought iron bars on the window with frosted glass. The room was decorated in striped formica in pink and beige with a dingy central light…thank goodness we had brought up some bottled water for the night. Graham muttered something about what he endures for my love of India, and I concurred!

The following morning we were up bright and early and packed up all our things in the hope that we would be moved to the modern wing. Thankfully when we returned at lunchtime this had been accomplished and we were installed in a normal hotel suite with functioning air conditioning and a reasonable bathroom and television and lighting. It was not good however, all the signs of neglect and decay were in this room too but we thanked the staff for the move.

Hampi in the early morning light was beautiful. Frankly there is so much to enjoy that I cannot list it all but I will give an idea of our favourite monuments. It is essential to try and arrive early whilst it is still cool because then by lunchtime one has seen most things. Then a return once again in the evening light is essential and one can revisit the Vitthalla Temple for the floodlighting which makes it beautiful in another dimension – but this only takes place at weekends. Naturally if one can spend three or four days it would be even better; that hopefully will be the lure with new hotel complexes being built in the area.

We started that lovely morning with the famous statue of Sasivekalu Ganesh which means 'mustard seed' Ganesh. This is a simple but beautiful pavilion with a benevolent huge statue of Ganesh on the way to the Virupaksha temple and it was looking so lovely in the morning light. I was glad to see that the ASI have landscaped the area around it and made it a pleasing feature. You must have gathered that I too love Ganesh so this was a good start, but I do not understand the epithet of *Sasive Kalu* which is supposed to be funny. In ignorance I do not know why.

The Virupaksha Temple has wonderful pillared corridors and an inner courtyard which others would find interesting; we however had recently within the year probably seen our fill of temples so gave it a miss, but situated as it is at the end of the bazaar street with its own great wooden chariot housed close by it is an obvious first point of call. In the middle of the river there is a boulder which sanctifies the flowing waters with sculptures of Nandi and Ganesh carved into the rocks. The monolithic statue of Lakshmi- Narasimha which is partially mutilated is a wonder; now situated in a walled enclosure it is quite stunning and one of the iconic images of Hampi along with the monolithic carved stone chariot; it stands 6.7 metres high, and originally it was a four armed figure of Narasimha, the man-lion incarnation of Vishnu, with the goddess Lakshmi perched on one thigh and a seven-hooded Naga, the snake god, curved protectively over his head. Next to it is the famous gigantic lingam which is in a pool of water. We had an interesting diversion at this point. A European man, with long pony-tailed hair, came along and leapt the gate of the Narasimha statue and proceeded to worship it ostentatiously whilst his female companion looked on. The old woman employed by the ASI as an attendant came to gently remonstrate with him but they seemed to end up rubbing noses which was all rather endearing! Graham and I were intrigued by the different sorts of people who were drawn to Hampi. I looked around at the coconut trees and country area and tried to imagine all this in the height of its glory. Young children started to gently pester me to buy postcards and I bought from a girl, it would make her day, and then of course I had to buy from the boy as well. Then along came a disabled lad riding a sort of modified tricycle and it seemed right to give him something...and then a very old man hobbled up and asked for money; well he was given some too. Why not; here we are privileged people with so many choices who had come as a 'leisure activity' to look at bygone wonders. These people exist amongst these ruins and eke out a living. They were all happy and I took a photograph of them together.

The Queen's Bath, the Krishna Temple, the Mahanavami Dibba or Platform, the beautiful Stepped Tank, the Lotus Mahal, the Elephant Stables, the King's Balance, the Vitthala Temple and the wonderful monolithic Chariot, the aqueducts, the view of Jaina temples with their stepped pyramidal towers on the Hemakuta hill, the Hazara Rama temple, the stone door, well, it just goes on and on. Just looking at the huge walls with their massive stone blocks is fascinating and slightly reminiscent of Chichinitza in Mexico; I felt there were quite a few similarities between this architecture and the Mayan wonders of Mexico.

Some buildings have a special attraction: I loved the stone carvings on every surface of the Mahanavami Dibba the enormous twelve metre high plinth on which the king would sit for great festivals like Dussehra. In fact the Dussehra celebrations here at Vijayanagar influenced the ones that have become so famous at Mysore. The Stepped Well or Tank is so beautiful and symmetrical with the carved joined stone aqueducts bringing water to it; this must have been a ceremonial bathing place for monarchs. The Lotus Mahal is a pretty building but they were clever enough to apparently pour water down its walls from the second floor which would then have the breeze blowing in and thereby creating an early form of air conditioning – that is the method used in desert coolers which are still very effective. I loved the Elephant Stables which are very grand and each stable has a dome that is architecturally different from its neighbour. The Guards Quarters nearby I think might have been elephant keepers' quarters. The area called the Royal Enclosure has been beautified with some nice landscaping, but in fact quite a bit more should be done to enhance the whole area.

The finest temple in Hampi is the Vitthala Temple built by Krishna Deva Raya and dedicated to Lord Vishnu as Vitthala. The slender pillars when struck give off a different noise and are therefore considered musical. People are asked not to keep trying them out as a sort of stone xylophone but inevitably they do.

We returned in the evening and wandered down to the river and watched young people either having fun or bathing or washing. It was rather beautiful and I was looking forward to the floodlighting of the temple. It was past six o'clock in the evening and the lighting is

Vitthala Temple at Hampi-Vijaynagar

supposed to start at about six thirty and last for two hours. Typical of greedy minor officials we were then told it was only starting at 7.30; some Germans nearby meanwhile were being hassled by a security guard and asked for entrance money. During the day one does have to pay to see the Vitthala Temple but for the evening light show it is free and advertised as such. They would not give in to the guard's demands and when I arrived I said we would go in and immediately was given the same sort of treatment. So I replied very firmly that in that case I would leave and as a government guest would have something to say about all this. Pratap joined in and then an Indian apologised and entered the fray; of course it was free and should start at 6.30. The guards had thought they could exploit the situation; I have seen the sort of shameful behaviour before. Suddenly quite a lot of people arrived and then the lights were switched on. As the sky turned blue and then black it was very beautiful. One of these days perhaps the authorities will produce a son et lumiere production on the weekends.

We had met a young Australian girl by chance and enjoyed talking with her. She had come to India to stand as the 'best friend' to a fellow Australian who was marrying a girl from Jaipur. This had been

The ceremonial step well at Hampi-Vijaynagar

a wonderful experience and now she was travelling round India and then going to do some speech therapy work in Bangladesh. Graham was concerned, she had walked all the way from Hampi Bazaar alone, but now was faced with the prospect of walking back alone in the dark – with just a torch. This was most unwise; as she said some groups of young men had called out to her along the way. Graham sought her out when we were leaving and offered to take her back in the car; I have read in the Indian press of foreign women or girls being mugged or raped and it is very unwise to put oneself in such a vulnerable position. Instead we went back together to the Bazaar and wandered into a few shops. We found what I wanted as a gift in one and then we parted company. I liked her immensely and hope her trip continues happily and safely.

We left Hospet early the next morning as we had a long way to go. I do not expect that we shall ever go back to Hampi but I most heartily recommend it to anyone really interested in visiting India.

Chapter Twenty

Crocodiles and Coracles

On our way west we visited Lakkundi. This small, modest village has temples dating from the 11th to 12th centuries – the Kalyana Chalukya period. They have been well conserved but I think are very little visited and are poorly signposted. There are in fact fifty temples but the most ornate and spectacular of these is the Kasi Vishwanatha Temple. I actually liked seeing such architectural wonders right in the middle of a normal village; they are no longer living temples but nevertheless life is going on around them and after we had walked around and photographed them we continued in the car and saw all the women outside their little houses together with babies and livestock. Sometimes it is just nice to find oneself in a living village with its place of worship or monuments that provide a focus and have stood the test of centuries. This village has a water pump, a water tank, electricity and I have no doubt television for the wealthier residents; its children do go to school; there is modern transport and it is a microcosm of the modern India that just happens to have a thousand year old group of temples within its heart.

North west of Hospet and Hampi is yet another wonderful World Heritages Site at Pattadakal, which is close to Badami and Aihole. All these architectural gems are quite close together but at the end of another long road journey. Further north from them is Bijapur. One day it will be possible I think to fly in and visit all these places but in the meantime the alternative is really only road; the rail link does go to Badami but even driving from Goa it is a long way and quite challenging.

Bijapur's most celebrated building is the tomb of Muhammad Adil Shah, the second son of Ibrahim II. The building is commonly known as the *Gol Gumbaz* or round dome. I am told it is the second largest dome in the world, second only to St Peter's Basilica in Rome, unsupported by pillars. Its most distinguished features are the seven-storeyed octagonal spires at the four corners and the heavy bracketed cornice below the parapet. It is an enormous cube of stone and masonry capped by a gigantic dome. The whispering gallery, which distinctly echoes the faintest whisper eleven times, is remarkable. Completed in 1659 this tomb stands in a formal garden and there is a small mosque on the west side. The second mausoleum of note is that of Ibrahim Rauza and it is often described as the finest Islamic building in the Deccan. It may have inspired the Taj Mahal in Agra. The Adil Shahi sultans made Bijapur their capital having defeated the Bahmani sultans who had Gulbarga as their capital during the 14th and 15th centuries. The Citadel is in the heart of the city and surrounded by a wide moat. Within its walls are many small palaces and halls and even outside the walled city the area is rich in monuments built by the Adil Shahi sultans. The Jami Masjid was begun by Ali Adil Shah I in 1576 but never completed. To this day the mosque attracts more than 2,000 worshippers during Friday prayers and is a truly beautiful building with graceful arches, aisles, halls, intricate designs and large onion dome. Writings from the Koran in gold are carefully preserved. Truly in this northern area of what is now Karnataka there was a veritable flowering of Islamic architecture right from the 14th to the 17th centuries.

Long before that however, from the 4th to 8th centuries, the great and powerful Chalukya kings who ruled the Deccan created architectural wonders that are breathtaking to this day.

Badami is another town with less than prepossessing hotels, but it is

Temple at Lakkundi

210

situated within a horseshoe of red sandstone cliffs overlooking a large lake. This was the capital of the Chalukyan kings and has a wealth of beauty in both cave architecture and temples. The land was called Karnata Desa or the Land of the Black Earth and to this day that is how the tilled soil looks, but with acres of sunflower and cotton fields as I described earlier. The Chalukyas became a major power after casting off the yoke of their Kadama overlords in the 6th century. Their kings have huge names like Kirtivarman and Pulakeshin II; Harshvardhana, the ruler of Kannauj who was one of the greatest emperors of ancient India tried to invade the Chalukyan kingdom in AD 641 but was defeated by Pulakeshin II.

There are four caves at Badami that are rich in carving rather similar to Ellora and Ajanta. Cave One has a beautiful Nataraja panel and Cave Two is distinguished by its frieze of Varaha, the boar incarnation of Vishnu, with a row of dwarfs carved beneath it. Cave Three has an inscription giving the date that can be chronicled as AD 578; it is large and very beautiful with a veranda with an enormous four-armed figure of Vishnu seated on Adisesha, the serpent whose five hoods protect his crown. The fourth cave has standing and seated Jain tirthankaras covering the walls. The whole area of Badami is like an open air museum but sadly it is not a place to linger because unless one is totally dedicated to temples and ancient carvings the hotel facilities are minimal and one is not inclined to stay long. I do seriously hope that either the Indian Government or that of Karnataka State looks at the potential here for tourism; there is a huge wealth of ancient beauty but people will not go all that way if they cannot relax and live comfortably whilst sightseeing. The temperatures, the journey and local terrain do not make it conducive to relaxation, so the authorities must encourage someone in a big hotel group to open something special and perhaps construct an airport nearby which would serve all these ancient places.

Aihole is a tranquil village on the banks of the Malaprabha River and this place is acclaimed as the cradle of Hindu temple architecture. There are hundreds of temples in the villages and fields nearby. The most impressive one is the Durga Temple with its semicircular apse, elevated plinth and the gallery encircling the sanctum. The Lad Khan Temple, which is one of the earliest built, was originally a royal assembly hall and marriage *mandapa* chosen as the abode of a Muslim prince – Lad Khan.

Pattadakal has a lovely location also on the banks of the Malprabha River and is the crowning glory of Chalukyan architecture and thus the UNESCO World Heritage Site; the name is a corruption of Pattada-Kisuvolal meaning Stone of Coronation and this is where Chalukyan kings came to be crowned. I find similarities with Mamallapuram in both size and exquisite architecture. Ptolemy, the famous geographer, refers to the place as Petrigal in his writings (c. AD 150). This is where one sees the blend of northern Indian Nagara style with southern Indian Dravida styles of architecture which, if you consider that this place is almost at the centre of India and thus became a melting pot and blend of the best of both. Temples as an institution only evolved in the Gupta period around AD 350, when the sacrifice-centric Vedic religion was replaced by a more personal form of worship which we now call *puja*. The old gods which had largely comprised natural forces and phenomena gradually took on anthropomorphic forms and these newly-conceived deities required to be housed in suitably ornate and splendid shrines.

In southern India where the great temples, as I have shown throughout this book, have whole communities and enclosed property, they own land and cattle and employ hundreds of musicians, florists, cooks and artisans; they had in fact become the nuclei for urban settlements. In medieval Europe this is exactly what happened around the great monasteries and cathedral closes; indeed in England in the 16th century Henry VIII was so angry with the Pope and guilt ridden because of his thwarted determination to discard a wife and take a new one that he shed his Roman Catholic loyalties and espoused a whole new form of Christianity that became the Church of England and gave him the excuse to plunder and decimate the wealth and power of the medieval monasteries. So much art and architecture was lost during that monarchical 'tantrum'. Here too in Scotland the Roman Church was largely discarded and the new Calvinist theocracy was borne. It too robbed our small country of so much beautiful church music and other religious flowering and probably added to the habitual taciturn and slightly melancholic character of many Scots.

We finally arrived at Dandeli via Hubli. The latter is another unremarkable but prosperous looking town which does have a train station. The terrain changed quite markedly and became altogether prettier with forestation and lush fields. This too had been another huge car journey and we arrived in Dandeli after a six-hour drive and found that the Kali Adventure Camp is very close by – just in time for lunch. We were so glad to arrive and relax and find a pleasant, spacious but simple room with good en-suite facilities. I do not mean to harp on about hotels but most of us are in holiday mode when we travel; we are not intrepid explorers, so we do want a bit of clean comfort, hygienic food and water and a pleasant ambience with amiable staff helping to achieve all this! The older one gets the less one wants to 'pig it'!

Taking the coracle back to camp at Kali

The Dandeli Wildlife Sanctuary is the second largest in Karnataka, sprawling over an area of 843.16 square kilometres in the Western Ghats of Uttara Kannada district. Kali boast that they are the only place south of the Himalayas where one can experience white water rafting for most months of the year. Certainly it had been a draw card for lots of young people holidaying in Goa who arrived the next day full of anticipation. Set on the banks of the River Kali the camp's tented cottages offer a very pleasant way to relax. We in fact were accommodated in the main building block but it too had a pleasant veranda and the high ceilings with fans gave us some coolness which was very welcome. Kali also belongs to Jungle Lodges & Resorts and is situated about five hours driving from Goa. The claim that it is a mere two and a half hours from Dabolim airport in Goa is wrong, because the most direct way is in awful condition and we drove the good road down to Karwar and then up into Goa and it took all of five hours.

There are many attractions with white water rafting, kayaking, canoe tours, canyoning and coracle rides. Mountain biking, trekking and bird watching, a visit to tribal settlements and an excursion to the Kavala Caves and Siroli Peak are also on offer. Naturally the most attractive activity on offer for us was going into the huge park and outer reaches of the Dandeli Forest to see animals.

We had two jungle safaris in the company of a very charming Indian family. There were two young sons who were so well behaved and articulate and good in the jeep. They seemed genuinely enthused about all the wildlife and knowledgeable with it; I felt so happy that here was a family being educated in the beauties of their own country's wild and wonderful places and its wonderful animals. We saw langur monkeys, gaur, two wild dogs, and the giant Malabar squirrels. Jackals, barking deer, hares, woolly necked storks, the Malabar Trogan, which is a rare bird, the famous Malabar whistling thrush, giant hornbills, the Nilgiri flycatcher – any amount of kingfishers, grey shrikes, a white-eyed buzzard, bulbuls, wagtails, moorhens and peacocks. The youngsters were longing to see a black panther for which Dandeli is famous but sadly we did not have that excitement.

However, on the second morning we set off really early in the dark and were speeding along one of the main roads and suddenly right in the middle were three men all sitting crossed legged and meditating. Naturally we had to come to an abrupt halt and our Indian friend remarked dryly that he quite understood that many people had faith in the divine, but that was taking trust a little too far! The villages we passed were rather attractive and we had so enjoyed climbing to a viewpoint to watch the sun set over the miles of Dandeli Forest which were covered in a misty haze the previous evening – that was very reminiscent of Scotland!

After breakfast we were invited mid-morning to experience a coracle ride on the Kali river which would drift over some gentle cascades. It was pointed out that the river had plenty of supposedly fish-eating crocodiles. We were not to be at all worried at that prospect! I reasoned that plenty of local folk appeared to be washing their clothes and indeed themselves in the river, so on this occasion man and beast had come to some sort of amiable arrangement; we entered the coracle and set off. I had seen the coracles at Kabini and photographed others enjoying going round in circles and was a little nervous about a fast flowing river. The Kali has optimum water levels because the dam further upstream dispenses water and the levels are monitored. It was a delight. The coracle operator knew exactly what he was doing and just told us to hold on firmly to the middle seating arrangement – it was only later that I realised that it was in no way fixed to the vessel. Within minutes we spotted a tiny crocodile and then a huge one that basked quietly on an island bank. In all we must have seen about ten crocodiles most of which were big...then they would slide into the river on our approach and one could observe the bubbles from their breathing until they submerged to a depth. Hmm, this was a fun experience but I thought that they did not in any way resemble the fish-eating crocodiles to which I was used, namely the Gharial. These animals looked like the ordinary Mughar and I could not see how anyone could declare them only fish-eating. Anyway we bobbed downstream and enjoyed ourselves and shot the tiny rapids and finally ended up at the appointed place about four kilometres away from the start. A great experience; the jeep had been sent to collect us and the dismantled coracle and drive back to the resort. It was one of those special experiences that we will always remember.

I think someone told me that there is also a local elephant camp but we had already experienced these delights so just rested and enjoyed the peace of the place. It was however interesting to receive an invasion from Goa with a mixed bunch of young and elderly Europeans, mostly British, who were not actually the average wildlife viewer. They had all been on a cheap holiday to Goa and tacked this adventure experience on to the end of their holiday with white water rafting the cherry on the cake.

Kali River Camp could be really wonderful; it just requires some enlightened improvements and vigorous vigilant management which sadly it is not going to receive as a government undertaking. What really annoys me is that in a place so close to a little town the food could be significantly better with masses of lovely fresh fruit on display or used for breakfast and as a refreshing dessert, but left to indolent Indian cooks the meals were really mediocre. The Indian guests naturally ate Indian cuisine as indeed did we, but the influx from Goa were given baked beans, sausages, bacon, fried bread and eggs and ate vast quantities of it whereas a plate of fresh sliced fruit followed by an omelette suffices on a hot morning for me!

We departed as early as possible for our final long journey down to Goa. The Western Ghats are quite high and lush and have their fair share of significant hairpin bends; these coupled with the ceaseless traffic of heavy lorries transporting iron ore all the way from around Hospet to the port of Karwar made the journey quite stressful. However it had started on a light note when we were driving along on the forest road and came upon a bunch of five men, two of whom were completely stark naked and each carrying a fly whisk; these men were Digambara Jains and I had never ever seen young men in India walking along the public road completely unclothed. From time to time in the hill regions of Himalayan foothills one comes across old holy men who are perhaps naked and covered in ash sitting near a shrine, but this was new to me.

Imagine chasing poachers in the black of night, sleeping under an open sky with big cats stalking prey close by. Imagine trying to do all this without appropriate clothing, caps and shoes. Then imagine trying to survive on a morsel of rice and a sprinkling of curry, and perhaps having to drink from jungle pools. Lastly imagine earning just Rs 90 per day as a 'monthly rated employee' with the Karnataka State Forest department and being paid once in four months. All this is exactly what the protectors of the forest live through and endure, yet they do not give up their fight against poachers and smugglers who can terrorise these poor individuals with state-of-the-art guns and ammunition. It can surely be said that these forest guards are the heart and soul of the forest department, be they in Karnataka or Madhya Pradesh, Tamil Nadu or Uttarranchal – anywhere that there may be a national wildlife park.

For some inexplicable reason forest staff are only paid their salaries once in four months, and whilst waiting for the next payslip they have to borrow from the local shopkeepers who exploit the system shamelessly; they are poorly paid and therefore feel undervalued and are very poorly equipped. Most guards trudge the length and breadth of the national parks and wildlife sanctuaries with outdated equipment. Apparently the Tiger Project Areas have upgraded the communication systems for their guards but all this makes for a shameful story and India can surely do better than this, particularly now as the country's increasing wealth and prosperity is there for all the world to see.

Karnataka's forests and wildlife are her priceless natural heritage. This state has some of the largest jungle tracts south of the Vindhya Hills. From the majestic evergreen forests of the Western Ghats to the scrub jungles of the plains this wide variety of habitats teem with diverse flora and fauna, but the human population must continually be educated and encouraged to understand that they all bear responsibility as custodians of their lovely part of India. All this coupled with the plethora of ancient beautiful monuments and historic places makes it a very special place; the people of India must however realise that just looking forward eagerly through burgeoning commerce and economic growth is not the total answer. I do hope the people of our age and younger realise how much we all need these wonderful wide open spaces, along with the animals that inhabit them. Conservation, preservation and careful husbandry are all part, or should be, of the new vibrant India.

I am however sometimes very depressed with the Indian ability to talk long and loud about what should be done – actions always speak louder than words. Imagine my dismay when I read that the chief minister of Uttar Pradesh, the state in which I was born and indeed the most populous state in India, has managed to start creating his own 'dream project' to build a leisure resort involving a whole new airport, and luxury resort in his home district of Etawah – a luxury resort in the midst of poverty and natural beauty of these designated wetlands. Generations of villagers in the farming districts of Etawah and Mainpuri have lived in harmony with the 3,000 sarus cranes (the world's tallest flying bird) which are the state bird of Uttar Pradesh. That area is home to a fifth of the world population of sarus cranes; standing up to six feet (1.83m) tall the birds are revered in Indian myth and folklore as a symbol of conjugal bliss. The cranes, which are some of my earliest memories of wildlife seen on train journeys, have a distinctive red head and neck and a collar of white feathers. The birds mate for life and males share brood-rearing responsibilities with females. Their courtship includes an elaborate 'dance' of flapping wings, bowing and jumping and calls between males and females. The cranes live in pairs and practice monogamy during their 90-year lifetime. Their perfectly pitched unison calls, elegantly danced duets and choreographed territorial displays have won them a place in both Hindu and Buddhist scriptures. Fossils of the sarus crane dating from more than forty million years ago make the bird among the oldest surviving creatures on earth. The Hindu epic the *Ramayana* opens with a hunter cursed for killing a sarus crane. Who knows maybe that legendary curse will descend yet again on the greedy self interested chief minister and his family who it is alleged has used the finances of the state to create this brash new family venture.

Local farmers who are just surviving above the poverty line are too scared to protest but forced sales have left them without incomes. "We hardly have food. We don't even have electricity or water. It's just the chief minister's wish..."

I weep for India when I hear of this sort of greed and venality.

It is time that we realised that the rich must learn to live more simply so that the poor may simply live.
(Kamla Chowdhry from Khadi: Spirituality and Sustainability)

Chapter Twenty One

Goa by Land and Sea

On this journey in 2006 we arrived in Goa by road having driven all the way from Dandeli, but on my first visit the approach was from the sea. The ship had anchored in the mouth of the harbour off Dona Paula on Christmas Eve 2003. It was an unreal feeling to be sitting on deck in bright sunshine and contemplating a lovely Christmas in warmth and sunshine. Sometimes Christmas these days can be challenging because after so many years of marriage one has arranged many family Christmases, and indeed in our family we had always provided our home as the family nucleus for the festival. This therefore was the first time that Graham and I would be away from our home. Increasingly it is considered a very commercial time of year and most of us feel utterly jaded by the time 'Winter Wonderland' has been played in a jingle fifty million times since the beginning of October!

The cruise line had arranged for a party of little children to come on board and give us a Christmas concert; it was actually just what was needed. As always small children are enchanting and the gravity with which they enacted the Nativity and then in full costume, as either one of the holy family, or as angels and shepherds or a Christmas fairy, they sang to us with such serious concentration and sweetness which just brought a little magic to the company. That night after a sumptuous dinner a few of us changed into something warmer and embarked into the tenders to be taken to shore and transported to the church of San Sebastian for the midnight mass. The drive to the church was interesting because one could see the area of the capital of Goa lit up and in festival mode just as in the west. The church had the usual slightly baroque stucco façade, but one did not enter for the service; instead chairs were laid out in the square in front of it and the congregation slowly came together for the service. The locals were dressed in their finery. It was a Roman Catholic Christmas Mass and accompanied by a lively band of musicians. Just prior to the start of the service a few fireworks were exploded and this seemed to excite the local pariah dogs, or indeed privately owned animals and a few of them rushed through the congregation and barked and performed which was quite amusing – I don't think the Goans were the least bit phased by this curious interruption. I liked watching all the little ones for whom it was well past their bedtimes and they gradually fell asleep or snuggled up to a parent or cried a bit. After the long service in which we were not really able to participate much as we are not Roman Catholic and did not even know their hymns, the congregation were so welcoming and urged us to come and talk to them in an informal party and offered us cake. It would have been lovely to chat with them but the tender was waiting to take us back to the ship and it was very late.

We spent the next day, Christmas Day, in the company of Indian friends who showed us round Old Goa. Goa was wrenched by the Portuguese from the Sultan of Bijapur in 1510 by Admiral Afonso de Albuquerque and thereafter the Portuguese established a permanent settlement in Goa. Their intention was that this should be a colony and a naval base as distinct from the fortified enclaves they had set up or tried to set up further to the south in India. However you research the Portuguese and their actions in Goa you find descriptions of the most appalling acts of cruelty and suppression, again all done in the name of Christianity. With the imposition of the Inquisition in 1560, that lasted till its suppression in 1774, many of the local residents were forcibly converted to Christianity by missionaries and it was indeed the latter who had requested that a deposition of the Inquisition come to Goa, which then became known as The Goa Inquisition, but its jurisdiction spread across the whole of the Portuguese eastern empire. Hindus were forbidden to practise their faith and even the Christian population lived in fear. Those who were judged guilty underwent the notorious *auto da fe* (literally act of the faith) in a public ceremony conducted in the square outside the Se Cathedral, and accompanied by the great bell in the tower; if they failed the 'test of faith' they would be burned at the stake. Those who were willing to admit their heresy at the last moment were strangled before the flames were lit.

Thousands fled to escape harassment and death and they settled in the neighbouring towns of Mangalore and Karwar in Karnataka. Goa soon became the most important Portuguese possession in India and rivalled Lisbon with civic privileges equal to those of the capital city. Portuguese were encouraged to marry local women and to settle in Goa as farmers, retail traders and artisans. A sizeable Eurasian community grew and a senate was created with direct communications with the king. By 1843 the capital was moved from Old Goa to Panjim.

The origin of the name is unclear but in the Indian epic *Mahabharata* there is a reference to the area now known as Goa as 'Goparashtra' or 'Govarashtra', which means a nation of cowherds. It has also been known by a variety of other similar names such as Govepuri and the region had been described in certain inscriptions and texts in the *Puranas* (old books – ancient texts). It became popularly known as Gove, which the Portuguese turned into Goa.

In the 3rd century BC it formed part of the Mauryan Empire, and it was later ruled by the Satavahanas of Kolhapur in Maharashtra around two thousand years ago. It eventually passed to the Chalukyas of Badami, who controlled it between the years 580 to 750 AD. Over the next centuries Goa was successively ruled by the various Deccan rulers. In 1312 it came under the governance of the Delhi Sultanate but by 1370 it was surrendered to Harihara I of Vijayanagar. The Vijayanagar monarchs reigned till 1469 when it was appropriated by the Bahmani sultans of Gulbarga, after which the area came into the hands of the Adil Shahis of Bijapur who made Velha Goa their auxiliary capital.

It is now India's richest state in terms of wealth per person and the language is Konkani. The Portuguese colony was forcibly annexed by Prime Minister Nehru's government in 1961. My first memory of Goa is just of the name, and it was explained to me as a child where it was and the reasons for its name being on everyone's lips. In the 1950s when I was small there were often quite savage riots in Calcutta (Kolkata) in support of the idea of annexing the colony into the country of newly independent India. On one memorable occasion I recall being in the car with my mother and our driver being stopped aggressively; fortunately he sped away because the favourite trick of the rioters was to drop a lighted match into the petrol tank. It was really quite scary and the rioters made all Europeans the butt of their anger and frustration, though of course we had nothing to do with it and were not Portuguese. It was a time in India's development when sometimes volatile mobs seemed to rule the city streets and set fire to trams if their university exams had not proved sufficiently easy or about some other vexation that they thought should be their natural right to acquire or achieve. It became a bit of a joke: "Have a problem burn a tram", which was treated with contempt by the European fraternity. Interestingly, in Venezuela where Graham and I lectured in 1986 in the University of Maracay, the dean told us that students were inclined to want to burn down his office if they felt they had not received a good enough pass mark, or indeed had failed! All round that wonderful university with its beautiful grounds there were the saying and teachings of Simon de Bolivar, the founder of Venezuela; such true aphorisms with

The Se Cathedral in Old Goa

which one concurs, but democracy is actually something that only mature responsible people can make work for themselves – developing countries take time to realise this and act accordingly. In 1961 I recall that Mr Nehru had some explaining to do in the United Nations and the fact that he had in 1956 declared that he would never commit an act of aggression and *that war, even a little war was a war*...and had now reneged on those words made him feel uncomfortable. He was made to feel even more uncomfortable in the November of 1962 when the Chinese army marched into Assam and we had to organise the mass evacuation of tea plantation personnel at a moment's notice. This was achieved with the efficiency and organisation of the Indian Air Force; the West at the same time was rather preoccupied with the extremely grave Cuban Missile Crisis between Russia and the United States. I used the word 'we' as I played a small part, despite my youth, in helping to organise the evacuation for a well known tea company called Williamson Magor, which I believe is now the largest family owned tea company in the world. Perhaps that too was 'a little war'? Certainly it was an act of aggression on the part of the Chinese, who in the end apparently ran out of ammunition. I think India learnt a great lesson on that occasion, one of shame and humiliation and shock at betrayal, and I am not shy in recalling it when I find Indian diplomats and politicians become a bit uppity and dismissive, particularly those who were not yet born in 1962!

221

Another view of the Se Cathedral in Old Goa

Walking round in the bright sunshine on Christmas Day in Old Goa, which is now a World Heritage Site, was delightful but slightly odd. That whole area is attractively laid out with large green spaces and flowering trees which were in blossom. People milled about either as church goers or as tourists such as ourselves, or indeed as pilgrims. The Se Cathedral at over seventy-six metres long and fifty-five metres wide, is considered to be the largest church in Asia – that is still the claim and I would not know how to research that fact. It is a large building and had a service taking place so we quietly stood at the back and watched for a short while. I could not forget the enormity of what had taken place outside the cathedral in centuries gone by. This is in fact the cathedral built by the order of King Dom Sebastiao which started construction in 1562, to replace the older church of St Catherine which had served as a cathedral hitherto. It took ninety years to complete the building; standing at the main door one sees the Senate House on the left and on the right was the Palace of the Inquisition. It is a very plain but pleasing building in European style but looks slightly lopsided as one bell tower collapsed in 1776.

West of the Se Cathedral is the Church of St Francis of Assisi which I actually preferred. A small chapel was built on this site by eight Franciscan friars in 1517; this was subsequently replaced with a church consecrated to the Holy Ghost and then that too was replaced with the present church in 1661. There are a number of other churches and chapels for those who are enthusiastic about religious buildings. The other building of great renown is the Basilica of Bom Jesus. It contains the tomb and mortal remains of St Francis Xavier, the 'Apostle of the Indies'. He became a legend in his own time with his ability to travel to the east and considering the conditions of travel in those days it was quite marvellous. He had been a pupil of St Ignatius Loyola, the founder of the Jesuit Order. Construction began in 1594 and the church was completed in 1605. The interior is simple but grand and the pulpit is quite superb. The focus of attention however is the tomb of St Francis

The famous blue and white decorated church in Old Goa

Xavier; the body was moved into the church in 1622 and moved again in 1659 to its present location to the right of the altar. St Francis Xavier's body was alleged to have remained intact after his death when he died on the island of Sancian off the Chinese coast in 1552. It was returned by ship to Goa, obviously in a coffin but was seen to be free of decomposition and therefore he was considered to be a saint; his body was embalmed by the viceroy's physician in 1556 and he was canonised in 1622.

Every ten years the remains of St Francis Xavier are displayed amongst much religious fervour for about fifty-four days and this is considered to be the most important Christian festival in the sub-continent; the last occasion was 2004/2005. The 3rd December is the saint's annual feast day and apparently a celebration worth watching and taking part in, even though one might just be a spectator and not a devout pilgrim.

223

It is a sombre fact that whatever the 'ideals' or 'spiritual' commitment, to give a generous gloss to the Portuguese ambitions, their wonderful new eastern capital had to be abandoned within a century and they moved down river because cholera continuously took its toll of the population. Recalling the awful cholera epidemics in crowded Calcutta in the 1950s every hot season I can have some sympathy. Daily the newspapers would record the number of fatalities of the previous day and the numbers were always in three figures.

The Church of Our Lady of the Immaculate Conception is a really pretty church painted white with careful use of bright blue in highlights and I took my chances with the traffic to obtain a good photograph of it. It was hot, thirsty work walking round all this however enjoyable on that Christmas Day, and I was very glad when we decided to relax and seek out a good hotel and some refreshment. Our hosts decided to take us to the Fort Aguada hotel which necessitated a drive to the other side of the Mandovi River and thus showed us in the passing quite a lot of interest on the way.

Goa's beaches are legendary and I could not begin to visit them all or write about them; one thing I am sure of is that in the years to come Graham and I will enjoy visiting Goa for a beach holiday and they are so well priced that I am sure it will become an annual occurrence. Some of the beaches north of the Mandovi River have been sadly overdeveloped and now resemble a 'Spanish Costa'; twenty years of endless development takes its toll and just like Spain no doubt the authorities in Goa will in time realise that people recoil from a concrete coastline, but it could be that those escaping crowded Indian cities are not sufficiently worried by over building – indeed they are so used to cramped living that as long as they are on holiday on a patch of sand with cheap drinks and food they are content.

The coastline south of the Mandovi is however a more peaceful world with wonderful five star resorts and therefore it attracts a clientele like ourselves who are more intent on 'chilling' than 'raving'. Goans speak of *susegad*, a term which translated means roughly 'laid back'. It originated in the Portuguese word *socegado* which meant quiet, so is not entirely accurate! Think of Goa as India's Latin Quarter and that gives a better, more accurate, impression of the ambience. We visited a friend's house and found the area enchanting; I can quite see why Europeans arrive annually to enjoy the good weather and good feeling that is all around. The old Portuguese architecture with iron railings and shutters and relics of a bygone era also slightly reminded me of the old mansion houses and mansion flats in Calcutta which were very much still in evidence in my childhood; all that has been bulldozed to provide ever more concrete chambers for the materially wealthy in modern Kolkata but modern air conditioned tower blocks will never have the charm of pillared verandas, lofty rooms and lazy punkas (fans). That has brought another memory to me of the colony of Portuguese Indians in Calcutta who in those days worked as managers and assistants in the big shops and grocery stores and now I understand that these people would have had to move around India to make a living as the Goa of my childhood was largely undiscovered and not a wealthy place.

On Boxing Day in 2003 we visited one of the fresh food markets, but I thought it was a terribly bad idea because in the heat of the afternoon on what was after all a holiday I knew that things would be far from fragrant and that people might indeed be worse for wear! I don't think any of the cruise passengers enjoyed the encounter and indeed the time would have been better spent perhaps visiting one of the historic Portuguese mansions like Braganza House that are open to the public. We then repaired to an emporium, which is where the famous emerald necklace was purchased so ostentatiously by the fellow passenger on the cruise ship. As shops go it was mediocre and unremarkable.

Goa has two bird sanctuaries and had we had more time I would have liked to visit them. The Dr Salim Ali Bird Sanctuary is in the centre on Chorao Island near Panaji and very accessible; between November and February it receives a huge number of migrant birds and though small in size is, I am told by similar enthusiasts, well worth a visit. Dr Salim Ali was a celebrated ornithologist in India and I grew up looking at his various books on birds, one of which is Birds of an Indian Garden; this was a rather basic book by today's standards but the pictures were interesting to a small girl and really all that we had in the early 1950s and I found it easy to learn to recognise the garden visitors from those simple illustrations and I still have it on our bookshelf and refer to it when necessary; indeed we found an updated version in the Malligi Hotel's bookshop! I cannot help but digress here to tell you about the bird watching experience we so enjoyed in Sri Lanka. People always speak of it as 'a garden island' but truly it is so and if you go and visit the area around Habarana and stay at The Lodge Habarana, or its sister establishment, one has the most amazing experience watching golden orioles, paradise flycatchers and every other exotic bird in the Asian spectrum. We also stayed at Kandalama which was designed to allow nature to come right up to the door; I found that hotel a little too minimalist and cavernous but nevertheless had lovely experiences riding elephants and watching wildlife really close up and would therefore still recommend it.

The Boarding Party is a book by James Leasor. This book tells the true story of the wartime drama that took place in Mormugao Harbour. Portugal and therefore Goa was technically neutral in World War II and had turned a blind eye to the use of their harbour as a base for German ships; the British authorities in Delhi were determined to put a stop to this and it fell to the members of the Calcutta Light Horse, a territorial army regiment based in Calcutta to sabotage the Germans. The Pony Club in Calcutta was administered from the offices of this famous regiment and I learned to ride in Calcutta through the Pony Club which was encouraged to use the horses at the Indian Army Remount. The officers of the Calcutta Light Horse who nearly all survived this daring encounter continued with their lives in Calcutta and I often rode my pony with their members in competitions called 'pairs'. The film of the book was called *The Sea Wolves* and starred Gregory Peck, Roger Moore, Patrick Allan, Trevor Howard and a host of well known names. Little did I know as a child of ten that I was riding round the ring and practising with men who had been heroes – it was something of which they never spoke.

Feni is undoubtedly Goa's most famous alcoholic drink. There are two types of feni, both of which are made from local ingredients. Coconut or palm feni is made from the sap drawn from the harvested shoots of a coconut tree. This is similar to 'toddy' of which I spoke in Kerala; and palm feni is available throughout the year. *Caju* (cashew) feni however can only be made during the cashew season in late March and early April. As in Tamil Nadu cashews are an important crop to Goa. Feni is made from the fruit or 'apple' of the cashew, whilst the nuts are laid out to dry. The apples are placed in a pit and trampled by foot to collect the juice. Both palm and cashew juice can be drunk fresh and is considered delicious but once fermentation starts it is another story; the liquor is distilled into *uraq* and this first offering is of medium strength (10% to 15% proof), but the majority is distilled twice and thus becomes feni. Goa's national alcoholic drink has an alcoholic strength of 30% to 35% proof. It is very good with cola or canned lemonade, but frankly in the heat I do not care for alcohol at all.

When we visited Goa by cruise ship in December 2003 we also made visits to the the Malvan Coast of Maharashtra which is just north of Goa. This coastline is dotted with pretty fishing villages, nice beaches and the most wonderful maritime forts. The first one we visited by ship, and indeed the ship had to stand off and we embarked on tenders and then again into little wooden hodi boats, was Janjira Fort. This fort is just off the beach of Murud; this was the capital of the Siddis of Janjira. The fort was built in 1515 by the Ahmednagar rulers under the supervision of their regent Malik Ambar. This fort is the only impregnable fort on the 720 kilometre Maharashtran coastline. The Marathas, despite their repeated attempts failed to subjugate the Siddi power, Shivaji attacked in 1659, followed by his son Shambhuji, who even tried digging a tunnel having failed to scale the fifteen metre high walls. There are two virtually undiscovered beaches called Nandgaon and Kshid a few kilometres away. Nandgaon is famous for its Ganapati temple and the annual fair held in honour of the god Ganesha every February.

The second fort that we visited is called Sindhudurg; this was built by Shivaji in 1664 at a site personally selected by him. Constructing a sea fort is a formidable task and 4,000 mounds of iron were used for casting and the foundation stones were laid down firmly in lead. Even today as one approaches the fort past a rocky reef, navigable through a narrow channel, one marvels at the transportation of such heavy material through such choppy waters. Within its precincts are temples holding the shrines of Maruti, Bhavani, Mahadeo, Jarimai, Mahapurush – all Hindu deities and also one of Shivaji – the only shrine to him in India. I should explain that Shivaji was a great Mahratta warlord and hero of India; this fort is still inhabited. We were fortunate enough to have a most elegant luncheon laid on for us cruise passengers on Tarkhali Beach which is quite close on the coast to Sindhudurg fort. The beach is a pleasant one with casuarinas and palms almost down to the water and the local hotel has a few very comfortable chalets on the beach in which we were invited to change. The lunch was served under a beautiful shamiana (an Indian word for a marquee) on the beach and the chairs and table cloths were all charmingly themed to make it appear amazingly sumptuous. The food was outstanding seafood and a selection of curries followed by Indian sweets and ice cream. Those of us who felt brave enough bathed and thoroughly enjoyed it. I was struck by the simple little war memorial at Malvan when once again embarking on the ship's tender. It is a pink tiled memorial set in an alcove and says:

"From this town 75 men went to the Great War 1914-1919 of these some gave up their lives." The cipher of G R I is engraved above.

I am always incredibly moved by something like that. What did the simple men who were probably fishermen know about a huge war being fought in Europe and yet they went heroically in the name of a distant emperor whom they had never set eyes upon?

Almost exactly a year later on Boxing Day 2004 the same cruise ship had offered luncheon on the beach at Tarkhali, but this time an enormous wave came in and swamped the shamiana; the guests thought it was just a big wave until someone in the party received a phone message on her mobile asking if she was alright, and then they

The Majorda Beach swimming pool close to a beautiful beach

learned the truth about the tsunami. The rest of the cruise had to be rearranged because of the devastation to Sri Lanka.

Gokarna is another beach resort about 120 kilometres south of Goa on the Karnataka coast. Hitherto it has not had any really special place at which to stay but since last year the CGH Earth Group have opened a small resort, which I am sure will maintain their excellent standards. The place has two beaches of renown called Kudle Beach and Om Beach – the latter so named because of its distinctive shape. The CGH Earth resort is on Om Beach and I think there is also to be a Trails of India resort very soon. All these places are reached by car from Goa to which a plane journey would be the most convenient way to travel. Gokarna has been a pilgrimage centre for ages; it is one of the most sacred Hindu sites in southern India with the Mahabaleshwara Temple, home to a revered Shiva lingam. Nearby is the Ganapati Temple honouring the god Ganesh. Near the temple are two enormous chariots which are dragged along the main street annually in February to commemorate Lord Shiva's birthday. The third temple is the Venkataraman Temple and about 100 metres south of this is Koorti Teertha, the large temple tank where the devout perform their ablutions along with the *dhobi wallahs* who are doing the town's daily washing!

Our visit to Goa in March 2006 was brief but very enjoyable. As I said we entered the state of Goa from Karwar travelling from Dandeli; Karwar is the location for a huge Indian Naval base which is being thoroughly modernised. South of Karwar are some lovely beach areas like Devbagh and then Gokarna as I have already mentioned. On this occasion we chose to stay at the Majorda Beach Resort. It is a truly lovely place and we received a warm welcome and enjoyed the whole ambience of the place. It is not as large as some five star resorts but has one hundred and twenty rooms of various kinds to suit everyone's budget. We had a lovely spacious cottage close to the outside swimming pool. This resort has had the very good sense to build an indoor pool as well which I could see I would use on a very hot afternoon. Graham and I liked its lush, well maintained garden with a path that leads to a very fine beach and that area of the coast is actually called the Majorda Sea. The Seafood Restaurant right down by the shore was excellent and so beautifully lit at night with nice touches that made it very romantic – the tiger prawns were delicious grilled with garlic! Every Monday night they have a special 'Fish Market' night and the area round the restaurant is made to look like a Goan fish market and guests can choose to buy their fish and watch it being cooked in a number of ways. I wish we had been there on a Monday night. Apparently this is such a popular event that people come from all the adjacent hotels to attend this evening. The hotel is only fifteen minutes by car from the airport which is very convenient and I can see us using it in the future for a leisurely holiday; certainly from talking to the British and Indian guests a lot of them are people who return

Hammocks on the lawns at Majorda Beach in South Goa

because they find it fills their expectations. One thing of interest was the amount of Russian or eastern European people on holiday with their families. Russians are increasingly a factor in Asian and Middle Eastern travel but curiously they are not very friendly to fellow guests and find it even impossible to smile at others which is odd, as we have some charming Russian friends who live in the Scottish Borders, one of whom is the most gifted artist specialising in animal paintings. Graham and I liked the spacious green lawns and the way the hammocks and easy chairs are spread out with thoughtful touches to provide cool drinks and snacks from a charming kiosk. Breakfast was truly an international affair outside in the Garden Café with so many different languages being spoken and the hotel also has a casino which operates throughout the day and night. Of more interest to me were the beauty centre and the Ayurvedic centre, both with up to date equipment in charming surroundings. Adults and children are well catered for with outdoor tennis, squash, table tennis and a computer corner. It is also so easy to walk on to the beach and eat at the beach shack restaurants as well as those in the small hamlet within walking distance on the landward side – this can make a holiday a great deal cheaper.

I had found it sad saying farewell to Pratap who had driven us so safely right from Bangalore, down to Bandipur, over to Kabini, up to Orange County, across to Hassan and beyond then right up to Hospet and Hampi and then across finally to Goa from Dandeli. We wished

Sunset on the beach at Majorda in Goa

him well and gave him a good tip and asked him to be careful driving back alone to Bangalore. I mean to send him a photograph of himself outside the Vitthala Temple at Hampi.

Looking out at the Arabian Sea as the sun set I had a good feeling of achievement. Essentially this last huge trip was the end of my many journeys up and down and round India to find the information that has been the basis of my three books. This had been a 2,500 kilometre journey by road plus the 3,000 kilometres by air down to Bangalore and then back from Goa to Delhi – a long journey by anybody's reckoning. I thank God for our safe arrival and all the wonderful experiences we had enjoyed along the way.

Chapter Twenty Two

Happy to be in Delhi

Springtime in Delhi is lovely; both in April 2005 and March 2006 I was able to experience it and on this occasion, just a few weeks ago, the temperature was amazingly cool and we even had some welcome rain. Coming from a snowcapped Scotland I did not really want the rain but it was so obvious how pleased everyone was and even I could see how it washed all the dust and dry leaves off the trees and encouraged spring growth.

Presidents and Prime Ministers have been beating a path to the capital of India for the last few months, not least the President of the United States, who received a splendid ceremonial welcome at the Rashtrapati Bhawan which some say took his breath away. That is music to my ears as I had foretold in my second book that India was going to forge ahead with a burgeoning economy which would make it a force to be respected all over the world.

We were fortunate enough to be invited to look round the new Parliament Library. This is a splendid building which blends effortlessly with the Indian Parliament Sansad Bhawan, itself of grand but simple design. We both marvelled at *Sansadiya Gyanpeeth* to use its formal Indian title and thought that Raj Rewal Associates had been very clever in their idea of housing two storeys of the building beneath ground so as not to in anyway dwarf or dominate the original parliament building designed by Sir Edwin Lutyens and Sir Herbert Baker. Every little detail had of course been thought out and now that the building has existed for a couple of years it has matured and will stand the test of time. It is gloriously light inside with huge interior courtyards and cupolas with an enormous feeling of space. I was not allowed to take any photographs because of security but I think most people unconnected to parliamentary life are not aware of it. Just exactly a month previous we had dined in our own Scottish Parliament, which I enjoyed but we found the building totally underwhelming and a bit poky and dark, particularly for our northern country where we experience so much grey

Aline Dobbie with India's young female generation outside Rashtrapati Bhawan

light during daylight hours. Moreover it had cost us, the Scots people, an enormous amount of money and most of our building surveyor friends declare it will be a headache to maintain and probably obsolete within forty years. The Indian Parliament's new library is built out of the familiar red and beige sandstone that is synonymous with the great buildings of New Delhi. The general height is restricted to the plinth of the Parliament below the circular colonnade. The roof of the library building has a series of low profile bubble domes sitting on steel structures complementing the existing domes of masonry on the Rashtrapati Bhawan, which is not far away. Our new Scottish Parliament complements nothing whatsoever, and is completely out of keeping with the monarch's residence The Palace of Holyrood House which resembles an elegant French Chateau. Truly our new building should be named First Ministers' folly. The Welsh have a new Assembly Hall which is superb and cost a fraction of our concrete structure with its roof of 'upturned boats' which is really only visible from a helicopter or the famous extinct volcano Arthur's Seat in the royal park alongside. It is worth noting that the information technology system that is operated within the Scottish Parliament is operated by an Indian firm with Indian IT engineers living in Edinburgh. There was through colonial times a Scottish Diaspora to India and other colonies, now it seems the reverse is true in so many aspects of our lives.

China seems set on dominating the manufacturing industry of the world, though I personally think people will find that India can compete very favourably in that respect too, but it appears that India has made its metier the wider services industry, with a particular focus on Britain. Naresh Goyal, the very successful founder of Jet Airways says that the United Kingdom is one of India's main targets for the obvious reason that our two countries have so much in common, in part because of the historical ties but also because we, the British, gave India English as a language. Goyal is one of the emerging breed of Indian billionaire entrepreneurs leading the 'onslaught' on British industry; he with about ten others may not be well known as yet in Britain but I am confident they will become very well known as India looks to broaden its dominance away from outsourcing over the next decade. As in most countries the powerful men at the top of industry all know each other and they have all worked together to promote 'India Inc'. It is worth noting that in 2006 India has twenty-seven dollar billionaires, more than twice as many as year ago. The Tata conglomerate is another that is becoming well known here in the UK; I have spoken of them before and lauded their philanthropic and entrepreneurial achievements within India but now they are a commercial force to be respected worldwide; Ratan Tata, chairman of the Tata Group is a man of world stature as well as widely respected within India – a man of vision but unassuming with it. He was named as one of the twelve founding members (along with Bill Gates) of Gordon Brown's (the British Government's Chancellor of the Exchequer) International Business Advisory Council. Here in Scotland it is quite normal to find oneself behind a Tata vehicle on our country roads and the local farmers approve of their durability; without knowing it millions of people here in the United Kingdom drink Tata's tea, because the conglomerate bought the famous Tetley's tea brand a few years ago. In the corporate world Tata Consultancy Services, Infosys Technologies and Wipro are the three Indian companies the world knows best, and they are competing with each other and are participants in a race to become the first company with a $10 billion revenue mark.

A visit to Delhi invariably starts with us visiting The Imperial hotel for tea and Indian *mitthai*. Graham and I love *ras mallai* and nothing could have been nicer than a beautiful pot of good Indian tea accompanied by creamy fragrant ras mallai. We had arrived two hours late from London due to a supposed 'technical fault' on Air Sahara and had to change on the run to reach the Parliament Library, now we were catching our breath and beginning to enjoy our arrival in Delhi. That evening we did a quick change and went out to another favourite – the Bukhara at The Maurya Sheraton, which was enormously busy with the arrival of Queen Rania of Jordan – she is a very lovely young woman. The restaurant was busy so we had to wait and I quite happily filled the time shopping in the arcade at Maharani of India who has so many wonderful clothes. The meal was as ever worth waiting for and we had missed lunch altogether so tucked in. Two days travelling and time spent in London then nonstop in Delhi demanded some sleep!

The next morning found us bright and energised for our visit to the Rashtrapati Bhawan, the President of India's palace. The site chosen for the Viceroy's House, now the Rashtrapati Bhawan, was on Raisina Hill which was seen as an Indian acropolis. The building, designed by Sir Edwin Lutyens, has a large court to its front and a Mughal style garden at the back. During February and March the Mughal Garden is open to the public on certain days.

Rashtrapati Bhawan has 340 rooms. Lord Irwin, it first occupant apparently kept losing his way. It is big and grand and everything was designed to reinforce the sense of the importance of its occupant. Now it is the presidential residence for state presidents, who are usually men who have distinguished themselves in their field and command respect. Sadly most of the wonderful furniture with which it was equipped 'walked' apparently during the early years of India's independence. That is a great pity because it requires I think to be seriously re-furnished to reflect the building's grandeur and indeed India's stature in this modern world sixty years on. People keep referring to the coming 60th anniversary as the Independence anniversary but I refuse any longer to do that; my term is the 60th anniversary of India's Nationhood. She was an ancient land full of art, culture, science, engineering, medicine, literature, spirituality and natural beauty. For a time this land of disparate peoples was colonised – a mere two centuries in a history that goes back to the dawn of time as we measure it; how can therefore one continue to talk of its independence, that is so patronising and I keep referring to nationhood.

Most students of history are used to grand and historic buildings, so I was particularly pleased to have this opportunity as I have enjoyed so many others the world over. However, it must be said that some respected private hotelier or interior designer should be tasked to equip and maintain the place in tip top condition. It maybe that the current incumbent because he is a bachelor does not realise how "frayed' it is at the edges. Moreover the lighting needs to be brightened and maintained. The Durbar Hall is the main ceremonial hall which lies directly under the great main dome. On our visit there were men seemingly cleaning something, but frankly the state of it was to be regretted and I wondered how exactly a week ago to that day people had seen their way in the gloom when President Bush visited and was formally received. India has so much in the way of soft furnishings and beautiful antiques and artefacts; this great wonderful building should become a showcase for all of that. Now I understood why it had been decided to give the state banquet in the Mughal Gardens as had been done when President Chirac had visited in February. The gardens have a fresh sweetness about them and I am sure well lit up were an enchanting venue for a grand dinner on a balmy Delhi evening.

There is a rather amateur museum of the past British rulers and their spouses and former viceroys and memorabilia pertaining to that era. It could be stunning and is interesting but nothing much is explained and when a party of young girls accompanied by nuns came into view they were entirely ignorant of all they saw with no explanations to educate them. I quietly started explaining things to them and tried to give them a sense of perspective about their country's recent history.

When we finally emerged out on to the forecourt they wanted to have their collective photographs taken with us and so we duly took theirs as well. Devender Singh, our driver, had driven us up to the entrance and was parked nearby; I also took a photograph of him posed in front of the grand building which pleased him. Understandably security is very tight and we had arrived within the same week of the bomb atrocities at Varanasi. From the outside the building is truly massive; its dominant feature is its dome which is said to have been inspired by the Buddhist stupa at Sanchi. The column in front of the building is surmounted by a star made of glass; it was presented by the then Maharajah of Jaipur and is called the Jaipur Column. I can see how impressive it must look when the full presidential guard on horseback as well as foot soldiers greets a visiting head of state. The view from the forecourt down the Rajpath is amazing and can compare with any capital in the world. Standing on the broad sweep of the grand steps at Rashtrapathi Bhawan looking down the length of Rajpath I felt a huge surge of satisfaction that India has become such an economic force, and that this significant status has been achieved within the 60th anniversary of her nationhood.

We also visited Teen Murti Bhawan, built as the residence of the British commander-in-chief in India; it became the official residence of Jawaharlal Nehru, the first Prime Minister of independent India. After he died it was converted into a memorial. The three statues of Indian soldiers on the roundabout outside (teen murti) give the building its name. Kushk Mahal, a hunting lodge built during the reign of Firoz Shah Tughlaq, is on a mound just behind the main building, and the Nehru Planetarium is also in the same compound.

Graham and I found the history of the independence movement very interesting and moving and we walked about the rooms and looked out on the lovely well maintained gardens on which peacocks strutted. Nehru was essentially a man who lived simply and this is manifested in his rooms which have been left just as they were when he died. Now however, I think they need careful renovation just to freshen them up. We were the only Europeans and there were a few

Teen Murthi Bhawan, one-time residence of Pandit Nehru

Indians walking round but for me it was especially interesting having been born just at the time of independence and then grown up in India in the era which is encapsulated within this building. Looking at the archival photography of India then and knowing what I have seen and experienced in these massive journeys around the whole country, (except for Kashmir where one is advised not to go because of British Foreign & Commonwealth Office restrictions, that if ignored would invalidate one's insurance), I know how proud he, Nehru, would be of his country and its achievements.

From Teen Murti Bhawan we went to the Gandhi Smriti. Mahatma Gandhi was assassinated by a Hindu fanatic on 30th January 1948 in the grounds of Birla House. On 28 January 1948 Bapu, as he was called in reverence, was in a pensive mood. He had a premonition of the 'final hour'. Sitting outside his room (which you can visit) in Birla House, which had been his home since September 1947, he observed to Rajkumari Amrit Kaur, "If I am to die by the bullet of a mad man, I must do so smiling. There must be no anger within me. God must be in my heart and on my lips". Two days later, on his way to say prayers as he walked in the lovely big garden he died a martyr's death, but exactly the way he had wished – with God on his lips. *"He Ram,"* were his last words. A man of prayer, he died in prayer.

I had visited Birla House previously in 1998 but Graham had never been and I knew he would find it moving and thought provoking. Moreover we had both visited Gandhiji's Samadhi at Raj Ghat. That is something which I recommend to everyone on a first visit to India; somehow its tranquil calm and good atmosphere (of which I spoke in my first book India: The Peacock's Call) are the antidote to the frenetic cacophony that is Delhi, its traffic, and large parts of India. In Birla House gardens where he was killed it is beautifully maintained and there is a path with stone footsteps showing how he walked out to his death. There is an eternal flame and a memorial stone or Martyr's Column on the spot where he fell inscribed with his last words and the date and time of his death. The carving is reminiscent of Gandhiji's scrawled handwriting. Behind the memorial is a red sandstone bench where Gandhiji would sit during his prayer meetings. Today, a beautiful large photograph of him at prayer is displayed above it. Behind it is a pleasant pavilion, decorated with frescoes that tell the story of Gandhiji's life.

I had previously liked the way that his life had been illustrated in an unusual way at this museum by using a series of small dolls' houses and terracotta dolls portraying the major events in his life. This is a good way of educating the very young of India and foreign children. Looking at his simple bedroom and his austere way of life one is constantly humbled by his achievements and what he so wanted for his beloved India. We would do well to recall his words now. They are dreams to which every India should aspire nearly sixty years on; as one who is sometimes considered Indian by virtue of it being the land of my birth, I find his words encapsulate all that I could wish for this great country.

> *"I shall work for an India in which the poorest shall feel that it is their country, in whose making they have an effective voice; an India in which there shall be no high class and low class of people; an India in which all communities shall live together in perfect harmony. There can be no room in such India for the curse of untouchability or the curse of intoxicating drinks and drugs. Women will enjoy the same rights as men. We shall be at peace with all the rest of the world. This is the India of my dreams."*

> Mahatma Gandhi

Earlier in the day I had been interviewed by a distinguished travel writer called Rabindra Seth. Rabindra was so interesting himself because he has worked for sixty-four years as a journalist and had seen and reported on the independence of India plus some amazing things like the Indian Army's presence in the UN forces in The Congo in 1962. He was supposed to be asking me questions but in fact I found all his reminiscences about India's men of history fascinating. We had talked at one of my favourite venues, the India International Centre which was as busy as ever. Naturally Graham and I had walked in and enjoyed the Lodi Gardens before that meeting. I love the Lodi Gardens and they were still looking so beautiful in their spring colours and the remaining flowers of the winter season. Here amongst tombs to long gone emperors, as ever the green parakeets screeched and darted about in between the ancient buildings; a solitary yoga devotee continued his meditation, boys played cricket and young lovers met shyly away from the watching eyes of their parents. I sincerely hope that the Lodi Gardens continue to give the people of Delhi a beautiful tranquil place in which to recharge their spirits.

Because I wished to develop a theme about looking at India between her 50th anniversary and her 60th anniversary I wanted to revisit some of the important monuments to Delhi's past rulers and see what renovations had been done and how things looked to me after nearly a decade since my last visit to them. Safdarjang's Tomb is not far from

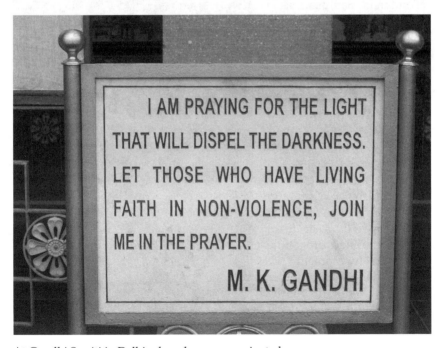

At Gandhi Smriti in Delhi where he was assasinated

the Lodi Gardens and I enjoyed our visit. It is looking good and the grounds are well maintained, even though the washrooms are the usual stinking hole. Again, this is obviously the meeting place for young men and women and the whole garden was filled with courting couples, behaving very demurely I might say. I found one young woman waiting uncomfortably, obviously her young man was late or not going to arrive and she felt very self conscious. It is a nice serene place and I think very beautiful with just the bird life and chipmunks, not least because the traffic snarls around outside but inside this garden area there is peace. Built in 1753-54 as the mausoleum of Safdarjang, the viceroy of Awadh, under the Mughal Emperor, Mohammed Shah, it has several smaller pavilions with evocative names like Jangli Mahal (Palace in the Woods) and Badshah Pasand which means King's Favourite.

Graham and I had taken the opportunity to revisit the Santushti Complex which is always very attractive; we had not eaten in the Basil and Thyme restaurant since May 1998 and it was as good as ever. Somehow we could not believe that so many years have passed since that occasion, but yes, we are grandparents twice over and God willing for a third time in the autumn when Corinne and Stewart have

their first child. I always recommend Santushti as a place to visit for first time visitors to Delhi because there are so many lovely shops gathered together in elegant surroundings that make shopping a real pleasure. We did however go on to visit the markets near Connaught Place because I was determined to buy some Punjabi shoes for our grandsons. We found them and in due course I hope they will wear them indoors, the shoes are a little big just at the moment.

Dilli Haat is another wonderful venue for tourist shopping, and indeed local Delhi-ites, if one is looking for dhurries, as I was, or fabric or bed linen and soft

Little Indian boy on his father's scooter in Delhi

Safdahjang's tomb in New Delhi

furnishings plus a host of cheerful crafts. It has been such a success that I read that a second Dilli Haat is to be opened in another suburb of the capital. Certainly on a pleasant, sunny Sunday afternoon it is an excellent place to visit. For foreign visitors the riot of colour amongst the stalls and then the buyers themselves must be a very pleasant assault on the eye!

We revisited Humayan's Tomb because I had heard that the Aga Khan's Trust had given funding for its renovation and restoration of the *char bhag* garden design. This had come about because a small band of right-minded people, including our good friend Martin Howard, had wanted to find a way to mark the 50th anniversary of 'Nationhood' for India. A number of ideas were put forward, but Martin's idea to have a renovation of the area around Humayan's Tomb won the day and the Aga Khan Foundation was approached successfully. It is absolutely beautiful now. Humayan's Tomb was by any standard a most wonderful place but its gardens on our last visit in 1997 were pretty disgraceful and only attended by some village women cutting the grass manually and that was probably for fodder for their own cattle – I photographed them and spoke of this visit in my first book. Now there are immaculate lush green lawns, rills of water and fountains

Humayan's tomb

tinkling. The paths are immaculate and bordered, chipmunks play hop, skip and jump amongst the masonry and trees and the whole ambience is now superb, moreover motor lawn mowers are operated by young male gardeners! The approach has been beautifully redesigned and one has to pay to enter, which is entirely right. I think on that occasion we just wandered into the area. Nothing can be maintained without funding and international visitors are used to paying at places of historic interest. The sum is now $5 each for non-Indians which is not too much, but I do think some thought should go into a collective ticket for the serious tourist who wants to visit many attractions, and young foreign visitors who are on stringent budgets.

The hotel which I had never had reason to visit but is much mentioned in European brochures is The Oberoi Maidens. This was built as a single storey structure in 1900 and is now a listed building located in what is known as the Civil Lines area of Delhi. Edwin Lutyens stayed in this hotel when he first came to Delhi to decide on the site of the new capital of British India. It is a delight and I can quite see why British visitors like it so much. The rooms moreover are so spacious and all the bathrooms are renovated. The pool is big and in quite gracious grounds and there is that air of 'the old days' about it. The management were very friendly and gave us a good tour; we particularly noted the lovely scent of lemon grass which was wafting everywhere as the oil was put in little containers with water and had a candle burning beneath it. A lovely touch, which we were to see used in The Oberoi, the group's five star flagship hotel in Delhi at the very end of our journey; Air Sahara cancelled our flight and behaved very oddly at Indira Gandhi International airport – itself an unattractive place, perhaps due to the fact that at that time they were contemplating the ill-fated takeover by Jet Airways which has since fallen through. Thank goodness for the cool and calm of The Oberoi Hotel, whose management were helpful and welcoming, and indeed for British Midland with whom we finally flew home two days later, having flown down to Mumbai to join their flight. I very much hope they will commence a daily flight from London to Delhi in the near future – reliability in an airline is essential!

The Qutb Minar complex is also looking very good with carefully landscaped grounds and careful restoration work. This too we had previously visited but had heard recently that renovation work had been completed and also that a nice woodland walk had been laid out at Mehrauli. This complex was crowded with Indian visitors on a sunny Sunday afternoon and it was good to see so many Indians enjoying their own heritage.

Delhi has new beautiful buildings about which to write too; the Akshardam temple, is a graceful new building in a large complex on the banks of the Yamuna river in New Delhi. Although loosely referred to as a 'temple' it is not a religious one in the true sense of the word, but rather a memorial and prayer hall built by the secular Swaminarayan sect. Their belief is in the innate goodness of human beings and the beauty of nature. The buildings are surrounded by the *narayan sarovar* (lake) on three sides. Water collected from 151 rivers, ponds and lakes from all over India has been brought here. The entire memorial is surrounded by sculptures in pink marble from Rajasthan. These sculptures depict the elephant in different situations, namely with man in domesticity, the jungle in its natural habitat and ultimately with the gods. In the jungle scenes it is shown as playing with and nursing its young and protecting them from other wild animals; on the mythological plane it is depicted as Lord Ganesha, among many other incarnations. At the entrance to the memorial the ten incarnations of Lord Vishnu have been depicted on the doorway

Looking at a modern day structure one has to commend the very new Delhi Metro. It is still under construction but what is already in use is state of the art and everyone is delighted with how clean and modern it is and the speed with which one can travel quite long

Tombs in the Lodi Gardens in New Delhi

distances. The entrances to the subway for the Metro are elegantly designed and blend in well with their surroundings, moreover people are not allowed to 'camp' in them, nor is one allowed to eat on the trains or consume any food or hawk or spit or do anything horrible in the underground system! One man apparently was given overall command of the operation and that is the way it has been achieved so efficiently and on time. I just wish he or some other like him would be given similar powers to rebuild the airports for Delhi, which are truly atrocious and do so much harm as the first experience for incoming foreign visitors and returning non-resident Indians or foreign-born Indians.

The CNG revolution in Delhi's transport energy system implemented by Indraprastha Gas Ltd is probably the world's largest and most successful anti-pollution exercise ever. Compressed natural gas (CNG) has transformed Delhi which was heavily polluted before at the time of writing my first book; even by 2002 I could see the improvements and commented upon it in the second book, but now there is a significant difference. The authorities are continuing to make plans to expand the piped natural gas business, introduce CNG railway engines, and make use of this fuel for their 60,000 strong light commercial vehicle fleet. They have created the world's largest eco-friendly CNG bus fleet and converted thousands of private vehicles to CNG. In a few years the Natural Gas network is expected to spread to Gurgaon, Lucknow, Agra, Nasik, Pune, Vijaywada and Hyderabad.

The bovine population has largely been removed from the streets of Delhi and the various little human encampments on the wide elegant avenues appear to have been removed as well. I do hope that the people were treated well and found decent alternative living quarters, but as a visitor I have to say this makes a vast improvement as the original grandeur of the capital city was in danger of festering under squatter camps and being subsumed by shabby squalor.

In my second book I touched on the vexed question of female foeticide. This continues to cast a shadow on India as a whole and indeed was a topic on the major BBC News last week. However, at last people are being arrested for participating in this needless cruel abortion of females. This selfish practice coupled with the 'bride bazaar' that continues to flourish amongst the poorer classes is something that sullies India's reputation, along with child labour and forced marriages.

Hundreds of government workers and social activists have been mobilised in Rajasthan and Madhya Pradesh to prevent the illegal mass weddings of under-age boys and girls. Most child marriages in India take place on two auspicious holy days: Akshaya Tritiya and Akha Teej. Police are often bribed to ignore such ceremonies, leaving the task of preventing them to unprotected child welfare workers who are often attacked physically. Apparently the chief minister of Madhya Pradesh caused outrage when he said after just such an attack that no serious action would be taken against those who forced children into such marriages. "Social customs are stronger than laws…" was his reaction which I find so reprehensible in a man of influence. It is only through the strict adherence to the rule of law that India can hope to control all these barbarities and engender universal respect. Remember if you will the words of Gandhiji that I quoted earlier in this chapter.

The men in Haryana apparently do not want daughters but they do want wives. Now I thought India was a land of mathematics; surely the men in this ancient country can work out that one cannot have one without the other. Not far from glitzy Gurgaon, which is growing like a rapacious insect, there are the thriving 'mandis' of flesh where the price of a bride is often less than that of a cow.

Disabled men who are unattractive often resort to buying women for as little as Rs 4,000; the money is usually pocketed by the middle person who inevitably is an awful grasping woman. Trafficking in girls from places like Assam and Bihar and Jarkhand is rife and what is worse, these men often share their woman out amongst their brothers. I know this is revolting and not an attractive side of India, but I cannot in all honesty write about the land and turn a blind eye, as so many do to these atrocities. They stain India's reputation badly.

In Haryana though the state government has claimed success in its efforts to correct the skewed gender ratio through awareness campaigns and incentives for the girl child; activists who work in the area are sceptical. Everyone knows that the various clinics have found new and subtle ways of fulfilling parents' desires to know the sex of their unborn child. Nothing has to be actually said, the doctor may just write something in red thus indicating a female foetus as opposed to writing anything down in a blue biro.

Now encouragingly in Karnataka there are new big financial incentives for couples to have female children. A very sizeable sum is to be settled on a female baby which will only be handed to her at the age of eighteen; no doubt the authorities are quite aware that someone will try and circumvent these rules, but it comes down to the old adage, "the Rule of Law must be enforced", perhaps with punitive measures that act as an example to all the other simple but unscrupulous and cruel, greedy people.

Another horrible subject I tackled in my last book I will briefly return to. The Arab racing syndicates buy small boys to work as camel race jockeys. In 2005 eighty-six children aged between four and twelve had lived a life of virtual slavery for up to seven years before being traced by welfare groups. Some were so traumatised that they could not remember their names or where they were from. Most of this happens between Pakistan and the Arab states. However India has its fair share of child trafficking too. It is thought that at least 1,700 Pakistani children are believed to be working as camel jockeys in the Middle East. In 2002 Pakistan made smuggling children abroad a criminal offence punishable by up to ten years in prison, but as usual the law is often flouted. In India it is often girl children sold in prostitution to the Middle East. When I wrote earlier in this book about the Arab states I cautioned that all that glitters is not gold and this sort of shameful practice sullies all that glitz and superficial grandeur that at first appeals to the unsuspecting tourist.

A positive step being taken in the United Kingdom is that the British Government has announced proposals that would allow the police to prosecute parents found guilty of compelling their daughters or sons to marry against their wishes. High profile British-Asian celebrities are to help promote a new campaign against forced marriages. There is however a vast difference between an arranged marriage and a forced marriage. The British Foreign Office has dealt with more than 1,000 cases of forced marriages since 2000. An overwhelming majority of the victims were under sixteen. I mention this topic because I do know that when these cases are publicised in the British press sometimes with the full tragic result of the death of a female, the rest of Britain, and I am quite sure Europeans, feel a total repugnance and this can have a very negative effect on how they see India as a whole. The British people after the tragedy of 7th July 2005 in the heart of London have some ambivalent feelings that can impact negatively on all the peoples of the Indian sub-continent, and now that India is surging ahead people will be watching to see whether her cultures and customs will change to reflect modern times; it will not be sufficient just to have a booming economy, a nation needs to be liked, trusted and respected.

Sadly I was wrong in my last book India: The Tiger's Roar to be optimistic about Project Tiger. Barely six months after that book was published evidence of the dreadful state of affairs surfaced and forced the Indian Prime Minister into action. 1,500 tigers have been poached in India in the past ten years, the most in the world. It is thought that 150 tigers, or the population in two national parks, are killed yearly. Six million rupees is what each poached tiger is worth. 2020 is when the Indian Tiger will become extinct at this rate. Only India and Indians can remedy this shameful situation, but as I said before, actions speak louder than words and disappointingly this Indian Government has shown itself not to want to have a total grasp of the situation. Inevitably so many in political life just do what is expedient and there is open discussion within intelligent Indian society and in the courageous free press about the venality of Indian politics. I salute all those who are working within India to try and save the situation. I wish I could do more. The tiger is a wonderful creature and a true emblem of India and if the country has a will to save it from extinction it can achieve it despite the difficulties – again it will require the rigid enforcement of the rule of law with at the same time a re-evaluation of all who work in the field of wildlife conservation, such as forest guards. It is so futile that the Indian Government is so reluctant to acknowledge the extent of the crisis. By April 2006 the most recent nationwide wildlife survey, the findings of which have yet to be recognised by Project Tiger, had yet to be raised at a meeting of the National Board of Wildlife chaired by the Prime Minister; conservationists allege it was suppressed due to pressure from the Ministry of Environment and Forests. The poaching continues unabated and yet these foolish people cannot see how the demise of India's tigers will hurt their tourism immeasurably. The tiger is iconic to India and as famous as the Taj Mahal – but even that is threatened by pollution which is the result of greed and inertia.

Sometimes I am so proud of India, but in this instance I am ashamed.

Were her leaders and famous men to truly work together they could stop this corrupt slaughter and put in place sensible ways of combating poaching. Furthermore I am confident that travellers and tourists would be only too happy to pay a realistic price for a permit to watch tigers as they do to watch gorillas in Africa. Distinguished conservationists and scientists in the private sphere are now ignored wherever possible. How truly sad and how bad can things become?

To look through a glass darkly however is not the way I want to conclude this book. India is going through her own industrial revolution. When Britain went through her industrial revolution it then went on to impact on the entire world. Though it must have been in so many ways a frightful era to live through for our country's disadvantaged, any research into the life and times of humble workers in the 'dark satanic mills' of Britain's then great industrial cities shows what hard, cruel and poverty stricken lives the majority appear to have lived. The First World War and then finally the Second World War led to the emancipation of millions of people from that grinding hard work and poverty. India's revolution is in fact both industrial and technical and hopefully the country will not find itself plunged into hostilities with anyone, let alone the whole world in the years to come.

By the end of May 2006 India will have 150 million telephones – approximately five million Indians are buying phones every month; by 2007 they too will have the opportunities to change their service providers and reap all the benefits that we in the West have with our telephonic communication. Mobile phones are evolving into mobile multimedia computers – truly in the last six years the changes in India have been amazing and all this now affordable technology allows the ordinary man to have realistic aspirations for his work and as a family provider. This can only be beneficial to the whole country, and coupled with other rare talents that are natural to Indians like having an ability to learn difficult foreign languages such as Japanese, this bodes well for the country's future. Japanese is considered a difficult language but Indians have shown themselves to be able linguists which has surprised the large Japanese firms; now many Indians are employed to interact between work forces in both the West and the East. The point I am trying to make is that there is no end to the talents of the Indian people and combined with a good work ethic and ambition they will make their country great.

Now it is springtime in the beautiful Scottish Borders and in our garden I can sit with the faithful Raju by my side amidst hundreds of nodding daffodils. The fruit trees and cherry blossom are flowering and Graham and I have worked to bring the garden back to its tidy beauty after a very long winter sleep. A pair of swallows have built their nest above the doors from the sitting room on to the terrace – that was after the two of them flew into the room and mercifully out again without any damage – they are happy with their new 'des res'! I think back to a few weeks ago and remember pools of pink lotus, jacaranda and acacia blossoms, coffee bushes in flower, parakeets, kingfishers, elephants and peacocks; the wonderful pack of wild dogs, grand Delhi, intricate carvings on ancient temples, the sun setting over Hampi; the beauties of all of southern India – the silence of gliding through backwaters, anticipation in the jungles, delicious food, the sunrise at Tikli, the sound of the sea, warm welcomes, a reunion with old friends, and the good feeling of being back in my 'other home'. India has so much to offer the foreign traveller and those within her borders are, I am glad to say, also travelling and revelling in her beauties. With her increasing success as a world economic power India's profile will continue to grow and all this by the 60th anniversary of her Nationhood; may God bless her as a whole nation.

Truly as I come to the end of three books on the Land of my birth I can look back on my life and know that I am so fortunate to have experienced this dichotomy of upbringing in both India and Britain; very sadly I did not have the opportunity to hear the Tiger's roar on this journey, but I did hear the Peacock's call and I know and treasure the knowledge that those long years ago as a baby of six weeks old I received the Elephant's blessing.

Aline sitting with her beloved cat Raju
in her Scottish garden, July 2006

Bibliography

Ali, Salim, *The Book of Indian Birds* (thirteenth edition) 2002.

Alter, Stephen, *Elephas Maximus, A Portrait of the Indian Elephant*, 2004.

Ashram, Sri Aurobindo, *The story of his Life and his Ashram*, sixth impression 2004.

Brown, L.P., *The Indian Christians of St Thomas, An account of the Ancient Syrian Church of Malabar*. Cambridge: The University Press, 1956.

Devee, Sunity (Maharani of Cooch Behar) and Rose, Aline, *Bengal Decoits & Tigers*, 1916.

D'Souza, Herman, Rt Reverend, *In the Steps of St Thomas*, 1983.

Holmes, Richard, *Sahib – The British Soldier in India 1750–1914*, 2005.

Ions, Veronica, *Indian Mythology*, 1967–1992.

Luther, Narendra, *The Rockitecture of Andhra Pradesh*, 2003.

Mayo, Katherine, *The Face of Mother India*, 1935.

McCann, Charles, *Trees of India*, not dated.

Ramachandra Rao, P.R., *Amaravati* 2002.

Ramachandran, T.N. & F.H. Gravely, *Catalogue of the South Indian Hindu Metal Images in the Madras Government Museum*, 2002.

Ramasamy, N.S. *Temples of South India*, 2003.

Roberts, Field-Marshal Lord, of Kandahar VC GCB GCSI GCIE, *Forty One years in India*, 1897.

Srinivasachar, S. & Satyan, T.S., *Hampi, The Fabled Capital of the Vijayanagara Empire*, 1995.

Times of India & Statesman Book Dept., *Wonderful India*, 1937.

Contacts and Details of Interest for those Visiting India

Aline Dobbie's own website: www.thepeacockscall.co.uk

Tikli Bottom (the gracious guest house close to Delhi)
Martin and Annie Howard
Email: honiwala@vsnl.com
Website: www.tiklibottom.com

Project Mala   UK Charity No: 801953
The Project Mala Office
Town Farmhouse, 25 Church Lane, Nether Poppleton
YORK YO26 6LF
Tel: 01904 786880
Email: info@projectmala.org.uk
Website: www.projectmala.org.uk

Butterflies Programme for Street & Working Children in Delhi
U-4 Second Floor, Green Park Extension
New Delhi 110 016 India
Email: butterflies@vsnl.com
Website: www.butterfliesindia.org

Future Hope UK (registered charity no. 1001769) Helping Kolkata's Street
    Children
6 Queensdale Place
London W11 4SQ UK
Email: info@futurehope.co.uk
Website: www.futurehope.co.uk

Future Hope India
1/8 Rowland Road
Kolkata 700020, West Bengal India
Website: www.futurehope.co.uk

Esther Benjamins Trust (UK registered No 1078187)
Refuges for street, jail and circus children in Nepal
Tel: +44(0)20 8877 2519
Wandsworth Business Village, 3–9 Broomhill Rd, London SW18 4JQ
Email: ebtrust@hotmail.com
Website: www.ebtrust.org.uk

Dr Graham's Homes, Kalimpong, India (charity registered in Scotland
   SCO16341)
Kintail, The Causer, Nethy Bridge PH25 3DS Scotland
Tel: +44(0)1479 821222
Email: dghukctsec@vcassie@fsnet.co.uk
Website: www.drgrahamshomes.co.uk

Wildlife Protection Society of India
S-25 Panchsheel Park
New Delhi 110 017
Tel: (Int. + 91.11) 4163.5920/21
Fax: (Int. + 91.11) 4163.5924

UK Support: WPSI (UK) is registered as a UK charity (registration
   no. 1074459).

Those who wish to make a tax-effective contribution can send cheques to:

Wildlife Protection Society of India (UK)
c/o Ms Helen Warren
Draydon Farm
Dulverton
Somerset TA22 9QE
UK

LifeForce Charitable Trust (wildlife charity registered in UK)
Email: lifeforcelink@hotmail.com
Website: www.lifeforceindia.com

Global Tiger Patrol (registered charity no. 328126 The Ranthambhore Society)
87 Newland St, Witham, Essex CM8 1AD UK
Tel: +44(0)1376 520320
Email: globaltiger@compuserve.com
Website: www.globaltigerpatrol.co.uk
Websites of particular interest:
                           www.worldwildlife.org
                           www.projecttiger.nic.in
                           www.sanctuaryasia.com

Discovery Initiatives Ltd
51 Castle Street, Cirencester GL7 1QD UK
Tel: +44 (0) 1285 643 333 Email: enquiries@discoveryinitiatives.com
Travel Operators for Tigers – Responsible Tiger Tourism set up in 2003
Website: www.toftiger.org Tel: +44(0) 1285 643 333

Responsible Travel
Email: info@responsibletravel.com
Website: www.responsibletravel.com

Alastair Sawday's
Special Places to Stay, INDIA
www.specialplacestostay.com

The India Tourist Office
7 Cork Street, London W1S 3LH
Tel: General Enquiries +44(0)207 437 3677
Tel: Brochure request: 08700 102183
Email: info@indiatouristoffice.org
Website: www.incredibleindia.org

The Ashden Awards for sustainable energy: www.ashdenawards.org

The Royal Burgh of Peebles website: www.peebles.info
The Scottish Borders website: www.scot-borders.co.uk